CONCORDE
A DESIGNER'S LIFE

CONCORDE
A DESIGNER'S LIFE
THE JOURNEY TO MACH 2

TED TALBOT

The History Press

Conversation piece, AD 2020

'Do you remember the time that we used to do New York in three hours?'

Cover illustrations. Front, top: Schematics of Concorde (courtesy of Julien Scavini/Wikimedia); drawing board (iStockphoto); *bottom*: Concorde supersonic aircraft commissioned in the 1970s, and withdrawn in 2004. (© LatitudeStock/Alamy) *Back*: Terry Brown and Ted Talbot at Hotel El Minzah, Tangier. (John Allan)

First published 2013
Reprinted 2014

The History Press
The Mill, Brimscombe Port
Stroud, Gloucestershire, GL5 2QG
www.thehistorypress.co.uk

British Library Cataloguing in Publication Data.
A catalogue record for this book is available from the British Library.

ISBN 978 0 7524 8928 5

Typesetting and origination by The History Press

CONTENTS

AUTHOR'S NOTE

In the balmy autumn 1956, when Britain had an aircraft industry which designed and built whole aeroplanes, we attended a meeting called by the Ministry of Supply to discuss the design of a Supersonic Transport Aircraft (SST). There were at least seven aircraft manufacturers and four engine manufacturers in attendance looking for contracts,* and many Ministry people looking for someone who might take them out to lunch.

This meeting resulted, some years later, in a beautiful aircraft and spawned a series of humorous, if scattered, episodes connected by a rather irregular path towards passenger flight at supersonic speeds. The action here is centred on Concorde, as the SST became known, its power plants and some of those who took part in this particular aspect of the adventure. The incidents involve colleagues – Brits and non-Brits – who formed part of a small team working within a very large one on the design, build and test processes.

One of the technical problems, of which there were many, could be expressed in non-technical terms as follows: at the height at which Concorde flies the possibility of encountering so-called air pockets, or any other type of upset, is extremely remote. However, should this 'remote happening' come to pass and the aircraft drops rapidly towards terra firma, then Granny, who had been relaxing in her comfortable seat in the cabin as she covered every mile in less than three seconds, now finds the world approaching rapidly from 11 miles below.

---

* Lest we forget:
Aircraft: A.V. Roe, Armstrong Whitworth Aircraft, Bristol Aircraft, de Havilland Aircraft, Handley Page, Short Brothers and Vickers-Armstrongs. (Fairey Aircraft and English Electric joined later).
Engines: Armstrong Siddeley Motors, Bristol Aero-Engines, de Havilland Engine Company and Rolls-Royce.

It was decided (at high level) that, as Granny floats gracefully up towards the overhead lockers, concentrating on not spoiling her new dress by pushing her ('I'm going to be a bit naughty!') gin, tonic, ice and lemon back down into its glass, she should not be distracted in this task by a succession of loud, shuddering bangs from the engines.

There were hosts of more technical requirements, but one of the same nature as the above caused many problems in the most technically difficult part of a technically difficult aircraft.

In order to avoid the many company mergers and name changes that have occurred over the development of this story, the firms given the British sections of the design and development contract are referred to as BAe (British Aerospace), of which Bristol Aircraft and Bristol Siddeley Engines (now merged into Rolls-Royce) became a part.

This book was commenced over thirty years ago as relaxation and escape from pressures. Perhaps the memory over these years is a bit misty, and for ease of telling some incidents have been coalesced, but be assured that all which is related here has a complete foundation in fact.

My thanks go to my ex-secretaries Jane Eves and Jackie Hewlett in the early stages for coping with some terrible writing (neat, but illegible), and to my granddaughter Aleisha, for helping me in the many times that the computer apparently did what I told it to do, but not what was intended. Also, on a more technical level, Duncan Greenman and John Lumley for digging me out of computer crevices.

I'm not sure how I feel about being dragooned into this exercise after twenty years of retirement by my colleague Colin Cruddas,* who quite frequently writes books about aeroplanes as a hobby. But here we are.

Above all my thanks and love have always gone to Ann for support in everything, and especially when the PC goes off along an unintended tangent and I am waxing eloquent at its infamy.

* *A View from the Wings*, Colin Cruddas (The History Press, 2012)

PROLOGUE

At the head of the long table that stretched down the briefing room sat the Chief Test Pilot, his Deputy and the other members of the Flight Test crew. They wore the 'heads are going to roll' expressions that they had picked up from their French opposite numbers. On the pilots' right sat the Flight Test Observers with their records of the day's flight – the 'ObsLogs' – waiting to correct the pilots' impressions of the sequence of events as diplomatically as possible without making it seem as if the pilots were wrong. On their left sat the Chief Inspector, the Ground Crew Chief and their assistants, waiting to find out what had stopped working, had broken or had fallen off. They were wondering if they had overlooked something, or whether they could pass the buck to the design office.

At the foot of the long briefing room table sat the representatives of the design team trying to look nonchalant, but inwardly itching to know how the tests had worked out. Post-flight rumours based on information from the man listening in on the VHF radio were not very promising. Could it be that there was something even more fundamentally wrong than the functioning of the pilots' seats and the location of their coffee cup holders?

The atmosphere, thick with cigarette smoke from those who had to smoke and of peppermint from those who were trying not to, was forgotten as the Chief Test Pilot delivered his brief: 'Then there was a bloody great row. Smoke on the flight deck. It sounded like World War Three had started!'

The Deputy Chief Test Pilot later added his sixpennyworth: 'Just like being in a train smash – and when all four engines surge it's like being in four train smashes.'

It was quite evident to the representatives of the design team present that the test pilots had been impressed when their first experiences of engine surge on the prototype aircraft at high supersonic speed crept up on them unexpectedly. The aircraft inspectors' eyebrows were raised in unison and they turned, as was their custom, to look accusingly at the design engineers. Few of the Flight Department had taken note of the warnings given to them about the effects of supersonic surges and were now wishing that they had done so. However, it was not the inspectors' fault, the designers had designed the thing and something had gone wrong, so it was obviously all due to 'them'.

Had 'they' got it wrong yet again?

'They' now realised that achieving Mach 2 – twice the speed of sound, or a mile in less than three seconds – had not been easy, even if relatively straightforward(!). It was the little bit extra, needed for performance combined with safety, that was going to be difficult.

For some years previously this design team had been suffering from a creeping awareness that there was no way in which a huge stampede of horsepower, in hiccups, could escape from the wrong end of the Olympus engines without some bright beggar commenting on the fact.

Even in the massive engine test cells at Pyestock, the National Gas Turbine Engine Test Centre (NGTE) near Farnborough, the surges from a single engine had shaken the very foundations of the cathedral-like cells and left an uneasy impression of brute power on the rampage.

Happily, in the current phase of test flying no pieces of engine or bits of aircraft structure had become detached and headed for outer space. I suppose, they thought, we had better tell the pilots of that possibility too, before they find it out for themselves.

The nucleus of this group of engineers who had conceived the power plant had moved over the previous years from positions in various aerospace departments round an inevitable spiral to their respective places in the new Power Plant Group by secondment or adoption. In the Aerodynamics Office I had moved from project studies on wing shapes and the workings of the power plants and was put in this group with strict orders to defend them from the aerodynamicists and their demands for even thinner, stronger structures: the poacher had been turned gamekeeper. Within a short time Jim Wallin, with his comprehensive power plant experience of civil and military aircraft such as Viscount, Valiant, Vanguard and VC 10, arrived from Weybridge to become the Chief Power Plant Engineer as the workload grew quickly. As a man from Weybridge he professed to be pleasantly surprised at the warmth of his welcome in Filton. However, manning the increasing workload still remained a problem.

Like myself, David Moakes had been roped in from aerodynamics to pursue the practical development of the intake and its geometry, and inevitably this grew to include a heavy involvement in the development and in-service support of the rest of the nacelle, including the engine, nozzle and thrust reverser and associated systems.

Back in the Aerodynamics Office, the genius that was Terry Brown had blossomed in any field that he took an interest in. With his friend John Legg they became the principals in the diagnosis and definition of the brilliant solutions to the demands of flexibility, performance and compatibility between the engines and their intakes as demanded by a civil aircraft.

On a completely different, but equally essential, discipline, the wide experience of Tom Madgwick on Fire Precautions was also imported from Weybridge, due to the lack of background at Filton in the current civil field. Others, although not formally in the group, became 'absorbed' and were regarded by all disciplines as full members for the duration.

To complement the Technical Office there was a large Design Drawing, Systems and Stress Office coping with the new technology and the differences between the two prototypes and the individual differences of the two pre-production aircraft (see Appendix).

This was the team, which now specified, assessed, modified and integrated the efforts of the British and French aircraft and engine companies whilst designing an intake and its control system to cope with every normal and abnormal happening in flight.

Each member of the technical nucleus was a superb individual in his particular discipline who had earned, by dint of his efforts, the quiet respect of his fellows. This respect was derived from the fact that, without exception, each one had not only a profound understanding of their own particular subject, but could also give as much as they received in discussions with experts in other fields.

Within a few years they had become an entity second to none, as they later proved when American and Russian engineers failed to achieve overall success in the same area of expertise. Both Russian and American engineers were generous enough to express admiration for the feat, but, of course, their respective politicians did not. Neither did ours, unless prompted.

Almost everything was new and in advance of most things military.

'Supercruise' (long duration supersonic cruise without reheat) is not a recent invention. Concorde had to be doing it from the start. The early Tupolev Tu-144 didn't incorporate it.

Fly-by-wire has only recently been adopted for civil airliners. Concorde had it from the start and it was carried on to its subsonic successors – versions of the Airbus series.

Electronic control systems for most engines are now the bee's knees. The Bristol Siddeley Olympus introduced the first one into civil power plants fifty years ago. (The Bristol Britannia had simple electric controls from pilot to engines seventy years ago!)

Disc brakes on aircraft were first introduced by Dunlop on Concorde, firstly with metal pads and then with composite units. The list goes on.

The aircraft accumulated more hours at Mach 2 than the rest of the world's air forces and will probably be unique for many years to come. Above all, Concorde is a thing of beauty, matched only by that gem of the thirties, the Spitfire.

Throughout the formative years of the project, and beyond, the designers were sustained by two common factors – a dry, Goon-like sense of the ridiculous, and a complete dedication to the project. The humour was worn as armour against incessant attacks on the British side from politicians, the press and trial by television 'experts'. Most of these 'experts' in reality knew very little about the problems, but were actively trying to further their own or their questioners' careers on the basis that the programme producers knew even less. I suggested to one producer who came to see me that she also talked to two more senior designers and the suggestion was summarily dismissed as they had already been interviewed 'but talked like engineers!'

The team's total dedication produced technical feats beyond even the normal expectations of intensive work projects when knocking on the doors of the frontiers of knowledge, but required no external pressures from any source to do so. The feat was still unmatched over forty years later in the civil or military fields.

It is unfortunate that in a project of this complexity it is difficult to pay tribute to everyone involved and my apologies go to that majority who are not mentioned.

The degree of dedication to the project was evident in the home life of those concerned, who, when with their families, found that their work was never very far from their thoughts. Honeymoons, holidays, weekends and evenings were planned or unplanned by it. Strange to relate, however, almost without exception their wives remained with their husbands, and the families appeared to be quite normal.

It is to these remarkable women, and to one in particular, that these stories are dedicated. This dedication is in the hope that, if they are still confused, it may bring some insight into the peculiar workings of their husbands' minds. Real engineers and real women – an unbeatable combination.

If, in the narrative, life is expressed in engineering terms, or vice-versa, just relax and accept the fact that this is how it should be. Don't fight it – in 'Engineering Speak' there really are male and female fittings which mate together.

All real engineers are creative artists.
Few, if any, so-called artists are fundamentally creative …
… and even fewer are engineers.

(Anon)

I

PROPOSITIONS

In my bachelor days, college, work and women had sometimes been difficult to combine and good chances had been missed. Whilst comparing tales of misery with fellow lodger Trevor Buxton, a hydraulics engineer, we had been gloomily discussing the situation. Our landlady, a rather delicate old dear, joined us. After her admonition 'never to get married too quickly' she abruptly changed course and advised us how to go about it – but suggested that possibly we should not 'go all the way'.

'The local vicar's wife has just started a club for people like you,' she said. 'Why don't you go down there on Tuesday and see what it is like?'

Go down there we did, but it did not look too promising.

Trevor was immediately commandeered by the vicar's wife and taken to one side of the hall. I was directed to the other. My group looked and sounded less promising than those opposite, so after a short session I excused myself and wandered across to the other side.

The vicar's good lady had by now latched onto Trevor and had been explaining that 'This was a Church of England organisation', and then enquired about his religion.

'I'm a Methodist,' said Trevor.

'And what are you?' she asked me as I arrived on the scene.

Not being party to the previous conversation I gave the obvious answer:

'I'm an aerodynamicist.'

It was not received with the awe and wonder normally expressed by the female sex.

But since that time things had changed beyond my wildest dreams when, at a blind date, a slim, golden-haired vision in a black dress had appeared at the top of a set of stairs in a midwives' digs. Things progressed well – very well! Soon it was time to venture forth to meet the new relatives-to-be.

The Morris Minor Tourer had been steered carefully along the route outlined by the Welsh railway porter at Fishguard Station. The first section past the ticket office and down the length of platform 2 to the level crossing between the two platforms was fairly easy. Platform 3 was a different kettle of fish as there was a difficult right-hand turn behind the waiting room, made worse by a carefully sited trolley at the apex of the turn. By swinging out towards the track, thereby frightening Ann and – I had to admit – myself, we completed the turn without losing face or paint. The car now rested in slings high up above the dockside, whilst the foreman in charge of loading the ferryboat sorted out his loading problems in a game akin to chess, but played with cars and cranes on the boards of a ship's hold. Roll-on-roll-off ferries had not yet arrived in the Principality.

The sight of 100 per cent of our capital swinging by on a single rope 40ft above the oily surface of the Irish Sea made me concentrate upon Ann's legs as they climbed the gangway steps onto the deck. They were a lovely shape, firm, soft and sensational – the legs, not the steps.

Stepping up the slope aggravated the sore feeling around the area where my appendix used to be. A recent operation to remove some stitches left by the first surgical procedure, done five years previously, had been only partially successful. At odd intervals the nether regions were still giving birth to hard black nylon stitches, put there contrary to hospital laid-down procedures one late night by 'one of the world's experts' practising the new keyhole surgery.

The Morris Minor, swinging gently to and fro high above the open hatch giving access to the second lower deck, was then lowered through the hole and turned to face the required direction before coming to a standstill on the baulks of timber now covering the lower hatch. It was then driven out of sight.

Having breathed a short prayer of thanks to the God of Crane Drivers we both retired to our respective cabins (although this was the late fifties we had been born well before the war, when things were done differently in some areas of life) to get ready for dinner.

Rising refreshed, we breakfasted in the early hours of a beautiful Irish morning in the safety of Rosslare Harbour. The ship had docked against the mole whilst the passengers were asleep and the car was already standing amongst the others on the quayside. The plan was that owners were to sit in their own cars and drive them onto a row of rail flatcars. These were then pushed by a small steam-driven shunting engine for their journey along the length of the mole to the landing stage.

There is always a first time for everything and this was the first time we had driven along a row of railway flatcars to the end of the train, to be followed in single file by a mainly rundown selection of Coventry's output. Once all cars had been loaded, the train set off on the short journey along the mole. Being first, there was nothing in front except a pair of buffers, the engine being at the other end. Sitting in a car on top of rolling stock, whilst being pushed by a steam locomotive was a new experience enjoyed by most of the drivers, judging by the way they hooted when starting and joyfully indicated right using hand signals at the junction of the tracks. When the train came to a gentle stop against the buffers of the unloading ramp, I for one realised that my right foot was pressed hard on the brake pedal. So, most likely, were the right feet of those behind us. The short ramp in front of the car was lowered and after starting the engine we drove slowly onto solid ground.

'I'll just give the car a rest,' I said. 'It's not used to this kind of thing.'

This was Ireland and time meant little. We parked and took stock of the activity surrounding us. Cars were manoeuvring, being loaded and departing. Some, like ours, were just sitting there.

Also just sitting, but this time on a bollard on the quayside and dressed in a long fur coat, was one of those travellers who had come on the first shuttle for foot passengers. She, too, was viewing the scene, but with an air of impatience. A young man who turned out to be her son came out of the nearby telephone box shrugging his shoulders whilst holding his hands, palms outwards.

'My son,' said her ladyship aggressively, turning towards the open window of the Morris Minor, 'has been trying to ascertain the whereabouts of a hire car reserved by us a month ago.'

'Oh – what is the problem?' I asked, feigning interest.

'There appears to be some sporting activity in Dublin and the car has been taken there! How do they expect to do business?'

It appeared that our new acquaintances had expected to be met by a hire car, but had chosen the wrong firm and the wrong week. Today, as they had discovered, was the day of the All Ireland Hurling Final in Dublin, and everything on two or four wheels had been mobilised to take the sporting populace to the stadium. Hurling, as played by the Gaelic male, is probably the fastest game played on grass. It is similar to hockey, but played with greater passion, to very few rules, the players being armed with semi-fragile war-clubs. Waterloo is reputed to have been won on the playing fields of Eton, but the whole campaign would have been over much more quickly if it had started at a hurling match in Ireland and carried on, using the same weapons, in Belgium.

The telephone conversation had indicated that anyone with any sense would have hired the car for the day before, and then kept it until the morrow – or better still, would have started their journey from somewhere else.

So we, of the Morris Minor, did the only decent thing. Once the car had got over its experiences on railway platforms, in slings, ships and on railway trucks, we loaded lady bountiful and the heir apparent into the back seats. As the boot was full of our own luggage, the new passengers' luggage was placed on top of the passengers themselves – no mean feat considering that the tourer was the two-door version. With the rear tyres flattened by the load, they were then driven to the hotel in the main square and off-loaded with all haste, before anyone could find out if there were any rooms free. Our car made all haste out of the town and into the welcoming countryside.

Compared to England the roads were a delight, practically empty except for the occasional wandering animal. It must be a helluva match, this All Ireland, we thought! It was the summer of '59, one of the driest on record, and the sun had turned the Emerald Isle into delicate shades of dusky browns, pale greens and yellows, but had not detracted from its appeal to the traveller. However, there was one drawback which had the effect of slowing down progress until one got used to the scheme of things: the road signs.

Each sign was in two languages, Gaelic and English, with the former uppermost. It was necessary, therefore, to concentrate on the signposts as soon as they came within reading distance and to skim through the names, rejecting the top one and every other one to save time. There was only one consolation – the first part of the journey through Wales to Fishguard had been infinitely more difficult. There were places where it had been necessary to stop in order to compare every letter on the signpost with every letter of the name on the map, in order to pick the correct vowel-less glottal-stopper.

Nevertheless, the 40-mile journey to Kilkenny passed quickly with only a few brushes with the local fauna. Few of these animals appeared to have any regard for self-preservation, and certainly had no knowledge of the rules of the road. Only later did we discover that the human inhabitants shared the same scant respect for the Highway Code.

Beyond Kilkenny, the Marble City, the road narrowed and twisted through hedgerows and farm entrances. A creeping suspicion began to form in my mind that the locals either had prior warning of the probable line of our approach, or that they had always, as part of history, stood gossiping by the roadside gates. Perhaps, giving them the benefit of the doubt, they were whiling away the time between morning Mass and the midday meal, whilst awaiting the start of the hurling match. Nevertheless there was a good proportion of smiling faces breaking off from intense conversations to bend forwards, peering towards the car windows, the owners smiling and waving their hands in greeting.

At last, about 4 miles beyond the town, we came to a gate leading to a whitewashed, stone-built farm. After passing through the open gate and entering the field, we crossed on the farm path to the white pillars marking the entrance to the yard. On the right stood the farmhouse shouldering a large stone barn. On the opposite side was a gated entrance to the orchard and between the two, on the remaining sides of the square, stood the low-roofed storerooms and pens.

We had arrived.

The arrival interrupted a work process being carried out by three players. The principal, in an advisory role, having a large sturdy figure supported by braces and a wide leather belt, and being protected from the elements by a flattish trilby hat, appeared to be directing work by jabbing in the direction of various items with the stem of a short briar pipe, the contents of which were held intact by a steel ventilated cover. The other two were obviously taking the part of the workers by the token of the tools they leaned on and the advice to which they paid lip service. One was Ann's brother, Donal; the other was their 'man', Willie.

As the car entered the portals and drove to the centre of the yard, the three pairs of eyes followed it until it stopped. The pipe was then returned to its proper place so as to enable him to see more clearly, and the users of the shovels leant upon these more firmly.

They took stock of one another, the owner of the pipe, John Wall, and the owner of the car. They both knew that they were to be faced with severe problems. The owner of the pipe's problem was that in the next few days he was going to be asked whether his daughter should be allowed to marry not only a Protestant, but an Englishman to boot. The problem for the owner of the Morris Minor was that he was going to be the one to do the asking.

Any likely tension was circumvented by a wisp of feminine perfection stepping across the yard from the direction of the house. Eileen, the eldest of four, had been despatched to Bristol on a fact-finding mission as soon as the news of the impending nuptials had broken. On her return her verdict had apparently settled any doubts.

'I'll marry him myself if she doesn't!' was her conclusion.

She now came towards us with a welcoming smile. There were four sisters in the family, all in the classical mould. Mary was a theatre nurse in America, and Ann became a midwife in England, as did Margaret initially. Mother, sadly, was not now with them.

With a shy kiss on the cheek the women were ushered into the stone flagged kitchen for tea and gossip. The men followed, the talk being turned to the forthcoming match wherein the local team, Kilkenny, were up against their near neighbours Waterford. Arguments were passionate and somewhat one sided, as they all supported the local side.

After the midday meal silence fell as the radio was switched on and the match commentator lit up the airways with the pungent brilliance of descriptive verbiage that few outside Eirin can match. At the farm a simultaneous translation and unsolicited comment service was at hand for the visitor who had not the slightest idea of the game, or the rules.

This lamentable omission was to be rectified the next weekend with an introduction to the incredibly fast game of hurling. From this visit it was possible to gain two lasting impressions – the first being the picture of two men walking up and down opposite touchlines with a bundle of clubs under their arms, handing them out to any team member who had broken theirs on the clubs, shins or heads of the opposing team. The second was of the volunteer ambulance men who walked around the outside of the spectators, not, as it may have been assumed, for their own protection, but in fact to attend to the higher casualty rate in the outer ring of spectators, who were disadvantaged by having the sight of the oncoming missile obscured until too late, when the row of heads belonging to those standing in front of them ducked aside. Or so I was told.

However, in the more structured arrangements at the arena in Dublin, events were coming to an end and Kilkenny had won. It was time to go into the city to meet the crowds and celebrate. In the main street we found a fair crowd lining the main Dublin-to-Waterford road waiting to celebrate victory with the returning supporters of the victorious team and to exchange good natured catcalls and banter with the supporters of the vanquished as they passed through on their way to celebrate defeat.

'Are the pubs open at this time?' I asked, as Sundays in those days had different licensing laws.

'Do you think that they would miss an opportunity to celebrate?' said someone. 'You can tell the pubs that are open by the men standing at the front doors telling people to go round the back! We'll go in this one.'

Inside there was an air of celebration, and the smell of cigarettes and stout. After an interminable round of introductions the serious business continued. As in any such company the volume of talk rose in proportion to the volume of stout consumed, until it was brought to a sudden end by an insistent shushing. Looking around, expecting to see someone being propped up to make a speech or give a song, no cause for the call for silence was visible to the untrained eye.

'What's up?' I asked.

'Shhhh!' came the reply.

A whispered explanation said that the barman had given the signal that the Gardai (Police) had just gone into the kitchen to check that the law was being upheld in terms of no signs of unlawful assembly and, presumably, no lowering of the specific gravity of the beer.

'Why the silence?' I enquired again.

The informant's face showed that only an Englishman would ask such a daft question.

'When they get back to the station they will be asked if they checked the pubs and heard any sounds of drinking on their rounds – and they can say no without having to go to confessions in the morning!'

Throughout the holiday it was possible to gradually get used to the subtleties of the Irish sense of humour, but yet almost impossible to sort out fact from fiction. I started to believe in fairies.

The week following our arrival passed very quickly. The cowsheds were wired for light, the family Ford Popular was inspected and tuned, and a new lintel was cast in place over the main door of the drystone barn. The wooden lintel over the door of the drystone barn had nearly given up in its fight with the elements and was allowing gravity to triumph. There was an urgent need to renew it before the rest of the facade followed.

'There's material in plenty for the concrete, but nothing for reinforcement,' said Donal. 'What we need is a substantial length of strong metal. What about using that rusty old horse plough lying in the hole in the hedge? It looks about the right length.'

'That keeps the pigs out of the yard,' said Father in a tone that brooked no argument.

A quiet discussion over a cup of tea and more of Eileen's cakes suggested a solution. Father had by then left to see his friends at the pub. The plough was removed from the hedgerow and replaced by hastily cut stakes. As the shuttering for the lintel had been erected previously, one side had to be removed in order to admit the plough. Once the boards had been replaced the plough was hidden from sight. Concrete was mixed by hand and ladled in over the top of the shuttering before being tamped down into the corners and crannies around the plough.

By the time that the world had been set to rights at the pub and the debaters had returned to their respective homes, the gap in the hedge had been camouflaged and the job was done. It was just a little unfortunate that during the tamping process the plough must have toppled slightly and leant against the inside of the shuttering.

It was also an embarrassment that the heavy exercise had caused the end of another suture to start to emerge from deep in my internals and poke itself out into the confines of my underpants, making me feel as if I had a thorn in my side. The original problem had manifested itself as a year's worth of multitudes of boils and injections, followed by a series of abdominal lumps diagnosed by three doctors as hernias. So I was sent to the hospital where the resident surgeon, a small Asian, diagnosed internal abscesses resulting from the initial operation. I pointed out that it was now three-to-one against this judgement, but he ignored the comment and said that he would get his colleague to form an opinion 'before they opened me up'. (The NHS was different in those days!) Away he went and a short time later in walked his colleague.

The unease of the immediacy of being 'opened up' when I was only expecting a consultation turned into sheer panic when in walked 'his colleague', the trainee doctor who had been Ann's previous boyfriend. We shook hands in an atmosphere of cold formality. As he prodded around he muttered 'hernia'. The thoughts of him and his boss armed with scalpels digging around in my nether regions whilst I was *hors-de-combat* made me think fast. In order to avoid an 'accidental slip' of the knife I corrected his opinion by telling him what the surgeon had said, right or wrong, thus probably enabling him to gain brownie points in his chosen career.

The first check on coming round from the operation was to feel under the sheet to ensure that all the essentials were present. They were. Several abscesses surrounding still-knotted sutures had been removed, leaving a bit of a trench. I was told that not all of the sutures had been accounted for, but the remainder would surface fairly soon, and was also told that my lifespan would have been quite short if there had been no operation.

Back at the farm I walked around the side of the barn to have a quiet look at the damage. Sure enough another of the little beggars was showing a small length of black suture.

Ann, there's another stitch appearing,' I whispered, taking her aside.

'Come upstairs,' she said. 'I borrowed a pair of suture forceps from the hospital before we set out, just in case.'

This type of foresight was to become the standard for years to come. I could never match it. The confidential whispering and the sneaking off upstairs must have sprung a few erroneous thoughts in the minds of the family, as that type of thing was not done so blatantly in the parental home in those days. Explanations must have followed later as the still-knotted suture became a prize exhibit for some time.

The next day was the day of 'the t'rashin''.

Early in the morning a magnificent steam traction engine arrived, towing a thrashing machine. It was set up in the rickyard with just about everyone issuing directions:

'Back a bit!'

'OK.'

'More!'

'Mind that girder!'

'Jaysus!'

The traction-engine driver, who had been there and done that many times before, took little notice of them, and managed to put the whole contraption exactly where it was wanted with far less fuss. Whilst this was happening more neighbourly help was arriving. I was introduced to the newcomer each time, and each, in turn, explained what was to happen and were somewhat surprised that I caught on to the process so quickly. It would have been ungracious for me to have explained that during the war, throughout the long summer holidays, I had worked on several farms in the Midlands, which had provided an apprenticeship. Anyway it earned me a few more brownie points.

Four days later, before a family audience, the shuttering on the lintel on the barn was removed. The new beam appeared flawless, except for an imperfection near one end, which looked suspiciously like a plough handle. Father took the pipe out of his waistcoat pocket and put it in his mouth in order to get a better look. He turned his head to inspect the hedge and then looked back at the lintel.

'The plough!' he said in disgust as he turned on his heel. 'I could have used that again.'

All too soon the time came for us to leave. With the baggage on board, together with another sample of Eileen's cakes and soda bread, and another apology for using the old plough as reinforcement in the concrete lintel of the barn – 'He'll never miss it,' said Donal – we left. It was only on the ship on the way back to resume our respective daily tasks concerned with midwifery and supersonic research that Ann said, 'Did you ask him?'

We had to do all the wedding preparations ourselves and the day passed stressfully as they always do. As it was February we decided to have the honeymoon learning to ski in Switzerland and so, following a journey by taxi, train, coach, plane and train, we arrived at Leysin. Here the sight of the first three passengers descending with difficulty from the funicular up to the hotel, due to the plaster casts on their broken legs, cooled our enthusiasm for learning to ski. We agreed to try it after a few days and were then saved from taking the risk by the snow rapidly thawing from the nursery slopes. We deliberately returned to the flat two days earlier than announced, but to no avail.

Our early return – to get used to being married – was interrupted by the Chief Aerodynamicist, Hugh Goldsmith, apologising and saying that George Edwards (GE), the 'God' at Weybridge, had told Mick Wilde, Hugh's boss, that he wanted an answer as to why we had got the design of the boundary layer diverter between the wing and the intakes wrong. GE's review was on Monday and it was now Thursday. I asked why Mick had not told me himself and Hugh just shrugged. Arguments about honeymoons began to simmer, but eventually I gave in with the proviso that future requests for days off – 'No! Not a day off!' – would be agreed promptly. Ann was beginning to realise just what this project meant to those involved in it.

Hugh and I travelled up the congested A4 to Weybridge the next day; the congested motorways had not yet arrived. I must admit that I was pissed off when we met the group that had mentioned our 'error' to GE and found that they had not gone into our background of work and had appeared to consider only the sizes of the Concorde and their TSR-2. When it was pointed out that our intakes were only 22in (outboard) and 10ft (inboard) from the wing leading edge and their aircraft fuselage in front of their intakes was much longer, plus the fact that our model testing showed that we needed to divert only two-thirds of the wing boundary layer to maintain intake efficiency, there was little more to say. Hugh asked if that answered their worries and would they please carry our answer to GE. He put it much more politely than I would have done.

Thereafter, whenever I walked under Concorde's wing I would look at the diverter and mutter 'you owe us a day of our honeymoon'.

2

EARLY WARNINGS

After two years as an engine fitter in the Royal Air Force and five years in college at Loughborough and Cranfield, job hunting had seemed easy as there were many firms with many projects. Unfortunately most of these were covered by the Official Secrets Act, so I was met with a statement that the particular firm had a very interesting project, but they were not at liberty to tell me what it was. So, being impressed by the interviewer Bill Strang, and offered two shillings and sixpence (over a gallon of petrol) more than any other firm, The Bristol Aeroplane Company etc. provided me with employment for nearly forty years.

At the beginning of the fifties the Bristol Aeroplane Company had been given the task of designing a stainless steel supersonic research aircraft, initially aimed at Mach 2 but eventually, with new power plants, to reach Mach numbers near 3. The engines for operating above Mach 2, the Gyron Junior type, had been specified by the Ministry for another, now discontinued, project and were made by the de Havilland Engine Company. At the same time, away 'up North' the English Electric Company were designing a fighter aircraft to fly at Mach 2, later to become the formidable Lightning. Both aircraft owed their provenance to a single Royal Aircraft Establishment report outlining possible engine layouts.

The Lightning had two reheated Rolls-Royce engines, developed from well-tried subsonic units, mounted one above the other in the fuselage, and equipped with reheat to enable it to get to optimum speeds quickly. It did, speedily and frequently. The Bristol Type 188 had its two engines mounted in the wings. Although designed for very high speeds there was a requirement to get there, but even with reheat it failed. The aircraft was to have aerodynamic refinements to help it along, rather than the brute force of the Lightning and its competitors. The main body of the aircraft was to have a coke-bottle shape to reduce the drag; the air intakes to the engines were to have limited variable geometry to optimise the performance still further.

On the other side of the Atlantic they were publishing reports on power plants that showed similarities to those of the 188, but from their shape it could be seen that they were aimed at Mach 3 plus from the start. There was no accompanying indication of the configuration of the aircraft. The American aircraft eventually became the renowned spyplane, the SR-71 Blackbird. The Type 188 was destined to join the ranks of the popular Ministry group under the heading Project Cancelled.

Sexy Shapes

The coke-bottle design for the fuselage, or to give it its more formal name Whitcomb's Area Rule, was, as was everything else, in its infancy and the theory for it to be known as Slender Body Theory was in an even more embryonic shape.

A TECHNIBIT

The draughtsman was asked to draw cross-sections through the body and wings at angles corresponding to each supersonic Mach number interval and plot the various areas onto the centreline of the body.

This gave a series of graphs with the appearance of a one-humped brontosaurus with bumps. These lines were to be laid on top of each other and smoothed and averaged out by changing the nacelle and body profiles. This series of graphs he presented to the Aerodynamics Office after drawing what he thought was a mean smoothed line through the lot. He would then be expected to add or subtract the differences from the areas of the current fuselage to achieve a result as near as possible to this 'scientifically' smoothed line.

In rising seniority three aerodynamicists – myself, John Flower and Mick Wilde – each drew what they were sure a better ('scientific') mean line should be. These were presented to the then Chief Aerodynamicist Bill Strang, who drew his own (and final!) version, saying that there must be a mathematical theory to avoid all this work, so find it!

This 'final version' was very similar to that drawn by the draughtsman, who left the office with a very smug look on his face.

He was back in a very short time.

'What accuracy do you want?' the draughtsman asked.

Remembering that he had witnessed the highly technical manner in which the final lines had been defined, it was deemed politic not to be too severe.

'About 5 per cent,' he was told.

He then disappeared for at least half an hour, it being the mid-morning tea break. He then returned, holding up the spaghetti of graphs as he leant over the top of the desk. He had found that, without any changes to the fuselage, he could pack all of the different Mach number graphs within the required 5 per cent of Bill's version. This would have produced a parallel fuselage, something with which no modern supersonic aircraft could expect to wear if it was to be considered sophisticated.

'We will have a better specification of accuracy when we have developed the theory,' he was told. 'Call you back!'

'Don't be too long because I will have to book my hours to Waiting Time!' was the response.

His was a veiled threat, as there was the usual purge on non-productive 'Waiting Time'.

The theory of slender body drag was in its infancy (and we were unaware that it would not develop satisfactorily for the next decade) so we had to think of something plausible, but satisfactory at the same time. The next day the draughtsman was told to make it 1 per cent with a maximum skin waviness of 1 degree. Well, why not?

Two years later, as I walked past the open door of the large hangars, which these days are now variously referred to as the Brabazon, Britannia, Concorde Hangars, or Assembly Hall, depending upon who was talking and when they joined the firm, I could see a very complex assembly jig under construction.

'What's that for?' I asked.

'It's the final stage jig so that we can get the correct profile that you required for the fuselage skin,' I was told. 'When we spot-weld this stainless steel it goes "twang" as we take it off the first stage jigging so we have to be very careful!'

The production people were beginning to learn that they should have challenged the design rather than accepted the challenge.

Steam Technology

As the design progressed, more designers were drafted in to cope with the increasingly complex technology in all areas. One such addition, put in a very responsible position, started a review of several critical areas. It was rumoured that his sole significant contribution to his last design was the seat of the toilets. He now wanted to relieve the new 4,000psi hydraulic system of the large load imposed on it as the undercarriage was raised. His eventual proposal involved a flash steam boiler wrapped around the turbine casings of the engines to supply steam to raise the landing gear, thereby putting no measurable load on the engine.

On certain aspects of drawing office activity, some things could move faster than others. The next morning there was a small gathering around one of the pillars in the drawing office, and these people were guffawing at a large, well-drawn cartoon hanging from it. As the day progressed word got around and engineers, secretaries, their bosses and others could be seen wandering in on some pretext or other to have a look.

The cartoon showed a drawing of the aircraft diving down, cockpit hood drawn back and Godfrey Auty, the Chief Test Pilot, with his hair flowing back in the slipstream behind a soot-streaked face. His shoulder flash showed his new title – Chief Stoker.

The new man, now referred to as Stevenson's Apprentice, did not last long.

Enter the Surges

The engines for the Type 188 were the de Havilland Gyron Juniors. The supersonic version of this engine had been specified for the Saunders Roe SR 177 rocket-plus-gas turbine interceptor which had been cancelled around 1957 in a White Paper declaring the passing of manned interceptor aircraft. The Gyron Junior had been specified in the cloistered surrounds of the MoD Procurement corridors and was to be designed to operate at Mach 2 plus. The results from the Number Two test cell at the National Gas Turbine Establishment at Pyestock showed that the Gyron Junior could operate at this condition, but only if the turbine stayed on the engine. One test was terminated abruptly when the turbine left the engine and tried to cut its way out of the test cell.

A TECHNIBIT

The Gloster Javelin was a twin-engine delta wing, all-weather fighter. It later blotted its copy-book by not appearing at the Farnborough Air Show due to the inevitable bad weather whilst the delicate Type 188 research aircraft appeared through the murk, happily hiccupping its way past the crowd. One of the breed was used as a test bed. However, there were indications that achieving this stage in the engine's development would not be without its trouble. Even though the Javelin's engine air intake was a smooth, round tube, the engine surged during ground running (surges are to engines what hacking coughs are to the asthmatic – only worse). When the engine does not like the quality of the air being thrust down its throat it releases all high pressure stored in the compressor in a series of high intensity bangs. The bangs startled us, as they did the pilot. It did not augur well for the 188, whose intake circular contained a cone held by five supports, between which are ten auxiliary inlets to open inward at low speed, behind which are ten spill valves to open outward at supersonic speeds. There was very little inside surface left to control the airflow. However, future extensive wind-tunnel testing showed how to get over these problems and provide a better air pattern than that of the Javelin. The reheat (called the afterburner by the Americans, who like big words) injected extra fuel into the jetpipe at the rear of the engine to give more thrust, and also gave problems later. The aircraft was ideal for teaching us what not to do.

So it looked as though the road to Mach 2 would be bumpy, but even then it was essential that the reheat system worked consistently, which it showed no signs of doing. The de Havilland team called for an urgent meeting at Bristol to talk reheat. They were very worried because the installed reheat would light consistently, but as the throttle was pushed through the maximum dry thrust gate to the maximum reheat stops, the flame either responded, giving full reheated thrust, or went out.

As the de Havilland designer was explaining the problem, the Bristol chairman called for Frank Crowfoot, known as the 'Bearded Wonder'. Frank came into the meeting and was promptly sent out again with the spare set of control system drawings; no explanation, but a command to 'look at that and tell us what you think!'

Within half an hour the conference room door opened and the beard was pushed through. Receiving a nod from the chairman, Frank entered.

'Funny thing,' he said. 'Do you find that when reheat is selected and the throttle is pushed forward, then sometimes you get full reheat and sometimes it goes out?'

There was silence until the de Havilland designer asked a questioning, 'Yes?'

'Well I'm not surprised, as it's built into the control linkage!'

It was now too late to modify the linkage already installed in the prototype for the ground runs, which were scheduled for later in the month. However, after studying the diagnosis, the engine men sent along 'Asbestos Harry' to supervise the runs. This gentleman appeared to be impervious to heat. With the engine running flat out he would stand many yards behind and to the side of the exhaust. He would then slowly lean over towards the jet and have a glancing look at the reheat flame in the jetpipe, his hair and ears flapping in the blast. Ear defenders were not mandatory in those days, and were therefore not used.

Should there appear to be a problem he would take a screwdriver out of his back pocket, remove a panel on the side of the nacelle, and insert a hand between the hot skin of the nacelle and the hotter skin of the jetpipe to pull the erring lever into its proper position. The aircraft would shudder as it felt the full kick of the reheat thrust. Asbestos Harry would lick his tingling knuckles and then give the thumbs up signal to whoever was in the cockpit.

This had to be classified as an interim fix!

Surge Alley

On the first take-off Godfrey Auty, the Chief Test Pilot, had inadvertently investigated the bottom end of the low speed envelope as the huge acceleration pulled his arm back and the joystick with it. Physical sensations had not been simulated by the chair, table and television setup. He found himself airborne and took over from there.

As the flight-testing entered the supersonic region, an area of surge was encountered at a certain combination of speeds and altitudes. This region became known as 'Surge Alley', and was not to be taken lightly. The effects were serious, as in more than one instance the aircraft suffered a simultaneous flame-out of both engines – quite a worry on a twin-engine aircraft with disproportionately large fuselage and nacelles and very small wings. In this condition one of the experts, who knew about these things, described the aircraft's gliding qualities as similar to 'those of a brick s★★★house'.

On the first incident Godfrey could be heard going calmly through the relight drill on engine Number One, but without any success. He then switched to Number Two as he descended rapidly, but with the same negative result. With commendable calm, even though ejection time was approaching, he reverted to Number One again, this time with success. After relighting Number Two he headed for home.

The time came for the Ministry pilot to assess the plane, which he did after a heavy briefing. His assessment was cut short as he ran straight out of Surge Alley. Godfrey immediately took over the flying desk whilst others were trying to turn up the 'engine out' drills in the Flight Manual. From memory he guided the pilot through the minefield until both engines were functioning again.

Stop the War

Aircraft being tested for spinning characteristics, or those whose potential characteristics were such that they should avoid getting into spins, were fitted with anti-spin parachutes located near the tail. The theory was that, when deployed, the parachute would straighten out the flight path and could then be released.

On one flight the anti-spin parachute fitted to the 188 deployed itself and could not be released. This left Godfrey with yet another unwanted problem. He was far from home and was having to use up fuel fast to counteract the drag of the 'chute. Prudence suggested an away landing at the nearest airfield with a long runway. Just in the right position was Brize Norton, an airbase manned by the American Air Force.

This base was being used by the Americans for their B-52 bombers in the heat of the Cold War, and at this time, way out over the Atlantic, a cloud of B-52s was approaching Fairford in the midst of a War Game.

Godfrey managed to get the aircraft, parachute and all, onto the long runway that had been specially extended to accommodate the B-52, although he missed the threshold. His braking overheated the brakes and, as the aircraft came to a stop, the heat was transferred to the wheels. In their turn specially designed fuses in the wheels responded to the increase in internal tyre pressure, and blew out. The aircraft stood on the runway with its tyres going flat. The B-52s were getting nearer, as was the rescue team from Bristol.

As the manager of the Bristol team reached the side of the aircraft, the largest African-American airman they had ever seen approached them. A similarly proportioned bulldozer followed him. The Americans' priority was made clear – the safety of their B-52s.

'I have instructions to clear the runway, Sir!' said the huge airman.

Negotiations to halt the 'war' until the appropriate tow-bar, wheels and jacking equipment could arrive were to no avail. The B-52s were very close. The worried serviceman was eventually persuaded that, if a rope could be provided, a pull would be better for the wellbeing of the 188 than a push.

In no time a rope was found, the 188 was removed from the runway and the war could proceed peacefully.

More Power

Several of the RAF top brass came to look at the aircraft as it passed through its build and test phases. With them came various adjutants, friends and others. One notable hanger-on, wishing to justify his jolly, asked a lot of questions, even though it became obvious that he could not understand the answers.

The Ministry had specified rather late in the design that fire extinguishers should be fitted to both engine nacelles. There was now no room at all for these inside and, in consequence, they had to accept large external bulges on the circular nacelles at about one o'clock, aft of the intake position. The eagle-eyed hanger-on spotted these bulges.

'What are they for?' he asked.

He received a long and confidential explanation of the 'fact' that the engines specified by the Ministry were short of take-off power and as a cheap supplement the firm had decided to split a Rolls-Royce piston engine Griffon in two, putting one six-cylinder block into each nacelle and coupling it up with the Gyron Junior. This fired his imagination, as he had said that he had been looking at one of the later marks of Spitfire earlier in the week and had noticed the bulges at the front of that aeroplane.

'I suppose…' he began again.

However, his informant had suddenly remembered an important test that was about to commence in the labs and had disappeared, which avoided any further embellishment on an imaginative theme.

Was it coincidence that the contract for the Bristol Type 188 was terminated after reaching a Mach number of 1.88? It had served one significant purpose, however – it showed us what not to do.

3

HELP FROM EXTERNAL SOURCES

On hearing of a proposal or a project most people have felt that they can immediately think of fourteen reasons why it is rubbish, or alternatively 'know' how it can be improved. The Concorde was no different and received many offers of help from non-experts and many shots across the bows from ill-informed and self-appointed experts.

Although most of the letters received were well meaning in intent, the 'superior' minds of the recipients gave them a collective label – 'The Nutters'. However, the Engineering Director insisted that we replied to every one – politely.

One senior executive spent many a non-productive hour rebutting statements from these worthies who had expressed their 'findings' on the air or in Public Investigative Hearings in various parts of the world. After a time, his total working life was devoted to this task as, although the complainant only had to make an unfounded statement in such a formal hearing, the company had to make a solid technical defence, or, as the complainant expected, look into the possibility of compensation for the supposed problem.

They were many and varied, and included the following:

- The adverse effect of sonic booms on the sex life of the bee population.
- The adverse effect of strong cosmic rays in the rarefied atmosphere on the sex life of passengers and crew.
- The adverse effect on people living around airports of the sonic boom caused by aircraft landing 'at supersonic speeds'! (To say nothing of the disgruntled passengers touching down in New York, and having finally to disembark dazed and shaken somewhere near Dallas.)
- The fear induced in the wild animal population around airports. Videos of antelopes on the airport at Nairobi continuing to graze whilst the more air-minded members of the herd looked up to watch Concorde take off did nothing to dispel this 'fact'.

- The effect of take-off noise from Concorde on the local buildings. Take the stained glass window of a church near the test base for instance: the vicar and churchwardens expressed worries, which were deflected when it was demonstrated that the window stood to have more damage inflicted by the bottom notes of the church organ.
- The noise that the Concorde made as it took off 'a few minutes ago' despite the fact that it was still on the ground, being delayed by some incident or other. These people were armed with timetables and would take it in turn to call in.

In the early days of operation the noise was similar to, but shorter than that of, a Boeing 707, Convair 880 or VC 10. At Fairford a visiting Pan Am flight engineer, used to these aircraft, watched the noisy, smokey prototype take off and commented that we seemed to have cured those problems.

And so on.

Sounds Fishy

Although the Engineering Director, Dr Russell (Russ), insisted that any letter from the public was always answered promptly and as straightforwardly as possible, taking into account the perceived technical background of the correspondent, he was not always as prompt in sending the letter down to the Project Office to be answered.

One night in an interview on the radio Russ had explained to a semi-technical interviewer the difficulty of designing supersonic aircraft and dealing with the aerodynamic effects of resultant shock waves. Suffice it to say that Russ was a (very good) structural engineer.

Over in a hotel in Wales a Canadian visitor had been listening intently, but with growing alarm, to this dissertation. At its conclusion he immediately put pen to paper to outline his considerable worries. For a few days the letter had languished in the pending tray until it was despatched down from the Olympian heights with an 'Answer this' instruction.

From the letter it was clear that the sender was seriously worried about the unknown effects of shock waves on the brains of the pilots. He thought that these waves, if not controlled properly, would cause the pilots to make random movements to the controls, thereby crashing the aircraft.

He was now in Wales advising the Water Board how to guide the salmon towards specially designed salmon leaps at the side of the electrical power installations. To do this he had researched the use of sending small pulses of electricity underwater across the river – his version of shock waves. At the end of his letter he said that he would delay his return to Canada in the hope that he could be of assistance.

A quick telephone call to the hotel ascertained that the writer had taken umbrage at not being contacted and had left in a huff that very morning, leaving no forwarding address.

The Punjab Cavalry

Several years BC (Before Concorde) India had been through the agony of partition, wherein those who were not of the right religious persuasion were encouraged to go elsewhere – or else!

In this era one of these newly designated countries was purchasing a fair-sized fleet of Bristol Freighters – this was a very functional aircraft consisting of a large elongated box with substantial wings, tailplane and pilots' cockpit on top. The wings supported two Bristol Hercules radial piston engines, from each of which depended the sturdy fixed landing gear. The one concession to streamlining was the rounded nose, which would open like a clamshell to admit the cargo, usually consisting of two cars (three in later versions) and their passengers or freight. A second version, the Wayfarer, was designed to carry around thirty passengers – corresponding to a British European Airways requirement (according to Russ who was our boss and had to be believed) that the aircraft should carry no more than thirty-two passengers, the capacity corresponding to that of the newly purchased airside passenger buses!

In their enthusiasm this foreign government had asked for alternative capability to be incorporated, versions which could carry bombs under the wings or a tethered field cannon inside the fuselage, pointing forward through a hole in the clamshell doors. The makers were reluctant to look into the possibility of these versions, although tests were actually made by dropping dummy bombs into the River Severn.

During the excesses of partition it was understood that these Freighters had been employed by being packed with 100 standing room passengers (the maximum permitted placarded design load was thirty-two seated, but what the hell?) in an effort to avoid bloodshed. An overloaded Freighter would bounce over the border to carry the human cargo to safety. The aircraft then stopped bouncing, the doors were opened and the passengers ordered out.

This exercise had left several impressions on one particular cavalry officer who had been assisting in the packing process. One was that the aircraft would have benefited from a larger wing to get it airborne, and a second was that there would have been fewer bounces if it had more thrust. His rational thoughts were expressed in a letter, together with a few suggested solutions. It was the solutions that took our attention.

If we could put another wing inside the existing one then, he suggested, using a system of wires and pulleys, the pilot could tell a re-mustered ground engineer to wind the inner wing out of the wing tip for take-off and wind it in again until it was needed for landing. Because of the helpful intent of this cavalry officer, and the fact that his employers had been good customers, it was difficult to work out how to let him down lightly. The main outer wing would have no room for supporting such a structure, nor would the fuel tanks in the inner wing have a happy life. Our response was to suggest larger flaps as an easier alternative.

The second suggestion was more difficult to deal with. For greater thrust he suggested that the ends of the engines' exhaust pipes could be opened out to give more 'push'. We doubted that solutions to 'Bernoulli's Equations for the Flow of Gasses' would have been on the curriculum of the Punjab School of Cavalry, so we let the apprentice have a go at explaining this one, assuming that his knowledge of aerodynamic theory would be closer to that of our 'helpful' officer.

The Mathematician

We knew it was impossible, but there it was in his letter, proven by detailed mathematical analysis.

The proposition was that if the outer skin of the Type 188 fuselage was profiled in a certain manner – a series of concentric waves extending around the periphery – then these profiles would produce thrust instead of wave drag at supersonic speeds. After about ten minutes' discussion we gave this one to the new graduate.

It took all of one afternoon and part of the next morning before he came walking quickly up the aisle between the desks with the 'eureka!' look on his face. Buried in one of the letter's inside pages was an equation wherein a plus sign should have been a minus and a figure 2 had been forgotten. All was well. Newton was not a charlatan.

The graduate had got himself a brownie point, but nearly lost it in persisting in wanting to try to explain it in mathematical detail to the top brass, from the initial letter had descended.

The Use of Parachutes

As the hopeful character's letter explained, he was sitting in the Cardiff Job Centre waiting for something to turn up when he suddenly had this idea, brought on by a recent TV programme on survival from crashed aircraft which inevitably followed the Concorde crash at Paris.

Why not divide the cabin into detachable sections, each of which was provided with its own parachute? When the pilot is in such a position that he thinks a crash is imminent he presses a button, which releases the sections and their respective parachutes.

This would be fine, assuming that the hostess trolleys have disc brakes and the passengers are strapped in and therefore not blown away as the front and rear of their section opens up. And that if they escape the effects of high temperature supersonically, the lack of a breathable atmosphere, or sub-zero subsonic temperatures, they should be safe. Unless of course they were too close to the ground, as it was well known by the cognoscenti that it did not matter what the pilot did in an aircraft, provided that he did not hit the ground whilst doing it.

The sensible solution, we concluded, was to put more effort into avoiding crash situations, not to make them any worse.

The Exhibitionist

The urge to pass on ideas was the same whether it was done by post or in person.

The Bristol 600 Exhibition, where the firm had taken up one of the stands on Durdham Down to show its contribution to the 600-year history of the city, proved an irresistible opportunity to one of the natives.

You could see it coming. Whereas the general motion of the crowd was a slow drift past, with an occasional slowing down to point at a particular exhibit, or to ask a question, this particular individual hovered in the background moving to and fro. He occasionally looked at a piece of paper that he was holding before looking again at the stand. Eventually he plucked up the courage and took a step nearer, but this time he had stepped into the flow of humanity and was guided out of sight. Within a few seconds he was back, but this time right against the stand, having moved up against the slower-moving human boundary layer. This time it was now or never, before his courage evaporated.

'I wonder if I could ask you a question?' he asked.

Not being sure if that was addressed to him or me I decided on the encouraging, 'Of course, Sir!' rather than the off-putting, 'That depends on you yourself, Sir.'

That was my first mistake.

He started on an explanation of how we could extend the range of Concorde to any distance we would care to choose by removing the engines and the fuel! Thoughts of supersonic gliders catapulted into the stratosphere or of perpetual motion machines dissipated rapidly as he continued to pile on the suspense. The engines would have to be replaced, of course (of course!), by grills similar to large honeycombs.

'No!' I thought, 'we can't use bees, however powerful, as we have not yet proven that the shock waves will not affect their sex life.' However, this train of thought was also wrong.

On the ground at suitable stations along the route, he suggested, we could place laser guns (this was getting dangerous!) which would be directed at, and follow, the honeycombs as the aircraft flew past, thereby heating these grills, which in turn would heat the incoming air, just like the engines now do.

It was pointed out to him that this type of technology was not quite with us yet, but this doubt was countered by a statement that there was an article in the magazine that he was holding that NASA were developing such guns to immobilise oncoming missiles.

Ah! Had he thought of what would happen if the aircraft hit a gust of wind? Its up-and-down motion would cause the gun to cut the wing off.

There was a second's silence whilst he consulted his notes and changed the subject. Had we thought of using hydrogen fuel instead of kerosene?

Yes we had, but the heavily pressurised cylindrical tanks that are required for liquid hydrogen do not fit easily into an aeroplane unless some of the passengers are removed and replaced by fuel tanks. 'By the way,' I said, 'have you read about the *Hindenburg*?'

'Yes, but…'

It was at this point that it dawned on me that his questions were all concerning propulsion and that the Rolls-Royce stand was next door.

'Rolls-Royce are the real experts on propulsion matters,' I said, looking for relief by speaking contrary to the traditional stance of an aircraftman's expressed opinion, 'and they would probably be able to give you a more authoritative opinion on your proposals.'

Somewhat reluctantly he moved away to begin another hovering approach on the R-R stand. By now it was lunchtime and, as I looked at their stand, I noticed that the representatives had departed to the hospitality tent, leaving an apprentice in charge. I felt sorry for him, but as I said to myself, duty done, it's lunchtime and my relief had arrived.

4

EARLY PASTORAL SCENES

On that particular Sunday, even before first light, the forces of occupation currently in possession of the partially derelict structures high up in the elm copse knew that their cause was not a just one.

The silence that usually heralds the dawn had been disturbed by an uneasy chuntering as they had tried to convince one another of the justice of their demand for *Lebensraum*. In the sloping field, which lay between the house and the copse, a small herd of bullocks, oblivious of the build-up in treetop tension but fully conscious of their own shortcomings, fattened themselves quietly in a munching procession, moving mindlessly from the unkempt hedge on the high side of the field towards the water trough on the lower boundary.

In hand with the pale dawn came the first of the rightful owners of last year's nests. Their numbers were few, such that the only course of action was to stand off at altitude in a holding pattern and exchange insults at long range. The chorus of rooks became a cacophony.

With the arrival of the second wave it was possible to take the offensive in more aggressive terms and the day began in earnest with discord in the treetops. After climbing to operational altitude the attackers descended in ragged formation, applying full power at the last minute to execute a series of screeching pull-ups just above treetop level.

Several repeats of this manoeuvre had the desired effect on one of the younger usurpers who, in a rising panic, applied emergency combat power and left the battle area in a prolonged dive.

In the house nearby, the owner rose wearily, stiff from Saturday's work on the new extension. Through the open dormer window the noise of the rooks had spoiled a promising dream.

'They must be Catholics or else they would still be in bed on a Sunday morning,' I mused as I peered out of the dormer window and looked across the field, in time to see one of the rooks detach itself from the war in the air.

With a sharp cry it dived towards the field, its wings partially retracted to give a higher speed potential. Sighting its landing area it started to turn on its final approach using control and guidance systems developed during a million-year programme, albeit at zero cost to the taxpayer. The wing-tip feathers adjusted to the optimum configuration for low-speed control. As the touchdown point approached, the trailing edge flaps were extended and the landing gear was lowered.

Its speed over the ground was reduced to zero by a short pull-up manoeuvre and the rook touched down lightly on a small tussock. It glared aggressively out of one good eye into the face of the leading bullock. Deadlock.

A second bullock, seemingly unaware of the niceties of international confrontation, ambled into the arena, its wet nose dripping a line of mucus onto the ground. The timely interruption provided the passive combatants with an excuse to unlock their gaze without either side losing face. The two animals butted each other lightly and resumed the fattening process, whereupon the rook, its spiritual batteries recharged, squawked derisively before climbing away at full boost towards the arguments in the branches of the elms.

Whilst the kettle boiled I paid the customary visit to the nearly completed room next door. If I was honest with myself I paid a visit at every opportunity. We were converting the original garage, which in its turn had been made as a lean-to by extending a roof from the surrounding blast wall to the wartime generating station (now the house). A large stone fireplace, made of stones dug from the garden, reached up to mahogany beams in the low ceiling. Wood panelling on the walls opposite surrounded a large picture window and reached round to the French windows at the end of the room.

The mahogany mantelpiece had been taken from the roof beams of the garage. During the war the crafty old farmer who owned the land had bought mahogany beams from bombed out churches in Bristol and had stored them in his barn. After the war he used them to convert the emergency generating station for the airfield into a small cottage – this one. Most of the beams in the house and garage were 6in by 2in mahogany cut from 6in by 6in church beams. Every wall was a blast wall. Thus the 8ft by 4ft window, which had been cut out of the garage wall to convert it into this living room, produced a massive amount of rubble. Hence the new terrace outside and so on. One job always led to another.

Through the French windows, beyond the patio, lawn and field, could be seen the copse of elm at the head of Brockley Coombe – the 'wooded valley of the badgers' as the Celts would have it. At the head of the Coombe was Lulsgate Bottom, the lowest section of the old Lulla's Yat, or the gate to Lulla's territory. I wondered what his reaction would be if the Old Chieftain could return to see the airfield now perched on the hill. He would probably be just as surprised as the crew of the German Junkers 88 bomber who were the first visitors to the new runway on this wartime airfield, after mistaking it for their own base at Lanveoc, near Brest. They were captured by the driver of a mechanical digger, parking in front of the aircraft.

A Ford Cortina GT in British Racing Green stood in front of my garage doors. It had been bought after reading of its performance in rallies all over the world.

'You too can own this car,' said the advertisement, showing a picture of the winner of the African Rally. From recent experience of the car's utter unreliability we had concluded that we had actually bought the one referred to in the picture, but only after it had completed several more rallies. Two days after taking delivery of the car I had had to depart in a hurry as usual to Toulouse and made the now familiar excuses over the telephone.

'I've got to go now. Will see you in a couple of days' time. Derek will deliver the car to the hospital.'

Derek Morriss duly arrived at the maternity hospital where Ann worked, followed by a colleague in his own car.

'Here it is,' he said, 'running beautifully.' Derek was a person who expected any new car to be free from fault and extraneous noise and insisted, no matter how many visits to the vendor it took, on getting what was expected. Why a man called Morriss expected Rolls-Royce performance from a Ford car I could never understand.

So it should be, Ann thought, since it was very expensive and only two days' old. On the way home she found that it ran easily, but on the drive into the hospital the next day it stuttered to a stop on the steeper stretch of the twisting Belmont Hill.

'Don't panic,' she instructed herself. 'It was OK yesterday. It must be your driving.' Slowly she restarted the car and struggled up the rest of the hill. Beyond that it was mainly downhill.

'Shall I call Derek or not?' she argued with herself. 'It was OK yesterday. Perhaps he will think that I'm too fussy.'

This state of affairs lasted for another day, with every sign of the engine expiring at every turn. On the third day she drove through the town in the rush hour to the airfield to meet the executive jet on its return from the milk-run to Toulouse. At the entrance gate the policeman gave instructions on how to get to the Rolls-Royce departure lounge. Unfortunately he left out the obvious bit (i.e. obvious to all those who worked there).

'Down the long hill, over the mini island, past the hangars, over the railway bridge and turn left near the Fire Station,' she repeated to herself. Obeying these instructions to the letter she finally turned left onto a very wide road.

'No sign of the Fire Station, but this is a very big works, it's probably some distance on,' she thought to herself.

In no time at all a Land Rover with a flashing light came up rapidly from behind, swung past, and came to a stop in front. The driver jumped out and ran back.

'What the hell are you doing?' he demanded.

'Trying to find the Fire Station,' Ann replied.

'Well you won't find it here! This is the bloody runway! Turn round and follow me!'

'I thought it looked a bit wide,' she reasoned.

She was right – it was built for the Bristol Brabazon and was about twice as wide as London's Heathrow. The Land Rover, sporting an illuminated 'Follow Me' sign, turned off the runway and pulled up beside two large fire engines.

'Now park here,' she was told. 'AND DON'T MOVE!'

After a short time the Hawker Siddeley HS 125 business jet arrived. Immigration and Customs formalities were completed and the passengers loaded themselves into their respective cars.

'Hello, love. Everything OK?' I asked.

As soon as the engine of the Cortina was started it was clear that all was not OK. Apart from the irregular running of the engine itself, the distinctive 'crack' of a healthy spark could be heard. The bonnet was opened quickly and it became clear that an ignition lead had come adrift from one of the spark plugs.

'So it wasn't me at all,' Ann mused.

So began a history of one of Ford's Friday-afternooners. On a memorable visit to meet a Ford representative, who had driven all the way from Dagenham to drive the car and see what all the fuss was about, the car was obviously embarrassed by its history of disasters and wished to be incognito when it met its Maker. The number plate fell off on my way to the dealer's premises.

'Sir,' said the representative, getting his pre-emptive strike in first. 'Did you know that you are motoring illegally?'

He nearly received the offending plate between the eyebrows. This was the week after the alternator support had cracked through and the belt had pulled the alternator into the fan. The latter had no option but to go through the radiator. This incident was only a few days after the car had refused to start and, in heavy rain, I had to ask Ann to come out to push. Going down the hill from the house the engine had finally coughed and started. Through the open window I shouted a 'thank you', not wanting to stop. However, I had to stop to put my raincoat on as the window refused to wind up.

As the representative drove the car forcefully down the Portway beside the River Avon to demonstrate that the problems lay with Ford owners and not with their cars, I told him to brake hard but said nothing else. The man braked as forcefully as he had driven. The car rose 6in in the air and threw its wheels at the ground. The river appeared briefly through the front windscreen before the car met its rightful piece of road. The slow drive back to the Temple Meads Garage was completed in absolute silence.

A month later the gearbox seized solid on the narrow, wet road leading down the Coombe. Skid practice at the Police Driving School, organised by the BAC Motor Club, came in very useful.

A letter to the Managing Director of Ford, England, had produced a response from the Publicity Director, who apparently judged the consumption of four gearboxes, three clutches, two halfshafts and two differentials in eighteen months, plus innumerable other faults, as being close to the norm.

'Sir, we note that the car is a 1963 model,' he apologised. It was obviously a bad vintage.

It was during the many return visits to the vendors that the sales manager, newly recruited from Steeles Car Sales down the road, joined the group discussing the latest GT fault. The foreman outlined the car's history to the newcomer. Whilst this was in progress, an assistant salesman leaned out of the office and announced that he had just persuaded a customer to get his new Cortina from here and not to go back to Steeles.

'What is his name?' he was asked.

'Morriss,' said the assistant salesman.

The new sales manager blanched.

'Not D … P … Morriss?' he said with emphasis on every syllable.

'Yes!'

He walked away quickly, muttering, 'I resign! I resign!', having recognised the very perfectionist who had delivered the GT to Ann.

Behind the Cortina, in the garage, stood a pale cream Morgan 4/4 which in reality belonged to my brother. The bodywork, suffering from the combined effects of dry rot, wet rot and woodworm had been rebuilt by brother Pat and myself last year, following a telephone appeal to 'Come up to home, (near Burton-on-Trent) to help him to finish it off, as he was planning to drive it to Spain on the following Monday, for a holiday with his girlfriend. It was then Friday.

On getting 'home' it was clear that the possibility of completing the job by Monday was a little optimistic: the only things on the chassis were the engine, transmission, steering bulkhead and wheels. The body frame was ash, but had to be cut from the lengths propped against the wall.

My brother Pat left on holiday on the Tuesday, driving the car. The Morgan Works would have been proud of us. They would have been even more proud if they had learnt that, during the same holiday, he had managed the final traverse over the Pyrenees on a supplement of a gallon of Spanish brandy – petrol stations being few and far between. It was almost as cheap as using petrol anyway. Now it was my turn to rebuild the Morgan's hotted-up Ford 100E engine, which had laid a smokescreen on the road after a piston disintegrated. Its many separate parts stood on the work bench.

At the far end of the garage, standing like rows of Chinese irregulars within the confines of the Forbidden City, young marigolds waited patiently for their release from the tray resting on the workbench. Two-year old Michael, at knee height, wanted to 'Help Daddy', and wasn't to be deflected from this aim. So I chose the marigolds as a diversion.

The process of digging out the tendrils of buttercup, interlaced with twitch grass, was a long process – hampered only by the persistent efforts of young Michael trying to reset the shoots in freshly dug ground.

'Throw all these bits of grass and weeds over the hedge into the field,' I said. 'No! NOT the marigolds!'

Eventually the flowerbed was ready for planting and the process of dibbing the holes and introducing the individual plants to their new homes began.

'Bring me a flower please,' I asked Michael.

The head of the flower arrived, held in a grubby fist.

'Come off,' he said in explanation.

The edges of his small mouth turned down and the blue eyes became moist. A noble compromise might avoid the storm, otherwise the all too familiar roar of his crying, akin to the sound of an Olympus with reheat, would rival the jets approaching the nearby airport.

'Daddy will divide them up, and you can bring them along in your bucket,' I explained patiently.

The initial sprint to the garage to get his small bucket was foiled by the gravel surface of the patio. As he fell flat on his ample stomach the roar started, cutting short an instant admonition to slow down. Young hands, scoured with gravel, were rubbed hard against father's trousers to mask any small pain. Then off he went, at the same rate as before, leaving an aggrieved parent telling no one in particular to 'slow down'. For some time afterwards the work proceeded smoothly, or nearly so.

'One more please,' I said.

'More' duly arrived and the process began anew. After the second expedition for 'more' a grain of suspicion grew out of the fact that the soil around the roots was of two colours. Still in a bending position, I looked behind to see the trowel being carefully inserted under a plant at the far end of the row and the young shoot put into his bucket.

It was time to give up.

'No more,' I told him. 'I'm going to mend the Morgan.'

Leaving the trowel and fork in the box recently vacated by the marigolds I wandered stiffly towards the garage. The garage was a large lean-to that we had built ourselves immediately after moving in. The foundations had to be cut through the tarmac surrounding that side of the house. When the tarmac became thicker than the concrete that was supposed to replace it, digging stopped and the blocks were laid on top.

It was during this period that the neighbour over the road in 'Green Tiles', a beautifully designed house with a steeply pitched roof, had been seen to be taking a keen interest. After a while he came across to introduce himself.

'I was very interested to see the drawings that you submitted for planning permission,' he said. 'They were well drawn.'

'Thank you,' I replied. 'But I'm surprised that you would take such a detailed interest!'

'I have to,' he said. 'I'm the Local District Surveyor! – I suppose that I had better sign up the Chit for approval of these foundations before anyone from the office comes round. Anyway, the tarmac is over two feet thick so it should be OK. Unorthodox but adequate!'

After that meeting he became good friends of the family, until a year later when he was taken flying to cure his fear of that activity. The cure was not a success.

For several days before the flight, my neighbour's young family had been winding him up with questions about the lack of a parachute, what to eat immediately before, and had he made a will? In consequence, when it was time to take his seat in the Auster beside his new neighbour, who was in the pilot's seat, his nerves were visibly twanging. The situation was made worse when the engine refused to start. These were the days of 'Switches off, suck in', whereupon the person swinging the propeller (in this particular case the diminutive flying instructor) gave it a few swings to suck the air/fuel mixture into the cylinders. As the instructor was not very tall, nor muscular, the swings were minimal, but usually adequate.

'Switches on. Contact!' I called out.

The propeller kicked over for a quarter of a revolution, the engine coughed in the wrong place … and then kicked back. No joy. The process was repeated several times with the odd insertion of a 'Switches off!' reverse swing to blow out any accumulation of unwanted excess fuel. Eventually we were rewarded with a healthy cough followed by a clattering roar as the engine picked up. The instructor tottered aside and staggered off to the clubhouse for refreshment.

After a wait to allow the engine to warm up properly I increased power to taxi the long distance to the take-off point. There we carried out the pre-take-off checks. By the time these were complete we had been in the aircraft for about twenty minutes, with the tension gradually building up in the passenger's seat.

'Close the window in the door on your side please,' I said.

The passenger raised his hand and pushed the catch forward. That was all that went forward, the catch had come off in his hand. Without a word he put the catch in my lap, with some difficulty opened the door against the propeller wash, and got out. He then walked to the nearby boundary fence, climbed over and set off home. However, that episode in our relationship was yet to come.

On a low, sturdy wooden box at the end of the garage by the window stood the bare crankcase and the many parts of the Morgan engine – a Ford 100E sidevalve engine with an Aquaplane head, ideal for pulling the sports car up muddy hills on trials. Maybe if I got it together it could take part in the Works Motor Club events. It might be possible if it wasn't for the family, the unfinished house, and my work on the Bristol Type 188 all steel research aircraft, and the new Supersonic Transport Aircraft.

Under the bench was a disassembled 1923 Levis two-stroke motorbike that I used to ride occasionally to college. I had bought this for ten shillings from my uncle after discovering it buried up to its rims in the earth floor of his garage. It had rested there for sixteen years, but after filling the carburettor with petrol the engine started on the first push. My uncle had foregone the ten shillings on finding that it was my birthday the following week. Maybe I could start work on it next year? (The rebuild started forty-two years later and is still waiting to be finished.)

The working parts of the Morgan engine had been cleaned and were standing in their proper order of assembly. Two years of working on aircraft engines in the RAF had instilled into my mind a rigid discipline of cleanliness during maintenance and my thoughts went back to Griffons in Spitfires, Merlins in Hurricanes and Lancasters, Gypsies in Tiger Moths and Centaurus in Tempest II.

The main cylinder block rested on the box in front of the bench, camshaft and crankshaft already in place. The newly ground surfaces had been lightly oiled and gave off the characteristic greeny-blue sheen. They had a pleasant feel under my exploratory fingertips. No grit, no burrs, no excuse for not starting.

Pistons, con-rods, shells and big ends were oiled, replaced, and carefully tightened and locked in position. From outside the garage came the 'Brmm Brmm Brmm' of the young Stirling Moss (who was the foremost racing driver of those days) pedalling a noisy toy car around the gravel paths and driveways. The tightness of the fit of each component was checked at each stage to ensure that the new components matched the re-ground surfaces. Beautiful – now for the timing gear.

A frown of annoyance passed under my receding hairline. The timing sprocket, which had been on the crankshaft when it was sent away, was now not there. The label, which had been attached and now lay on the floor, said 'Mr Talbot. 100E', so I had picked up the right one, but obviously the part had been removed before the grinding process and I had not noticed that it had not been replaced.

Revisions to the SST's intake, suggested by the French against everyone's better judgement (except that of the Boss) had been on my mind when I had made a last minute dash to collect the disassembled engine. Blast it again!

Without this component the assembly process could progress no further and so the partially assembled engine with the four cylinders exposed was left standing on the box, its smooth grey oiled surfaces picking up green and blue highlights in the morning light.

'Coffee!' called Ann's voice from the kitchen.

'It's about time,' I thought.

We had a cup of coffee and thought things over. Side-stepping the low-slung flurry of arms and legs, which had been activated by thoughts of food and drink, I walked to the back door with Michael, shouting 'Boots off!'

To me the coffee and biscuits were very welcome after the morning's exertions and frustration. To my son, it appeared to be no more than a continuation of the stuffing process. The smells wafting from the kitchen promised another culinary triumph for the midday Sunday meal.

Following the refuelling process two pairs of gumboots were fitted to two pairs of feet in double-quick time, but the getaway was foiled by the fact that the smaller pair were on the wrong feet.

For the next twenty minutes nothing disturbed the digging. Peace had been declared in the elms and the erstwhile combatants were practising glides, turns and power-off approaches, oblivious to the undercurrent of menace to some other small family unit contained in the distant call of a cuckoo.

'Look, Daddy, garden!'

My son's voice appeared to come from the garage.

Putting down the fork I walked round to the entrance. Everything was just as before, but more had been added. Each open cylinder of the Morgan engine had been filled with a mixture of building sand and soil, as had the valve chest. Soil had been packed in and watered so that it must by now be inside the intricate labyrinth of oil-ways that wended their tortuous way through the walls of the casting. Three tufts of twitch grass and groundsel stuck out of the soil in an exhausted fashion and showed no signs of being revived by the generous dose of water that was being poured over them.

'Why did you smack him?' Ann asked.

A shaking finger pointed at the residue of mud and distressed weeds.

'How else am I supposed to teach him not to do things like this?' I replied.

'Keep an eye on him, of course!'

Ann inspected the mess. 'You can rinse it out, can't you?'

Some questions just cannot be answered. Seeing that this approach was not likely to spread the soothing balm as intended, she changed tack.

'What did he use to carry the water in?'

'That saucepan over there, under the car.'

'No! That's my milk pan! Just wait until I find him!'

In later life it was almost impossible to get Michael to do any gardening, no matter how big the bribe or the threat. However, in hindsight this was probably pre-ordained as, in the RAF, he did take to the maintenance of aero engines.

5

ENTER THE POWER PLANT

When the British and French first came together to design a supersonic transport, as described by Kenneth Owen* and Sir Archibald Russell,** there were two similar aircraft proposals, but different in one significant respect. The Brits put forward a six-engined long-range proposal – Europe to USA. The French proposal was for a four-engined medium-range aircraft. A two-for-one compromise was reached with two four-engined aircraft of reduced capacity. The structural difference now lay mainly in the provision of fuel tankage for the two variants. This difference may help you to realise why the crews of the eventual version had to fly with the thirteen fuel tanks labelled one to eleven. Tanks 5a and 7a completed the set on the long-range version.

Gradually the French medium-range version fell by the wayside following the decision that it would not be allowed to fly supersonic over inhabited areas, but we were very glad that the French engineers (and their politicians!) stayed the course to help with the design and construction of the British version of Concorde. It was too late in the design to revert to the original six-engine proposal in order to make, say, Frankfurt to Washington a feasible proposition, and so Paris to Washington became the limit.

The design and build of Concorde was divided between the two countries. The Brits got most of the non-conventional bits – the flight deck and the droop nose; the electrics; the fuel system and the power plants, amongst others. It was the emerging technology of the latter which caused the most difficulty and became the principal concern of this particular group.

In all this activity the brilliant contribution of the Bristol Siddeley Olympus engine and its design and development teams must not be forgotten

* *Concorde: New Shape in the Sky*, Kenneth Owen (HMSO, 1982)
** *A Span of Wings: An Autobiography*, Sir Archibald Russell (Airlife Publishing Ltd, 1992)

(even though we did not offer that praise at the time!). This part of the story is described in detail by Sir Stanley Hooker.*

It was very convenient having the aircraft power plant and engine teams located only a runway apart, us at Filton, Bristol, and the other team at Patchway, Bristol.

A TECHNIBIT

Power plants are known as engines to most travellers, but in the case of this aircraft there is a lot more. A complex variable air intake, a complex two-spool engine with a reheat system, a complex convergent, divergent nozzle and nearly a ton of associated control systems *all* working together at or near their peak of efficiency in harmony with the aircraft, the pilot and the atmosphere under *all* conditions, at *all* times (*almost*!). If the harmony broke down there could be a hell of a series of heart-stopping repetitive bangs (surges) from one, two or all of the engines – which would be very bad for customer relations.

In 'cruise' the incoming air passes from intake entry to engine face in one hundredth of a second, losing nearly 1,000mph on the way and increasing its pressure fivefold, thereby delivering 75 per cent of the power plants' total thrust (a Rolls-Royce figure – not mine).

It is essential to appreciate that, in order to achieve a satisfactory performance, both engine, intake and variable exit nozzle are operating close to the narrow peaks of their efficiencies and the margins were small. The intake control system is having to hold the leading shocks just forward of the cowl lip in cruise for optimum drag, airflow stability and efficiency purposes.

Surges occur when either the innards of the engine fail or the intake fails to supply a sufficient amount and/or distribution of air to satisfy the engine demands. The intense internal pressures are released and coughed forward many times per second. In consequence the intakes are built like battleships.

At the start of this barrage the operating lane controlling the air intake has to sense the incipient failure using engine compressor speed as the indicator and take the appropriate action to spill the unwanted air in order to minimise the effect on the aircraft. In addition, should that control lane fail in the process, the second control lane has to take over immediately and finish the action.

However, at speeds above Mach 1.6 it was impossible to ensure that the disturbed airflow in front of the adjacent engine does not cause that engine to surge in sympathy. The result was that the Concorde was certified aerodynamically as a twin-engine aircraft above Mach 1.6.

* *Not Much of an Engineer*, Sir Stanley Hooker (Airlife Publishing Ltd, 1991)

Remember, this is 1960s technology applied for the first time to a civil aircraft. Laptops and mobiles were only in the inventors' minds' eyes or sketched on their drawing boards – and Concorde was drawn in pencil on bigger boards. Calculations were carried out using mainly 6in and 12in slide rules and electro/mechanical adding machines.

6

GRAMMAR IN SEVERAL LANGUAGES

The first formal meeting of British and French technical minds brought together to discuss the virtually uncharted fields of supersonic power plants for long-range civil aircraft took place in the Grand Hotel, Paris. Twenty or so experts in their respective fields had been brought together to share any relevant (and in some cases, irrelevant) knowledge.

In such a gathering it was essential that someone would take charge so that there would be a recognisable end product. In the minds of everyone present there was no doubt that only one person in this august gathering could give instructions that would be accepted with the minimum of dissent on both sides, and that person was Pierre Young, the Chief Engineer Olympus from Bristol Siddeley (now Rolls-Royce) at Patchway, Bristol. There were two telling reasons. The first was that he understood the subject and was prepared to learn more. As these people were not politicians, this specification was accepted. The second reason, more telling than the first, was his fluent command of French and English, both good and bad. If there is any factor that can produce instant recognition and respect in a gathering of engineers it is the facility to swear in more than one language.

His introductory speech in two languages suggested that no useful progress would emerge from such a large gathering and that it would be more beneficial to break up into small groups to discuss separate technical items. Such foresight was greeted with enthusiasm, until the point was reached where the groups had been nominated and had gathered into clusters, preparatory to being directed to their separate rooms. Apart from Pierre, few, if any at that time, spoke a second language with any facility. Technical translators capable of coping with this new, and thus far immature, technology were few and far between, and not present. In the early stages of the project there had been no time to revise old school lessons. Mr Young's presence was requested by almost every group leader. The response was always the same. 'Not me,' said Pierre. 'I have my own meeting to attend.'

I had made an attempt myself to have the use of Pierre's services. The response was the same, but with the additional comment: 'Your French was good enough to order three beers last night – try it out on the instability of plug nozzles!'

I looked at Pierre, and then at my two new colleagues. There was no need to know their names to realise that they were foreigners; they were sallow-faced and taciturn. They smiled weakly at one another. Sallowface shrugged and so did I. Taciturn studied his hands whilst Pierre addressed him in French. Pierre's face looked slightly puzzled as he replied.

'I'm sure you'll manage,' said Pierre, moving quickly away to join his own meeting.

Clearly there would be no help from that direction. All three of us shrugged again in unison. Here was the first indication that a common line of contact could be established without words.

In a sombre dark-green room, seated at a rickety table, the more sallow-faced of the two specialists started to talk in what was taken to be French. Gradually it was possible to pick up the odd word, but not the sense of their speech until I realised that the speaker was saying that neither of them spoke English. My mind went back to lessons painfully learnt and quickly forgotten sixteen years before at my grammar school, which nestled under the shadow of the castle at Ashby-de-la-Zouch. I offered a silent prayer to the image of the rotund, bespectacled French master, whose name was Sammy: 'Sammy, help me.'

As if the prayer was answered, Sammy's words came back from the distant past: 'Don't *tell* me, lad, write it down in your exercise book!'

That's what was needed – paper! Sheets of it.

The standard pad of BAC paper worked its miracle. Sallowface sensed that he had been getting nowhere with his explanations and produced a pencil with which he sketched the details of a jet engine. He then named each item in French, writing each name on the sheet and carefully repeating the word, waiting for a nod of understanding before proceeding to the next. When he had completed the labelling he handed the pencil across the table. His hands shook slightly all the time and it appeared that he was of a nervous disposition. Taking the pencil I wrote the English equivalent under each word at the same time as saying it out loud (this being the correct way to address foreigners). Having finished, the pencil was handed back to its owner, who nodded his approval and smiled at his companion, a rather sombre individual who nevertheless had followed each move with the greatest interest. This sheet of paper was then laid between the two parties so that we could refer to it in whatever discussions might follow. They then proceeded to write the symbols for pressure, temperature, density and speed of the gases as they flowed through the various parts of the engine towards the nozzle exit. Again this sheet of paper became a reference item. Several more sheets were produced.

The atmosphere in the room had changed. It became apparent that there was a will on both sides to succeed in exchanging as much information as possible in order to assess the background and ability of each other's organisation. The language of mathematics was common to all – this had been realised days before when I asked the technical library at Filton for a Japanese report. Everything was in Japanese symbols except for an 'e^x' in the middle of the first page.

Sallowface raised a smile, which completely transformed his features. He spoke rapidly to his colleague – in German!

So that was it! The names should have given some indication, although there are a lot of Germanic names in France, particularly in Alsace. These two men were Germans who had been brought to France after the war. Their wartime technology had advanced faster than that of the Allies and, even with less advanced materials being available, had produced remarkable technological results. With some of their colleagues from Junkers, Bramo Fafnir, Daimler-Benz, BMW and others, they had formed the technical nucleus of the embryonic French jet engine industry. Others had gone more willingly to America. They had gone less willingly, but in greater numbers, to Russia to perform a similar function in those countries (the main German aircraft factories were relocated in the East in an effort to avoid the bombing).

It was now clear why the French spoken by these two gentlemen sounded significantly different to the two-thirds-forgotten pronunciation battered into us by dear old Sammy some sixteen years – or was it sixty years – or so before. Here was a new factor, which the school and college text books had not considered and which explained Pierre Young's final remark before he left to go to his own meeting. One year of conversational German at night school, again mostly forgotten, was not much use to me any more than my minimal French, but nevertheless it broadened the communal vocabulary. However, it was not possible to carry out a long conversation using 'Ja!', 'Nein!' and 'Was ist Das?' My previous year's Italian night class, pursued with the intent of finding out what Maria Callas was singing about, did not take the explanations much further either.

Nevertheless, the determination to communicate, which existed on both sides, carried the discussion along at a furious pace, especially when a waiter, bringing mid-morning beer, appeared through the door, apologising for lack of coffee, which had not been ordered in sufficient quantity. Pages of notepaper were filled with drawings, graphs, equations and words.

Vaguely remembered tenses were of little use and so the question of whether a test had been done, was being done or will be done in the future, was settled quite quickly by a raised eyebrow. This was the signal for a smidgeon of Pidgin hit-or-miss Latin to creep in – *factus est, sumus, serat* – sometimes negated by 'non' or the thumbs down.

By the end of the day all three of us were both elated and exhausted. Sallowface had blossomed and Taciturn was smiling as he reported the results of our discussion to the combined session held in the late afternoon. Pierre translated with some difficulty.

'I don't know how you managed,' said Pierre as the Filton party left for the hotel. 'His French was bloody awful!'

'That was nothing compared with his Latin,' I agreed. 'He had no idea what the Roman phrase for "instability of plug nozzles" is!'

The creases in Pierre's face deepened further into crevasses as he smiled.

'They were great engineers, those Romans, so I suppose that they had a word for it, although I can't think of it at this moment!'

In the evening following that memorable first day, the BAe group was wondering how to tackle the cafés of Paris for a meal when the representative of Franco-Britannique, the engine company's agents in Paris, arrived to announce that he would take the party out to dinner and show them Paris. We made the mistake of accepting his offer of a lift in his car instead of going by taxi. Monsieur H, it turned out, was an ex-rally driver who took delight in telling tales of his exploits and demonstrating his techniques as he drove through the Paris traffic.

In those days Paris drivers were allowed to sound their horns at any time, there were no restrictions as there are now. Mr H appeared to have a very simple rule: when he was in the car he sounded the horn. To do this he used hands, splayed fingers, wrists, forearm or elbow to produce a long continuous note on a horn whose Gallic tone encouraged stray dogs, cats and pedestrians to move bodily aside. The remaining parts of his anatomy played rapid symphonies on the gear lever, accelerator, clutch (except where demonstrating clutch-less changes), lights, brakes, and cigarette lighter, as he weaved in and out of the 'circulation'.

His most impressive demonstration was one that reduced us all to a white silence. It was a tour of the Etoile, around the Arc de Triomphe. Here he demonstrated the art of demanding the current rule of priority over the traffic approaching from the left (*priorité-a-droite*) by driving in a series of straight lines until he came close to apprehensive pedestrians on the opposite pavement, and then turning sharply through a right angle on the handbrake to continue across the oncoming traffic around the monument. This technique allowed us to observe that most of the other drivers enthusiastically used their car horns, following Mr H's example, whilst using their non-horn-blaring hands for signifying disapproval.

All at once there was a squeal of brakes and then a silence. Mr H had got out.

Our shattered nerves revived enough to allow us to realise that we had arrived at the restaurant of his choice and that he was standing on the pavement beckoning us all to alight. As we extricated ourselves one by one from the compacted mass on the rear seat and emerged into the gloom, we could not help but notice that we were in one of the more disreputable areas behind Les Halles, the French equivalent of Covent Garden. Rain clouds were beginning to gather above us and we all shuddered at the thought of a return journey on wet cobblestones at Monte-Carlo-Rally speeds, chauffeured by a driver who, by then, would have dined well.

'*Le voilà*!' announced Mr H, giving a gesture that would have been well received in any music hall.

High up on the corner building the standard blue-and-white street sign, covered by the dust of ages past, indicated that our party stood in the Rue Bachaumont. We looked at the dilapidated exterior of the restaurant with the sign hanging above the door, which told all who were ignorant of the fact that they were before the portals of the restaurant 'Aux Crus de Bourgogne'.

De Gaulle had not yet arrived to lead the French recovery with his edict of 'clean up or be cleaned up' and so the exterior of all French buildings were still suffering from a tax system which appraised a person's wealth by assessing the appearance of the outside of their property. In true Gallic response to this approach most of the houses and less important shops, no matter how exotic they were on the inside, had poverty-stricken exteriors.

With some trepidation, we filed in one by one behind Mr H. Inside the scene was transformed and could have come from any Renoir painting. There were small, thin-legged square tables covered in red checked cloths, with paper squares on top, stood on a shining black-and-white marble floor. The tables were tightly packed together, affording any man an excuse to rub shoulders, or whatever he fancied, with any lady sitting at the next table, and something he could do at the same time as rubbing knees with his companion. A few ferns stood in pots on high stands in the corners formed by the walls and the waist-high divisions around the room. At the left of the entrance was a marble-topped bar behind which stood a dark-haired woman with a very pale face. She was in the act of dispensing drinks to an ill-matched pair who had arrived just before our driver had stopped outside, sounding his horn. At the end of the bar was the entrance to the kitchens, from where we could hear a clatter of pans, plates and tongues. Where they could be seen, the walls in the main body of the restaurant were a sombre red; otherwise they were hidden by gold-rimmed mirrors and cupboards. One thing that we later discovered to be a good omen was that most of the diners appeared to be locals. However, as far as we could see there were no unoccupied tables.

'Messieurs?'

We looked at the striking woman who had addressed us. She was just over 5ft tall and the same size wide, dressed in a short-sleeved plain black dress, with no stockings and black sandals. The set of her jaw indicated strength while her black eyes gave a suggestion of past hardship coupled with a sense of humour. Well-rounded, muscular arms supported an ample bosum, while her curly hair was black.

'Messieurs?' she said again as we parted to let Mr H through.

'Madame,' he said in French, 'I salute you and your beauty.'

Madame's eyes narrowed as her cheeks lifted in a broad smile. A brawny arm relaxed from its supporting role and gave him a playful punch. He staggered slightly as the hidden force of the blow registered on his slight frame and he masked any suggestion of pain with a smile.

'The table for six?' he said, raising his eyebrows and looking around the room, indicating that every table was full.

Other diners were beginning to take note and look at one another with conspiratorial amusement. Waggling fingers and nods appeared to highlight our difficult predicament. At this point each member of our party was anticipating a return to the car prior to enduring another lap of the 'race' to some other establishment. Perhaps a better alternative, we considered, might be to go hungry until tomorrow. A slightly more appealing prospect was to walk to the nearest French equivalent of a fish and chip shop.

'A votre service,' said Madame, indicating a spot across the small restaurant that was protected by a sea of diners.

We looked surprised. So did Mr H. So did the other diners.

'L'armoire?' said Mr H in bemusement.

We looked more surprised and so did everyone else.

The *cupboard*?

Madame waded between the diners at their tables in a manner reminiscent of Humphrey Bogart wandering up to his waist in swamp, towing the *African Queen* behind him (in the film of that name). Just like that determined vessel, our party followed, pushing close in case the human swamp through which we were passing closed in on us and blocked the way. In a small clearing before two large doors, Madame stopped and opened these wide, pushing some seated diners towards their soups until the doors were fully open. Inside the cupboard was a narrow table, which occupied the full width. On the far side one could see the tops of three chairs.

'*Voilà*!' said Madame in the manner of a conjurer producing the rabbit.

'Alphonse! Trois chaises!' she called out, using the same hand with which she had indicated the table to snap her finger and thumb in the direction of a small, bent, balding gentleman, who was surrounded on three sides by a large apron, which was at that minute emerging from the kitchen, attached to Alphonse. This man, showing a remarkable turn of speed and strength, brought two chairs held shoulder high, each grasped by a leg. He then returned for the other. Diners ducked low as he passed by, but Alphonse had obviously done his party trick before and tut-tutted at each guest in turn for showing such a lack of confidence in his abilities.

Hats and coats were handed over and three of our number inched carefully into the cupboard past one corner of the table, whilst the other three of us sat down in a line on the outside. There was a round of applause from our 'audience'. Madame bowed and Mr H, wishing to re-establish command, asked what his guests would like to eat. The response was immediate – but it came from Madame, not from any of us:

'Langouste et Coq au Vin!'

Her swift glance round the table defied argument, but Mr H tried, bless him, but to no avail. Twenty seconds later he compromised on Langouste et Coq au Vin pour tous.

Many years later that lobster and chicken in wine remain amongst my treasured memoirs; the lobster by virtue of its succulent freshness and the coq au vin because of its 100 per cent-proof alcohol gravy.

Our lubrication started with an introduction to Kir, a white wine and blackcurrant liquor aperitif, followed by a leisurely stroll through white and red wines accompanying the various dishes until we arrived at plum brandy with the coffee and *l'addition.*

Mr H had insisted on a bill to pacify his masters, Franco-Britannique, whereas Madame was rather reluctant, as she apparently had no respect for paperwork (and also possibly for the taxman). However, she totted up the meal on the paper sheet covering the red tartan tablecloth and, tearing this section off, handed it over. His argument about the authenticity of this document was cut short when Madame produced a large rubber stamp from the depths of her cash desk and stamped the piece of paper with force that started a peal of Grandsire Triples from the glasses on the counter which stopped Mr H in mid protest.

For the remainder of the Concorde activity in Paris, 'Madame's' became the venue for an evening meal of quality for the Aerodynamics and Power Plant departments. In their turn the firm's accountants had to be satisfied with expense forms supported by evidence from torn-off bits of paper tablecloth authenticated by illegible rubber stamps.

Honour and the accountant being satisfied, the party was offered another round of plum brandies on the house and, with handshakes all round, staff and diners included, we weaved an unsteady way out to the car. As we moved through the doorway in somewhat wavy single file the last man raised a hand and said, 'Coats!'

To a man the procession wheeled on its heels to re-enter the hostelry, only to be faced with a pile of coats, supported by the bandy legs of Alphonse, who was weaving his way to the entrance.

'Ze Crazy 'orse,' said Mr H, with a dramatic but slightly slurred gesture.

'Surely you mean clothes horse?' said one man, looking at Alphonse.

'Non, non ze nightclub "Crazy 'orse Saloon" is our next 'aven of call!' he replied.

'He means "port",' said another.

'Good idea!' said a third, heading towards the bar.

But at that moment, almost in unison, our befuddled minds experienced a glow of recognition. There were slightly confused memories of the article on nightclubs in the *British European Airways Magazine*, which we'd read with relish on the flight from London. Each face indicated understanding.

The line wheeled out again, the last man patting Alphonse on the head in a 'thank you' gesture. We poured ourselves into the car whilst smothering the protests made by Yeo, a practicing Methodist, who thought that he ought not to approve of any near-sinful pursuits. The horn sounded as the car pulled away, but the thoughts of getting closer to the realities of the flesh which had been seen exposed on those airline photographs acted as balm to the agony of being driven across Paris again by a well-lubricated Frenchman. Fingers were tightly crossed and those who had had no time to commune with nature crossed their legs – both actions performed so as to avoid any accidents.

Our arrival at the Crazy Horse Saloon created no greater stir than that caused by the arrival of any well-dined bunch who had arrived late and who could not take their eyes off the barest of attributes being demonstrated by the sensuous body on a hammock on stage. While we were being ushered through a packed audience to our seats at a very small table in the inadequately lit auditorium, our progress was punctuated by our apologies and some whispered 'Shhh!' responses; two of our reserved stools had been requisitioned by members of other parties.

For most of the group this was their first experience of French nights in the flesh, so to speak. Silent appreciation (punctuated by the occasionally whispered 'Cor!') spoke volumes for a series of spectacles that should be sensed and experienced, rather than written about. Even our disapproving Methodist Yeo was now silent.

As in mathematics, it seemed that appreciation of beauty was the same in any language.

7

TWO WRONGS EVENTUALLY RIGHTED

The big meeting to decide the shape of the Concorde air intake to the engines was to take place the next day. Work had been going on for months in the wind tunnels on both sides of the Channel with the objective of selecting the optimum design. The French had concentrated their efforts on a two-dimensional model to look at shock wave location and to achieve the highest efficiency possible with this configuration. This they had achieved, but with a profile on the outside which it was thought would give a high drag resistance. The Brits on the other hand had done more work to develop a compromise geometry on three-dimensional models that gave a lower efficiency, but with a lower external resistance.

As in all these early decision assemblies there was to be an over-attended meeting of engineers, project directors, Ministry officials, and others from both countries, who had to make a decision on which one to use. The Brits went there to discuss matters, whereas the French had already decided.

A preliminary meeting of the British designers and their Ministry counterparts was to be held that evening in the designers' hotel, always assuming that they would be able to arrive in France.

Their non-arrival was a real possibility because most of the south-west of England was fogbound, except for the airport where I and the other design engineer were waiting with our wives. The wives were looking forward to a day in Paris. The men were not. Bristol's Lulsgate airport, standing on top of the hill, facing towards the Atlantic, had a habit of sticking its head into cloud when all the airports serving it were clear or, alternatively, standing out in the clear when the others were fogbound. In either case no aircraft came in or went out. The site had been chosen during the war as a base for pilots who were training to fly in foggy conditions. The first aircraft to land on its new wartime runway was the Junkers Ju 88, which had got lost.

This day, however, was one of the clear days when the uninitiated would be demanding to know why nothing was happening in this gorgeous weather. The receptionists would be patiently replying that the aircraft was fogbound in Cardiff and would then be asked why the pilots could not bring the aircraft over to Lulsgate and start from there. The patience of these women was remarkable.

Eventually, about three hours late, the aeroplane came in from Cardiff to take us to Le Bourget. Urgent telephone calls across the water rescheduled the afternoon meeting to the evening. Dinner would come afterwards, if there was time. Mick, the senior of the two of us, had asked his French counterpart, Etienne, to book suitable rooms for the two nights, but, as usual, there was a difficulty. Paris was locked into a 'show fever' and in consequence all suitable accommodation was already taken up. Thus, so as not to disappoint our wives, Mick had taken the route of desperation and booked the Penthouse Suite in the Hotel Prince des Galles, Avenue George V.

The Sud Aviation (later Aerospatiale) works driver was unusually deferential as he picked us up from Le Bourget and pulled up in front of the portico. As we entered, we understood why. Luxury lay all around, especially when we left the lift and were ushered into the vestibule of the suite. The deep-pile carpet of the entrance lobby and sitting room supported large armchairs and settees. On the marble mantelpiece stood two large crystal vases full of gladioli. In front of these were two cards inscribed 'Devoted Yours, The Management'.

On each side of this room were two bedrooms, each with two double beds and two bathrooms containing a 'his' and 'hers' of everything, including bidets and loos. As we absorbed all this luxury Mick quickly assessed the missing essential item: a kettle. He picked up the phone and gave his order: 'Four teas'.

Within a few minutes there was a discreet knock at the outer door. It opened and an elegant tea trolley was ushered in by a gentleman in white tie and tails. He gestured towards the contents and raised an eyebrow. The trolley supported a silver teapot, cups and saucers, and a small silver tray containing some finely cut lemons.

The eyebrow was lowered as Mick sent him back for the milk.

The French Head of Aerodynamics, Etienne Fage, announced his arrival for a 'quick word' (little did we know that this was to be the norm for years to come) before the meeting. Unknown to the rest of us he had been carrying out some tests in the Suresnes tunnel 'to clarify the drag problem'. He had tested an aircraft model with the two different nacelle shapes and had come to the conclusion that the French proposal had, contrary to all expectations, shown less drag resistance than the contender. It was the answer that everyone wanted, but went against all logic. The pencilled graph, with only two points defining his proposal and one less defining the other, looked preliminary to say the least, but, despite arguments from his own side, Mick accepted it (as was also to become the norm). At the same time he accepted the argument that the intake itself, on a two-dimensional model at a much larger scale, had shown no small instability (Small Buzz) as the leading shock reached the cowl lip. Surprisingly the designer of the intake, Jacky Leyneart of ONERA, was not present at either meeting so no further questions could be asked about its performance.

Within a short time the British Ministry experts had arrived and the meeting started, but not before they had made many a pointed comment on how the aircraft manufacturers were spending the Ministry budget on accommodation. They themselves had booked their 'pensions' in the suburbs many weeks before as they were not allowed such luxury and took a dim view of such extravagance. BAe promised to have a strict word with their French counterparts.

With much muttering the French geometry was accepted.

Meanwhile the two ladies had been sitting in one of the bedrooms, drinking white wine and eating crisps.

As compensation Ann and Mick's wife were taken out to sample the Paris nightlife. Mick led the way. The meal passed cordially and it was decided we should go to a nightclub, but which one?

Mick walked in front with his wife, with Ann and I, arm in arm, following their lead. Within a short time I felt another arm pulling me quite strongly in another direction and detected a heavy scent as a voice was saying: 'M'sieu! Chez moi! Hey! Big boy!' This last comment convinced me that my new admirer needed spectacles, so with a struggle, for the person was quite insistent, I disentangled myself from the clutching arm and we continued on apace. By now Mick was completely lost and chose the nearest club. The neon sign outside said 'The Indifferent (formerly the Fifty-Fifty)'.

Inside it was quite clear where the name originated. The nightclub owner tried to attach himself to Mick, which made me feel strangely superior. From our point of view the floor show was enough to foreshorten the evening, with male strippers, wearing two fried eggs as brassieres and flaunting feather boas around their nether regions, tried to raise a laugh, amongst other things. The drinks were half water – a fact that had most probably been the principal motive force in changing the name. It was an expensive hour's worth of amateurish entertainment.

At the formal meeting the next day the French intake geometry was adopted as the mainstream activity and was taken away to be blended in with the engines and the aircraft profile. It was quite a few weeks later, after much questioning of other French colleagues, that the two critical items of information given in the penthouse that night were found to be not strictly correct. The drag resistance figures had been derived from a model in a small wind tunnel and the minimal graphs were suspect. It would have been difficult to believe them even if they had been derived from an 8ft tunnel. In addition the isolated larger-scale tunnel results on an intake model at that time showed that the amount that the engine speed could be reduced at cruise without instability was not small – it was zero. But those results had not been made available at that time. However, in retrospect it formed a basis for future work, although it required intensive efforts over several years to go part of the way towards achieving a satisfactorily low external drag resistance and good engine tolerance. By the time it was finished it became a compromise between the two original solutions.

Later, when in airline service, we managed to sell a complete replacement of these early intake lower lips for the whole fleet based on improvements of economic performance. The lips were thinner, with a less abrupt external and internal curve achieved with minimal change to the higher performance of the chosen intake. Two wrongs gradually became a right.

Hugh, our Chief Aerodynamicist, had arrived hurriedly to reinforce the technical group at the formal meeting and in consequence had needed a bed for the night. He was rented the settee in the penthouse suite to make the expenses chit look more acceptable. But, as usual, things were never straightforward. During the meeting Mick was told that he was wanted in Toulouse the next day. That evening, the discreet French chambermaid had come to the natural conclusion that he was moving out, and so moved Hugh's overnight attire into the vacated space in his bed. It didn't stay there long. The kit was soon returned to the sitting room and a second sortie to Paris nightlife was planned.

Following a meal at a nearby restaurant, the four of us paid a visit to the Follies. Not having booked a table we were seated in the outer periphery until a waiter came across and offered to move us to a more central location. Scarcely had we sat down than we were offered a third table adjacent to the stage. Here we were almost in the middle of the action, with the boobs of the be-feathered girls doing press-ups at the front of the stage hanging over us like delicate wobbly stalactites. None of the party had any idea of the reason for the moves and put it down to a waiter misinterpreting the instructions of a maître d' who had been bribed by some now dissatisfied diner.

Once the show had come to its spectacular end the stage beside the table was lowered to become a dance floor. We danced for a short while and then decided that after a mentally tough day enough was enough. However, there was no chance of a quick getaway. As the stage had descended it had taken the strap of Vivien Wilde's shoulder bag with it. The bag could not be moved. A protracted negotiation with the management began, as they could see that any move to dislodge the dancers might precipitate an exodus, with a consequent loss of sales of drinks. However, they eventually acceded to the request and made the following announcement:

'Would the patrons please leave the floor temporarily? It must be raised as the English wish to leave!'

In the full glare of public scrutiny, we left.

It was well after this phase in the design that even more serious problems emerged. These difficulties concerned expenses. If there was one crime in our organisation which was considered to be worse than wasting several million pounds on a duff design, it was that of not accounting properly for the last three and fourpence on an expense sheet.

When it came to the mathematics of expenses some were far behind others in that art. Some could return not only with the correct residue in line with the allowances, but with the extra allowance of duty free which, in practice, had cost them not a penny. Then there were the others who weren't so successful.

One day my telephone rang.

'It's Penny Telling on the phone, Eric the One's secretary,' said Jane (my secretary). 'She says it's something to do with expenses, but won't say what.'

'Thanks Jane,' I replied. 'Put her on.' There followed a rapid bit of thinking. When and what had I last submitted?

'Hello Penny, How can I help?'

'By talking to John Legg and getting him to submit expenses for his last three months of trips to Toulouse. Eric has found out and is on the rampage!'

Eric Hyde (known as 'Eric the One') on the rampage? That was something to behold, especially when he had lost control. Dancing on the table was yet to come, as was throwing heavy chairs about and knocking chunks out of the carpet. But, nevertheless, he had his ways of making a point, even if some of them were irrational in other people's eyes.

Penny always acted as the buffer between Eric and the lower echelons in the many times of stress. On one of these occasions she had been heard saying, 'I'm not one of your men. Don't shout at me like that!' before ushering some poor unfortunate out of the office with a final terminating statement of 'And I'm now going to the loo!', which effectively cut off any more tantrums and allowed a cooling off period.

'Will you have an urgent word with John, say like now?' Penny now asked me. 'He wants those expenses on his desk first thing.'

This was going to be difficult. The team was off frequently at short notice to the South of France, Fairford, or somewhere equally out of reach. To many reasonable people the aircraft came first and expenses came way down the line. To others the small beans must be counted accurately, as any efforts to correct a technical error, which might cost millions, could be ignored, if it happened to be located in some other part of another bean counter's budget.

'That's a wee bit difficult,' I explained to Penny. 'John's wife has just phoned to ask where he is and I've found out that he went to Toulouse on the shuttle last night. I suppose that I'll have to get him to send in a travel application form for that journey when he comes back. By the way,' I continued hopefully, 'Are they going to renew the idea of giving Terry, John and myself our own bank account in Toulouse, to be topped up after we submit an expense sheet?'

'I doubt it, it would never get topped up. Now, on another aspect of the same problem and before Eric gets around to it, I should have a look at yours if I were you. See what you can do? Bye!'

After a telephone call to the BAC office at Toulouse to get them to warn John, I called my secretary Jane Eaves, who established that, yes, there was a file full of my travel applications, and no, not all of them had had expense claims submitted against the French francs issued against them.

'Why not?' she said in response to the next question I asked her. 'Because you haven't given me any returns. For how long? Umm ... Fourteen months!'

It did not look good.

After half an hour of rummaging through drawers, briefcase pockets and travel bags, a pile of meal chits, including several pieces of torn-off paper tablecloths stamped 'Aux Crus de Bourgogne' began to emerge. It looked as though things might be salvageable until I noticed that some of the francs were of the old denomination. De Gaulle had introduced his New Francs about a year before. My frustration was getting near to boiling point. And this pile of travel forms accounted for quite a lot of pounds.

That evening's search of cupboards, suit pockets, and nooks and crannies at home unearthed the odd cache, but not nearly enough, until it dawned on me that the journeys had been undertaken with others whose meals had been paid for and others who might still have a shared bill. It took about a week to sort out the mess of bills that had been shared, and unshared, in old francs, returned old francs, returned new francs, and air tickets bought because of missed connections. At last a semblance of credible order was established with creative accounting applied only where other means failed. My expenses were submitted for approval to Eric in small batches. There was no series of explosions, neither large nor small.

'How is he taking it?' I had to ask Penny eventually, since there had been no mention of expenses at the daily morning meetings which took up a large part of our time, and where everything relevant and irrelevant was discussed.

'They go in at the bottom of the pile, or I sign them,' she answered. 'Just don't give me this problem again, please!'

8

CONNOISSEURSHIP UNDER TEST

The project was gathering momentum month by month. Even the Works Maintenance Engineers had taken on the collaborative effort with some enthusiasm and had provided new bi-lingual taps in the washbowls in the toilets. One was labelled C for 'Cold' and the other was labelled C for 'Chaud'.

However, by this time the basics of the specification for the prototype and pre-production aircraft had been agreed, even to the configuration of the convergent-divergent exhaust nozzles. Unfortunately the weight problem would not stop raising its ugly head.

Bristol had recovered from a hasty complete redesign of the method of suspending the engine and its surrounding nacelle underneath the wing, labelled Operation Twist, as the initial design would have broken the wing itself as soon as the aircraft tried to fly. The French referred to this panic as their 'Revenge for Waterloo!'

Morning meetings of the Nozzle Working Party at the French engine company SNECMA were always a hard grind. Early in the project any multinational events discussed in a mixture of English, French, Welsh or Breton usually involved some form of discord; French against English, Breton against French and Welsh against everyone. The technique for dominating such meetings universally adopted on the Continent was that the home team would stonewall all morning. They would ensure that the visitors were given the chance to lubricate themselves thoroughly at lunchtime in order to shake off their frustrations, and then, in an attitude of *bonhomie*, would get them to agree with the home team's approach in the afternoon. Sometimes, however, the midday meal at the Le Morvan in Villaroche stiffened people's resolve and failed to produce harmony throughout the afternoon.

This particular meeting was no exception. The engine nozzle weight had increased. Air loads had been reviewed. Items that had been entered twice in the weights chart accounting were reduced to one of each, and stressing calculations had been revised by the instruction for those involved to find better, lighter answers, albeit legally. The stumbling block was known as the Ratchet Principle – any attempt at weight reduction usually led to the weight going up, because some component, previously omitted by oversight, or whose weight had been underestimated, was now recognised and therefore had to be included.

Frazzled and worn at the edges, the whole party climbed into cars and, with our French hosts driving, we completed the journey at Monte-Carlo-Rally speeds to meet 'La Patronne' at the restaurant Le Morvan. This comely woman would see the cars coming and, without being asked, would line up glasses of Kir for the British and Scotch) for the French on the counter of the bar. Then, having called her daughter to serve, she would stand at the entrance to the restaurant to shake hands with each person as they entered. After a suitable chatting interval the entire party would sit down at one of the long tables under the glass-roofed conservatory facing the road. Vines and ferns grew inside and outside, hanging low over the expectant diners, British and French alternating, and all sitting in wicker chairs. Another serious business of the day was about to begin. Food and wine presentation was never over-elaborate, but there was always plenty of it, and it was very acceptable. Under the meal's influence conversation was accelerated, starting in each person's native words, progressing to the other's tongue and, as food and drink was imbibed, gradually becoming what passed in the speakers' minds as fluency in the unfamiliar languages.

Occasionally, however, there was one particular problem. As the meal progressed and the wine increasingly affected certain people, so Welsh John became more argumentative, with more than a hint of his usual aggression. The lunchtime conversation was about the excellence of French wines.

'You foreigners,' Welsh John said, cutting the French to the quick since they were on home ground. 'You foreigners call yourselves connoisseurs (here, in a minor way, he was wrong as they call themselves *connaisseurs*), but you cannot tell the differences between wines – in fact you couldn't tell the difference between red and white if you were blindfold!'

Conversation died instantly.

'I never drink too much to get *blindfod*,' said his offended French colleague. 'I can drink a lot, but I never get *blindfod*!'

'Non, non, mon cher Max,' said one British expert, who was fluent in 'Franglais'. 'Il ne dit blind drunk, il dit *blindfold* – ne peut pas voir comme ca.' he continued, putting a napkin over his eyes.

Max, who had a long lugubrious face reminiscent of Fernandel, the French actor of *Don Camillo* fame, turned the sides of his mouth downwards, at the same time dropping his lower jaw and saying:

'Quoi?'

Max took a deep breath. He took another, his head went back slightly and the air was filled with rapid French arm-talk accompanied on the mouth.

'He says he can!' said the linguist, airing a superfluous knowledge.

'Right, boyo,' said Welsh John, who knew that he was probably on to a winner, as even this moderate amount of drinking had almost certainly temporarily destroyed the other diners' palates. 'Let's try it.'

John collected five glasses, filling each with the remains of the red or white wines: three whites, two reds.

''Ave a go boyo,' said John, pointing in a dramatic Welsh manner to the glasses, using a gesture which his compatriot the actor Richard Burton would have been proud to imitate. Max looked at the glasses, then at John's pointing finger, but only briefly because his eyes were then covered with a napkin by a grinning Breton man who had moved up rapidly to stand behind them in readiness. Bretons are regarded by the French in the same way as the Welsh are regarded by the English, and the feelings are mutual. What is it with these Celts?

At the first sip one could see the doubt setting in below the blindfold. A second sip and a sniff did not allow Max's state of indecision to change.

'Rouge,' announced Max as he put down the glass of white wine.

A hiss of indrawn breath rose from the French.

'Obviously a blind guess,' said an Englishman, *sotto voce*.

The tasting progressed to each glass, with much sniffing of the bouquet and swilling around within distended cheeks. Removing his blindfold with a flourish, Max looked around for approval.

'Two out of five,' announced Welsh John in a very satisfied tone; a score with which all present had to concur was close to random guesswork.

Max looked around apologetically, as, even before his mask was removed, he was already prepared to accept that perhaps his score was not likely to be 100 per cent. He raised his eyebrows, his shoulders and then his upturned palms.

'I have a little cold,' he apologised. 'It affects the senses.'

There were murmurs of sympathy all round.

However, in order to restore the honour of *La France*, Madame was summoned.

'Encore du vin, blanc et rouge,' was ordered, and, since it was all in a good cause, we thought 'to hell with the expense chit.'

The next patriot to the defence of *La Patrie* owned a few strips of vines in a very small vineyard, but despite this, he failed just as miserably.

'It is not good wine,' he said.

La Patronne, who had stayed to find why the number of bottles had risen above the normal quota, bridled and folded her arms across her ample bosom, expelling a protesting breath through pursed lips. Realising his gaffe the unfortunate fellow tried to clear the air.

'Perhaps the cork …?' he said, putting his head on one side and raising his eyebrows above a mouth with the beginnings of a smile. This observation had the effect of pouring hot oil on an otherwise inflammatory situation. Madame exploded and stamped back to the kitchens. Almost invariably she could be seen sniffing the cork before permitting the wine to be served! Hastily, the next Frenchman stepped into the breach, but to no avail.

'Bien, we will see how the English can do it!' said Max.

'That lets me out,' said John. 'I'm Welsh.' And he retired to a seat at the back of the room to take no more part in the contest that he had been instrumental in starting.

In this atmosphere of challenge to *l'honneur* there was no way that the English could back out. They had the French attacking at the front, the Breton on the sidelines, and the Welsh ready to make sure that there was no retreat.

There were not enough fresh glasses on the sideboard so, being familiar with the layout of the restaurant and on smiling terms with the staff, two of us repaired into the kitchen to find some more – as well as another bottle of red. On the counter were some newly washed wine glasses, which looked the same as those in the restaurant. However, on closer inspection, these had hexagonal stems, whereas those used for lunch had round stems. We quickly poured the new bottle of red into three of these and used our own remaining restaurant glasses for the white.

Not surprisingly, the English did very well, two out of three getting 100 per cent. The remaining one couldn't be notified which stem represented which wine without giving the game away, and he would probably not have remembered anyway. Besides, three out of three would have looked suspicious, a thought that salved our consciences.

After a quick taste and pronouncement on each and a neo-Gallic shrug to say how easy it was, 'time' was quickly called and we cleared the glasses before anyone had chance to realise what happened. Not to put too fine a point on it, Welsh John seemed to be a little piqued, as did the French.

'We really must get back to work as the plane leaves from Le Bourget this evening,' one of the English party said.

Le Bourget was on the opposite side of Paris and the Boulevard Peripherique around Paris was not yet complete. (By the time the Boulevard had been finished it was of little use as, like the M25, it was always jammed and the French and other important airlines had switched to Orly anyway.)

'But how do you do it? Was it good luck? By smell or taste?' The questions came thick and fast. My answer had been prepared in double-quick time:

'It is a gift of an excellent palate inherited from my ancestors. I have a French name as you know and my ancestors came from Guyenne. Connetable Talbot was governor of Guyenne in the 1460s. We are descended from that branch of the family.'

This was said with some confidence, because we had ordered a bottle of Chateau Talbot at dinner in the hotel the previous evening. The diamond-shaped label at the back of the Chateau Talbot bottles gave a potted history of the French branch of the family. I decided it was more politic in the current circumstances to take this approach than my family's more probable history, wherein the real ancestor was in the English camp a few decades earlier. Never having heard of political correctness, and in line with the tendencies in that era, he had been a leader on the side of those who set fire to Joan of Arc. However, he did not get the chance to attend that ceremony as he was in charge of the one of the few battles that the English lost in the Hundred Years War, due to his impatience to fight and the remaining (perfidious?) English commanders turning up too late to provide any support. John Talbot and his son both lost their lives on the battlefield.

Being almost the last battle in the Hundred Years War it is a cause for celebration by the French, since they had difficulty in remembering the date of the previous battle that they won. They now celebrate it yearly, with a magnificent pageant, having changed the name of the town back to its original one of 'Castillion' and adding 'La Battaille' to ensure that no one forgets. Perhaps our French colleagues were too polite to mention that or not too good at history.

'And where are you born?' I was asked, my questioner mistaking his tenses.

'In a little village called Ashby-de-la-Zouch.'

'How are you spelling it?'

I showed them my passport in the name of John Edward Talbot and waited.

'Mais, un Passport Britanique?' There was no way that my inquisitor would drop the subject.

'That's because my parents have lived in England for a long time.'

Not a word of a big lie so far.

'My father left France for the first time in 1919,' I said.

The 'first time' was inserted as an afterthought, as I quickly realised that things would get complicated if my French questioners realised that my birth was a decade later. However, it was the truth, father only left England again after the First World War to go on holiday to Wales.

'I am not possible to find Harssby de la Zouch on this map of my diary!' said one Frenchman.

The noose was getting tighter.

'It is north of Caen, in Normandie.' I was still sticking to the truth, but being economical with it. 'Let me have a look – why of course you can't find it, the scale is too small. Look, you cannot even find Villaroche on that map.'

'But Villaroche is a small town!'

'Exactly! And so is Ashby-de-la-Zouch!'

This was technically correct, although slightly misleading. Happily we had by now completed the second stage of the high-speed car journey back to the works and the subject had to drop whilst we focused again on other weighty matters.

Two years later Roger Ferraud, my 'inquisitor' at the wine tasting session, was transferred to Rolls-Royce, Bristol, as it was now re-named, in the role of the SNECMA Technical Liaison Representative.

As part of the initiation process he was introduced to those various Rolls-Royce sites that had some connection with the Olympus engine. Unfortunately, for this exercise one such site was in Hucknall in Derbyshire. On his return from the tour he crossed the runway to Filton from his new office at Rolls-Royce. Bursting in through the office door with a triumphant gleam in his eyes, he pointed an accusing finger and declared, 'You are not a Frenchman!'

'Why do you say that?'

'I have just been taken to the Rolls-Royce base at Hucknall, near Derby,' he said, pausing for dramatic effect. 'And I have passed through Ashby-de-la-Zouch on the way!'

'There are lots of Ashbys in this world!'

'But only one that was given to the Zouch family after the Normans had beaten the English!'

He obviously enjoyed both victories equally and had done his homework, so it seemed to be a reasonable gesture to offer him a bottle of whisky to buy a conspiratorial silence.

It would have been un-English and unkind to have mentioned that at the time of the Norman Conquest the Normans had also beaten the French.

True to his word, the exact location of Ashby-de-la-Zouch remained as much of a mystery to the French as it still is to most inhabitants of this Sceptred Isle. For a comfortable time afterwards the remainder of our French colleagues still continued to offer the occasional glass for a *Connaisseur's opinion*.

9

ARRIVAL OF THE VULCANS

It is symptomatic of the company supplying the engines that they always want an aircraft devoted to the sole purpose of testing their new engine, whether a suitable aircraft is available or not. If the intended recipient of their product has not yet flown they will improvise, using some other design. Occasionally this can lead to a protracted investigation of a problem associated with the new non-standard installation and not found on the intended one. The Type 188 Gyron Junior engine in the Gloucester Javelin testbed had been a typical example. However, this type of testing can sometimes demonstrate significant, serious and potentially disastrous problems.

A Vulcan bomber, No XA 894, fitted with the standard versions of the Olympus engine had been provided to test the Bristol Siddeley Olympus 22R for the TSR-2, the developed engine that would become the precursor to the Bristol Siddeley 593 of 38,000lb thrust for the Concorde.

The Olympus 22R engine and reheat system had been fitted in a nacelle under the belly of the Vulcan. Above it, in the empty bomb bay, the engine company had installed a fuel tank to supply the extra engine. At aircraft displays this Vulcan was even more impressive than usual as it flew past the spectators on the test engine alone, with the others shut down.

One day at Filton the aircraft made a different impression as it stood on the hard standing to the north side of the runway for one of the many engine tests. The Flight Test engineers were at their usual stations within the front section of the fuselage, forward of the bomb bay. An umbilical cord connected the instrumentation in and around the engine to a mobile caravan on the side of the hard standing, from where it was being monitored by the support team.

My office window on the other side of the runway was directly opposite the engine test bay and a hand-on-chin thinking session was begun the moment that a large cloud of vapour erupted from the stationary aircraft. The bang rolled across the runway as the vapour caught fire. The red-hot turbine of the test engine had become detached from its shaft and had shot upwards through the fuel tank. The disc then passed through the structure and described a large arc as it moved over the runway to land near the Bristol Type 188 standing at the far end. The flames rapidly took hold of the main body of the aircraft, but it seemed an age before the test crew dropped down the ladder and ran towards the caravan that was standing a short distance away from the wing tip.

After a few minutes, which seemed like an age, the firm's brand new, high-tech fire engine arrived and parked down the slight slope of the hard standing in front of the Vulcan. The fire crew disembarked and went to get an update from the test crew in the caravan. Whilst this was in progress the fire had been busy weakening the shell of the port wing fuel tanks. A cascade of fuel dropped onto the hard standing, where it ran downhill and flowed under the firm's new fire engine. The flames followed.

By this time the situation was not containable and everyone became bystanders. Telephone systems in both Bristol Siddeley and BAe became overloaded as the electronic grapevine swung into action. Crowds of office and manual workers from both firms on either side of the runway gathered and began to seek better vantage points. 'Oohs!' and 'Aahs!' floated on the air as incident followed incident.

As the tanks weakened, the additional fuel began to affect the port landing gear structure, the main engine supports and the wing spars. The landing gear on that side collapsed as the magnesium it contained added a Guy Fawkes effect to the bonfire. The aircraft now leaned to the port side and the two main engines released themselves from their weakened supports and fell to the ground, the enclosing wing skins and doors having been consumed by flames some time before. It was now possible to see through the gaps in the wing spars where the intake and exhaust ducts had been accommodated. Now being denuded of any protection it was only time before the spars themselves in turn weakened and the wing separated from the fuselage. This allowed the remaining starboard wing and engines to tip the remains of the aircraft over the starboard wheels onto the wing tip.

Eventually the crowds dispersed and the various managers tried to estimate how many man-hours had been lost and were still being lost in the many discussions now continuing at the workplace. The wreckage was left to the test crew's fitters to remove while reports were compiled for those at higher levels to criticise and have endless meetings, so as to apportion the blame. The fire engine crew had to dig a defensive ditch of excuses in which to take cover.

Somehow, much later, the Ministry allocated a second Vulcan, No XA 903, for a similar application on the embryo Concorde engine. There must have been a spare aircraft on the books and they wanted someone else to be responsible for writing it off.

The then current Bristol Siddeley test pilot went to collect the unfamiliar aircraft and, at the same time, learn the basics of flying the machine under instruction from a Ministry test pilot. The omens were not propitious.

There had been a plan to do a few hours' dual instruction before landing at Filton. However, the weather decided against it and the decision was to cut everything short and to land at Filton as soon as possible. This would have been a good plan if the visibility had been favourable and the Ministry pilot had not touched down halfway along the runway. Realising his error he immediately applied full power and headed back to the murk. By jettisoning the braking parachute, which was still in its bag and had not had time to deploy, he gave some of the observers the idea that this was the first of the crew baling out.

At co-operative NATO exercises with the USAF the Vulcan had always impressed the American observers with its ability to head for the heavens directly after reaching take-off speed, even with a full fuel and bomb load. However, this aircraft had not had time to reach the placarded take-off speed, and at the consequent higher drag of this attitude, the early versions of Olympus engines could only perform miracles. The aircraft hung on the thrust of its four engines without gaining much height.

At the end of the runway, immediately over the airfield fence, were the well-named Runway Garage and the A38 Gloucester Road, whose motorists it serviced. Years before the garage had had to face a Lockheed Constellation which, after getting things wrong, managed to stop short of demolishing the petrol station by hanging over the back fence.

This time the errant aircraft passed very low overhead and lost an aileron and a wheel or two to the lamp posts beside the A38, and lost more parts to the old air raid shelters on the other side of the road. However, the Runway Garage was not unscathed as the force of the blast from the four jet engines blew over a petrol pump and also collected a car from the A38 and deposited it on the forecourt. One can only guess at the insurance claim submitted by the unfortunate owner of the car.

Standard insurance claim form questions would have been: 'What was the speed and direction of the other vehicle?' and 'Did the driver of the other vehicle stop and exchange insurance information?'

It was rumoured that the unfortunate driver had previously had an altercation with another delta aircraft – a Gloster Javelin. Following this latest incident he must have been giving serious thought to mounting an anti-aircraft gun!

The only clag-free* alternative airfield was RAF St Mawgan in Cornwall. Here the BOAC Boeing 707s were putting in some practice and one of their number, hearing of the Vulcan's predicament, offered to do a close inspection of the damage prior to landing. For both Vulcan pilots this inspection was almost as hair-raising as the aborted landing, since the BOAC aircraft performed two passes in front and almost at right angles, but nevertheless the reported damage was fairly accurate.

The aircraft was repaired and flew to Filton to be fitted with a simulation of the Concorde nacelle and an early version of the Olympus for Concorde. Later engines were significantly different from this prototype.

A TECHNIBIT

Later engines had five instead of fifteen inlet guide vanes, a zero staged compressor, a low pressure (LP) instead of high pressure (HP) fuel system, annular, not cannular combustion chambers, and revised LP and HP turbines. The nacelle was an approximately straight version of the banana-shaped Concorde nacelle.

Again the aerodynamic experience gained was questionable.

When I asked their Chief Engineer, Olympus, by then Mike Beanland, if anything remained of the original design on the current Olympus, he said: 'Yes, the outer race of Number 2 bearing!'

* Aero-speak for conditions that stop flying such as fog, heavy storms etc.

10

SEARCH FOR A PERMANENT BASE

It was a glorious summer Sunday in the late 1960s and there was no better way of spotting an unsuitable site for the next house than flying over the countryside, preferably in a Tiger Moth. It was always an instinctive action born of the time sitting in a glider, to be looking over the side for suitable landing grounds. Thus it was automatic to register likely or unlikely places in which to live. The area north-west of Bristol lay under a haze of orange and grey-white smoke carried from the industrial installations at Avonmouth by the prevailing Westerlies. This area was, therefore, one to be avoided whenever a change of abode might be contemplated. Turning east, another no-no unfolded. The 8,000ft runway built for the Brabazon, and now awaiting the advent of the Concorde, provided a flight path, which, as we were now in a position to choose, would also be a good area to avoid. Should we decide to move, we would not choose to live there either.

And so, we went back to base at Lulsgate Bristol Airport with its short runway, limited by the A38 at one end and a steep drop towards the coastal plain at the other. This location was not an ideal site for an airfield, as had been proven many times when living beside it for several years and commuting across the city from home beside a frequently cloud-covered airfield to work beside a frequently cloud-free airfield on the other side. It was the steep rise from the coast which produced the low-lying hilltop cloud. Combined with the then lack of modern approach aids at the airport, these two factors produced high blood pressure in the cockpits of commercial aircraft and in the hearts of casual observers.

On one occasion the overnight British Midland Argonaut arriving from Majorca had awakened us as usual at seven o'clock one Sunday morning. As this aircraft was the only one on the morning schedule it was possible to go to sleep again under normal conditions. But not this particular morning.

The four Merlin engines were at full bore and coming close. Dashing to the window it was just possible to see the blue-painted fin flash by the end of the house as the aircraft climbed under emergency power, trying not to meet the Coombe road which rose almost as rapidly underneath it.

Looking across towards the airfield it was apparent where the problem lay. A gentle wind was blowing from the east, hence the unusual direction of approach. The sun, rising in the east, had been reflecting across the thin layer of residual low cloud on the top of the hill straight into the eyes of the pilot. With no useful aids, but with good fortune for the health of passengers and crew, he had erred to the left of the required path instead of hitting too hard on the approach to the runway, and was now climbing up over the slightly lower valley through which ran the road up the Coombe. The noise of the aircraft diminished, happily unaccompanied by any explosion, but after a short interval it could be heard again on the approach. This time a white Verey light shot up through the mist from the direction of the end of the runway. And then another one after about ten seconds, and this was repeated as the Argonaut approached.

Very little information could be elicited from airport staff about this incident, but as there were no explosions, nor obituaries of note, the aircraft could be assumed to have landed safely, and that the person firing the Verey lights had managed to dodge out of the way in time, despite having to cope with a red-hot pistol.

A second incident gave more serious food for thought.

Ann, enjoying a morning 'lie in', was awakened by the ringing of the telephone, and when she answered a voice, full of concern, asked, 'Are you all right?'

'Yes, why do you ask?' she replied, gaining thinking time.

'Well I'm told an aircraft has crashed near you,' came the reply.

She put down the phone, got out of bed and went over to the window. In the field just over the road, wheels up and propellers bent, sat a Vickers Viscount resting on its belly. By then passengers had been shepherded away by stewardesses and airport staff. Still befuddled by sleep she picked up the receiver again.

'There's one here which looks as though it has come in for repairs,' she said to the worried friend who'd phoned.

After the third incident, the crash of a helicopter nearby at the village of Felton, we decided that someone was trying to tell us something. The house, wherein we had produced two sons, was much changed during the eight years while we had lived there. A lot of hard work had been put into it, but we decided to put it on the market and to look elsewhere. But where? To one of us an old farmhouse would have been ideal; to the other, brought up on farms, a brand new modern house would be the first choice. Taking the choices in that order, the local doctor, a fount of information, was approached by direct assault.

'Are there any local farmers, who, to your knowledge, are finding their work too much for them and are likely to be selling up?' I asked him.

'Christ, man, I can't tell you things like that! Think of my professional ethics, it's just not done!' he replied.

'Rather than putting it that way then, can you think of some poor chap who could be helped out of his final years of drudgery and pain, by someone offering him a way to settle down with a sizeable sum in his pocket?'

This 'Good Samaritan' ploy produced the required result and a few days later we knocked on a local farmer's door.

'Please excuse us for disturbing you,' I began, 'but I'm looking for a farmhouse in this locality and I wondered if you knew of anyone who was likely to be selling up?'

A series of rapid expressions crossed his face: surprise, suspicion, relief, and finally a wary welcome.

'What a strange coincidence,' he replied. 'I'm having to give up farming and I've put this place in the hands of the local agents.'

A telephone call to their office elicited the fact that the farm was to be put up for auction as an entity and not in separate lots. This posed a significant problem, as there was no way I could raise enough money to buy a whole farm, even if some of it could be sold off or hired out to a local farmer. Neither was there any chance of persuading my wife Ann, who was a farmer's daughter, to look after a small farm and two very young children while I was designing aeroplanes in Filton, Toulouse, Tangier or wherever. The alternative of buying the house from someone who wanted the land alone was then pursued.

Ordnance Survey maps have other uses than providing information for navigators during car rallies. The local one gave the names of the surrounding farms, and a painstaking search of the telephone directory produced the names and numbers of the owners.

'Excuse me for disturbing you, but I wondered if you were thinking of buying Old Farm and selling off the house itself?' was what I said in the first of my calls.

There was an explosion at the other end of the line.

'How the hell did you know? I've only just heard about it myself and decided to do just that!' came the welcome reply.

Bingo! First time!

After some discussion the boundaries and a price were decided upon and the forthcoming auction awaited. Business precluded my attendance at the auction and so afterwards I made a telephone call to the agent, who told us that he had sold the house to an acquaintance at a figure about five hundred pounds above our bid!

Bang went our dream of an old farmhouse with massive rooms, barns and a great potential. From now on our first objective would be to concentrate on selling our current home, so we could buy a new one with no need for modifications. Things moved slowly in the house sales market until, as always happens, everything happened at once. During one of my regular trips to Toulouse our house agent's representative telephoned Ann to say that a prospective buyer was coming down by train and would she meet the train, show her round, and give her lunch? ('She is a vegetarian by the way!' they explained) and then return her to the station? Estate agents have changed very little in the way that they earn their fees.

The fact that my visit to Toulouse had developed into a trip to visit a friend, who was holidaying with his own and his brother's families in Spain, these two being our property conveyancer and agent respectively, meant that Ann had to deal with the situation entirely on her own and throughout the process she was bereft of advice. This fact probably helped the transaction, but not the reception when I eventually returned, three days late because the managing director had commandeered the communications aircraft in the meantime. It was difficult to understand how she had coped with the situation, feeding the prospective customer (a vegetarian) for a whole day, driving her to the station and nursing a child with colic. Yet she had succeeded in selling the house at the same time. And so the house was sold and we had to move out, meaning that alternative accommodation had to be found immediately.

By dint of ignoring what was said by the agents renting the various properties, and talking to the owners directly (the two stories were always different) we rented Rose Cottage. This belonged to the local doctor and was situated just off the main street of West Harptree, a village under the foothills of the Mendips. The daily ride to work was long but enjoyable. Along the road beside the Chew Valley lakes, up over Dundry with its marvellous views of Bristol, the Avon Gorge and Brunel's magnificent example of the engineer's art, the Suspension Bridge. Then down into the Gorge itself and under the Bridge, followed by a stiff climb over the Downs to Filton.

Every weekend we sallied forth from Rose Cottage to view some of the hundreds of desirable residences described in the pamphlets showered upon us by various estate agents. Very soon we got used to the language and could sense trouble when words such as 'compact' were used to describe gardens, rooms or garages or when 'offers were invited'. Each time we looked, shuddered and drove away, very often amidst protests from vigorous under 5-year-old youngsters, who liked the idea of playing in a rubble-filled garden or watching the diggers, heavy lorries or trains passing close by.

Each time the subject of finding a home was discussed, after a weary day, with the children bathed and in bed, the talk returned to a sign indicating future development on a hillside overlooking the 5-mile-wide Bristol Channel at Portishead. The view was magnificent, with the Welsh hills forming a backdrop on an ever-changing vista. A maximum tide fall of 45ft twice each day produced endless variations on a theme of river traffic. Large and small ships passed closer to the shoreline than anywhere else in the vicinity and rounded the lighthouse on Battery Point, just as John Cabot had done centuries before when he set out to discover the mainland of America before Christopher Columbus made landfall on a set of Caribbean islands. Sunsets produced columns of reflected fire on the water, and these varied in hue from minute to minute.

A trawl through the local estate agents eventually produced information that could be acted upon and act we did, and were one of the first families to settle on this new estate. Our choice fell on a plot high up on the hillside, right up in the left-hand corner of the building site, where the house would be protected from the Easterlies by a copse of trees and the sound of noisy traffic would be ameliorated by being at the end of a cul-de-sac.

It would have been too much to expect that the house would be ready for occupation in time for the start of the school term, and, in consequence, each day Ann took Michael the 12 miles to his new school in the morning and returned to bring him back the same distance each evening. The return journey was broken by a visit to the site to inspect the building activities and to report any digressions to the foreman. This poor unfortunate had only one set of plans for two types of house. These were identical in that both designs had a sitting room, dining room and kitchen in that order, but one type had the sitting room at the eastern end, the other type had the sitting room at the western end. As we had asked for the stairs to be changed around, with consequent modifications, the chaos could be predicted and predictably it happened. The stairs came down to the hallway from the living area (the house was also upside down) and then led down in the direction of the bedrooms, but ended in a brick wall where the door should have been. Removing this wall and supporting the structure above by the insertion of a concrete lintel (a supportive beam) rectified this problem. However, our heads were constantly colliding with this masonry, either because the lintel was positioned too low, or because the stairs were wrongly placed.

A telephone call from the foreman, who now had a bigger car, informed us that the electric hot air system had been designed to the wrong dimensions and, in view of the urgency, would we accept a conventional water radiator system instead? I told him that a radiator system was what we had asked for in the first place. We then did a few heat-exchange calculations to convince the designer that the size of boiler had to be twice that which he was proposing. He was basing his design on that of the 'electric hot air expert' who had unsuccessfully tried to explain to me his version of heat exchanger dynamics.

Many visits and design changes later, the message arrived to say that we could move in. Arrangements were made with the electricity, oil and water people, and also with the warehouse where the furniture had been stored. A postponement by the builders then caused the preparations to go into reverse and the furniture went back into store. Once more a date was fixed and once more it was postponed. The net effect was that our family felt totally unsettled, the builders became more defensive and the furniture movers became almost apoplectic!

A third 'positive' date was fixed and the circus was set in motion again. This time, when the postponement came, the removal men refused to put our furniture into store again and announced that they were delivering regardless. There was no alternative but to tell the builders that we were coming and, as good as our word, we arrived.

All the furniture, apart from one settee, two chairs, two beds and a dining room suite, were piled into one bedroom of the new house. There were no fireplaces, no tiles on the floor or the bathrooms, no water and no electricity. Outside there were no paths, no neighbours and no roads to speak of. The children judged it to be ideal.

Electricity eventually arrived via cables swinging through the trees from the road down below. Water was provided by a tank on wheels located high up the hillside to provide pressure, and a hose connected it to the water system somewhere in one of the holes in the collection of craters which served as a front garden. Each day the new water main under the potholed roads was flushed and tested for bacteria. Each day it failed the test. Eventually, one Saturday morning there was a knock on the door.

'It's passed the test, Sir,' said the Water Board engineer. 'We are going to connect you to the mains this very morning!'

Visions of dirty children being washed in hot baths instead of lukewarm bowls, hot baths for ourselves, and other hot baths just for the joy of staring at them, passed before our eyes. The connection process took about half an hour, after which the man from the Water Board wished us 'Good day' and packed his tools. After the men had left, we lit up the new 'Wallflame' boiler and waited impatiently for it to heat the water. Excitedly we speculated as to who should have the first bath? We decided that it should be the children. The children decided otherwise as they didn't want to have a bath. In the meantime someone ran cold water just to gaze at its beauty. About half of bowlful of lovely water arrived before it dried up to a trickle and then stopped.

My frantic call to the Water Board ascertained four facts. One: the mains had passed the test. Two: the house had been connected to the mains. Three: the engineers must have forgotten to turn on the hydrant at the end of the road. And four: Bristol City were playing the League leaders in a Cup match and all the Water Board fitters were City fans and had gone to the football match.

During a waterless weekend, apart from that fetched by hand down a muddy track from the tank on wheels at the top of the hill, bathing was minimal until the water supply valve was opened up on the following Monday.

Things started to look much better until Ann opened the newly delivered local paper. The main article concerned the proposal for the new River Severn Barrage with its principal feature being an international airport runway down the middle of the estuary.

'Where would that be?' she asked me.

'There!' I said, pointing out of the window to the river directly in front of our house.

We would have been less concerned had we known that various proposals of this kind would be cancelled for the umpteenth time forty-odd years later. There is still a 45ft tide-fall going to waste.

Meanwhile, the builders continued to build the house around us and, when the tilers and carpenters had finished, work started on a DIY basis to construct a modification to provide an armour-plated playroom, despite all my protestations before leaving the last house about 'No more work ever again on extensions'.

Two of the playroom's walls were formed by the untreated brick of the house proper and the entrance hall, while a third was formed by a wooden plank tongued-and-grooved inner wall attached to the garage; the fourth wall, with a large south-facing window, was added. Unfortunately, I built this wall out of breeze blocks (the modern equivalent is a concrete masonry unit, or CMU), and it was ready to be rendered.

Within a day Ann was faced at the front door by an irascible housing inspector, complaining rudely and forcibly about the infringement of local regulations by newcomers to the area. Judging by his accent he was of Welsh descent, and he pointed out that the wall should have been built of brick and should not be rendered, even though rendering was permitted on the rear walls of the houses. With some difficulty Ann refrained from telling him to get back to his side of the River Severn.

In fact, the finished playroom was not used much during the daytime, as the children found trenches in which whole wars could be fought, there were woods to explore, scaffolding to climb and planks to paint. Other houses around us took shape at a more leisurely pace than ours, since the builders were not under pressure. New neighbours were scarce in those early days.

The extension had to be finished for Michael's fifth birthday, since several of his new friends had been invited for a celebration. Their parents had been warned to send them in their oldest clothes, but parents being parents Michael's pals were decked out in their Sunday best, one even doing a fair imitation of Little Lord Fauntleroy (a fictional character noted for his sartorial elegance) in a velveteen suit bought specially for the occasion. Before full control of the party could be established the children were outside in the trenches having a fine old time with improvised weapons. When feeding time was called they trouped in, but not before thirteen pairs of muddy shoes were removed. These were painstakingly cleaned whilst the food was consumed.

As soon as the stuffing process was completely finished, with Little Lord F mopping up anything which remained, the youngsters' shoes were donned again and off they went to the trenches, so afterwards thirteen pairs of shoes were again cleaned, as were several suits, with the velveteen one receiving special attention.

When Michael went to school each day, my youngest, Richard, had no one to play with and would make friends with the builders, watching them and copying their actions by building ragged walls with half bricks and mortar applied liberally with any small piece of wood, tile or plastic. This imitative tendency was to land him in severe trouble. Another house had been finished further up the hill, but as yet no one had seen the new neighbour until one day there was a knock at the door. A small chap in shirtsleeves, waistcoat and cap stood there uttering a peculiar laugh.

'Is that yours?' he said to Ann, and with a wild laugh pointed to Richard, who was wandering up the road, crying in a particular way, which we recognised as his style of weeping when he's suffered a severe ticking off, rather than when he's been suffering physically. It was a bubbling kind of cry in repeated sequences, which spoke of hurt feelings that anyone should find harsh words when he was only trying, as he often did, to help. Ann looked at Richard and then at the man. Both were under some form of stress but it was not obvious what had caused the confrontation. She decided to move carefully.

'Yes, he's ours,' she said.

There was a silence punctuated only by Richard's approaching bubbling cries. The man's strained laugh stopped abruptly, his face reddened as though he was affected by high blood pressure. And then the safety valve blew.

'WELL,' he bellowed. 'HE HAS PAINTED MY CAR!!'

'I beg your pardon?' Ann said politely.

'THE LITTLE BASTARD HAS PAINTED MY CAR!' he roared again, surprised that the statement had not been accepted at face value. Richard, seeing an angry face again, accompanied by a pointing finger which left no doubt as to whom the anger was directed, opened his crying throttle as a form of defence. The tick-over of a cry became a full-bore flow.

'Let's go and have a look,' said Ann, rushing forward to pick up Richard before his accuser could carry out any threatened intent of doing him a mischief. The small procession started off down the unmade road with the small man walking in front alternatively addressing the gods for bringing down such misfortune upon him and then laughing in a wild-eyed manner. Following behind, Ann stumbled over the brick ends and gravel of the ballast forming the basis of the road, trying to calm Richard whilst not losing contact with his accuser. In what was eventually intended to be a forecourt, they came across two cars. One, a bright new red Ford Escort, gleamed under its first coat of polish, except for areas where the contents of a paint-brush cleaning can had been applied not too expertly at about knee height. It was definitely no improvement to the Ford stylists' basic colour scheme, although, as Ann remarked, these go-faster flashes were now appearing here and there on production cars, but, it must be admitted, they were applied by professionals – in most cases.

'Look at that,' said the owner of the waistcoat. 'What can you do about that mess? I had just finished touching up a few places on the house that the painters had missed and gone in for a cuppa. And that little devil must have picked up the brush…' Here, words failed him.

'I'll try to scrub it off,' said Ann desperately, 'or perhaps Ajax cleaner, or turps, or…'

'No I'll have a go at it,' he snapped back. 'It may respond to immediate treatment.'

'Or perhaps my husband will pay to have it repainted?'

'And what about the minivan?' said the man.

Behind the Escort stood a grey minivan, which also showed evidence of the amateur's freethinking application of a rapidly drying paintbrush. From the look on Ann's face, Richard, even at 1½, realised that he had not done things that good little boys are expected to do and, despite all the modern concepts of correct upbringing practices for children, knew that he was in for a good rollicking, both physical and mental, when he got home. He opened the taps again and let the neighbourhood know that all was definitely not well. It was probably this that broke the deadlock.

'I'll let you know,' said Ann's new acquaintance, hastily cleaning and drying the offending paintbrush, which he had been using to touch up the paint on his new house.

We did not realise for several months that he happened to be one of the local postmen. He never rang the doorbell, not even at Christmas.

Richard only took to art in his early twenties, producing pen drawings, exquisitely detailed, of mythical knights, demons and dragons. To this day, for some reason or other, no one could persuade him to paint them.

Other troubles hit us like a series of waves pounding the seashore. It transpired that the road layout was in the wrong place by 15ft, which, naturally, cut this same length of land from our plot. This culminated in a meeting of solicitors, one of whom was seen standing 15ft inside the wood on the other side of the hedge running beside the house. With his arms outstretched like an old-world prophet, he declared that the hedge had moved from that position since the old original plan had been drawn.

'They do move, you know!' he said, nodding his head earnestly.

This legal expert could find no supporters, even on his own side. It was then that he studied the map more closely and realised that not only had his client insufficient land to justify his side of the bargain, but he had also sold the access to the large plot next door to us. Neither this character, nor any of his partners, was a happy man. Unfortunately for them he had also sold some of the land opposite to us at the same time. He left the partnership soon afterwards and moved abroad.

To the south of the development, another group had started to build some garages for the bungalows higher up the hill, where the two-wheeled water tank once stood. From the front window we tried to work out how the cars were going to enter the garages, as we now owned most of the area where the forecourt might be. It appeared that the man behind this latest building had been sold land from the wrong plan. The last episode had taught us that it was better to tackle problems head-on as soon as they occurred. The foreman, it transpired, was Irish, so, since Ann was the same nationality, it was left to her to chat him up and reconnoitre the lay of the land. By the time she had finished, our family knew more about the situation than the firm's boss did.

A letter duly arrived explaining in detail that, as the builder of these bungalows, he had undertaken to ensure conformity of design of the gardens in front of the forecourts and as: 'Your family had expressed an interest, would you describe your intentions in order for us to be able to follow suit?'

Our response to this letter mentioned a Japanese Pagoda, some exotic trees and plants and other refinements, which had the desired effect of fixing a time to talk. The builder had ascertained that I worked in the aircraft industry and approached our neighbour to see if he knew us.

'I told him you were one of the Whiz Kids at Filton,' reported the neighbour a day or so later. Pierre was the Bristol Siddeley person charged with the design of the Concorde engines.

Being armed with a psychological advantage and with a background knowledge of the cost of moving the foundations, negotiations were a bit one-sided. It was with a feeling of one-upmanship that we approached the forthcoming meeting. The boundaries were redefined anew, and compensation costing slightly less than rebuilding the garage foundations several yards back into the hillside was agreed. Then an awful thought occurred to us.

'Maybe we should have waited until he had built the garages completely?' Ann said.

We were learning, which was all to the good as the lamp post episode was soon to follow.

'Why are you digging a hole in my garden?' Ann asked the two men wielding spades in the patch of land in front of the forecourts. The plot of land was ours, connected to our house opposite by the vendor's other mistake on the land stretching across the end of the cul-de-sac.

They looked up in surprise and then stared at one another.

'We are putting a lamp post in, just like the others down the road,' one of them said.

'But that is our garden and no one has asked permission to do that!' Ann said. 'Would you please fill it in again!'

This they did and they promptly left. Ann awaited developments.

The development arrived that afternoon in the form of a polite council official, who arrived at our door.

'Good afternoon, Madam,' he began. 'I understand that you stopped my men putting a lamp post in the plot of council land opposite.'

'That land is ours and has been so since we arrived,' Ann explained.

'All of the plots in front of the forecourts belong to, and will be maintained, by the council, I assure you.'

'That may be so for the other plots, but that land belongs to us. Wait a minute while I get our plans.'

This last statement threw him completely. A lady householder who understood her plans? He would have to step warily. Ann returned with the plans and to his chagrin she was right and, what was worse, when he returned with his colleague he was proved to be wrong, as her plans outlining the land that we had bought predated his. However, the regulations required a lamp post.

'Surely madam, you would like a lamp post opposite,' he appealed to her. 'Just think of those dark nights.'

'No! I've lived in the country all my life and never had lamp posts around! They will only light up the house at times when we might want the house lights out. Anyway, why should we give you permission to install a post when you have just refused us permission to enlarge our sitting room windows on the basis that they would be different from the other houses in the road? The windows can't be seen from anywhere except in our garden. Our current window cills, which I assume that you approved, are so high that we can't see the view unless we stand up against them! All the other houses, built after ours, are now having them installed at different heights to compensate.'

Again he departed, to return a few days later, agreeing that we could install larger windows but there would be no written permission.

'Thank you,' she said, with a smile. 'Now you can install your lamp post. But there will be no written permission.'

Forty years later, the equivalent windows in the other houses are now of all shapes and sizes.

11

COMRADES *V.* NARROWBOATS

It is an unfailing source of amazement how one remark can set the scene for years to come and another can either undo or confirm that same scene. Take boats for instance. What started it all in the first place was a comment made by Ann.

'We never take the family out at the weekend,' she said, 'as we are either working on the house, you are working on the plane, or you are away from home.'

Which was true. And what added fuel to the fire was a moaning session with my colleague Terry.

'How the heck can I get out of these incessant calls from Mick or Jim to meet me on Saturday or Sunday to talk power plants?' I said to him. 'They don't seem to realise that the whole team, bar a few, take loads of work home to keep the programme moving, especially when the top brass don't seem capable of terminating useless red herrings such as the "magic holes".'

A TECHNIBIT

The 'magic holes' sensed pressures for a system, which, the French claimed, would save having to rely on a lot of computing power. For a few years, despite strong protests up the line, the group had to try to design two new digital Concorde intake control systems whilst maintaining an analogue prototype. Eventually the French system was tested in the French Pre-production Aircraft 02. In certain circumstances the system proved to be uncontrollable. It followed the idea of multi-vane auxiliary air inlets into history.

'Why not come for a trip on the narrowboat this weekend and get away from it all?' Terry asked me. 'Meet me at the junction of the Grand Union and Oxford Canals at Braunston on Saturday. You can then borrow the boat any weekend if the rest of the family like it.'

Being a boating enthusiast he had assumed that at least one member of the family would like it.

'What happens if they fall in?' I said.

'Provided that they don't fall into a lock they can walk back,' he reassured me. 'The canals are only about 3ft deep nowadays.'

'What happens if…'

'See you on Saturday,' said he, walking away.

At home there were very mixed feelings. Richard, now 7, and Michael, 10, were very enthusiastic.

'Does it have sails?' Michael asked. (Errol Flynn – had swashed his buckles across the television screen the previous Saturday morning.)

'Does it have guns?' Richard enquired. (*The Guns of Navarone* – an all-action war film – had been on TV recently for the umpteenth time.)

'Is it safe?' Ann struck a note of caution in contrast to the boys' enthusiasm.

However, whatever the reactions over the next two days, we were galvanised into action on the Saturday when we made an early start and bounced up the Fosse way towards Braunston, near Daventry, little realising how significantly Daventry would figure in our lives in the next few months. Be that as it may, we were now driving up the old road, used by the Romans to bisect 'Albion' into north-west and south-east sectors. One could imagine the centurion sitting back on his horse and shouting down the ranks of one of his cohorts: 'Pick up the step, there! Boudicca will think she has a walkover if she sees the rabble that you are at this moment!'

'This road must have been beautifully straight in those days,' I commented. 'No planning permission sought or required, no environmentalists to contend with, no notice taken of previous landowners.'

Concentrating to brake for another tight bend ahead broke into my reverie. The automatic driving responses had been abruptly re-engaged.

'Never mind the Romans,' Ann said firmly. 'Just look at the road and please stop blasting the Saxons for neglecting it and the Victorians for putting the kinks in it with their railways. They didn't drive so fast!'

'Mummy I feel sick,' came a plaintive voice from behind us.

'Now look at what you've done,' Ann scolded me. 'No! It wasn't the Saxons' fault his stomach's upset!'

However, despite the Saxons' lack of engineering skills and the engineering exuberance shown by the Victorians, our tribe arrived safely at Braunston in Warwickshire. At the Rose and Castle pub the car park was full of activity that was mainly associated with the canal lying alongside. Boats stretched in both directions on each side of the canal. Roses and castles abounded in profusion on the upper works of those boats, which were obviously old, and were even more in evidence on those which were very new. Some had been painted with love and affection by talented artists, copying the old traditional decorative patterns, which the hardy boat people had evolved throughout the eighteenth and nineteenth centuries. These stylised flowers represented the examples of natural beauty that surrounded the original hardworking boatmen's families as they passed through the countryside, whilst the castles, pictures of wealth and peace, represented impossible dreams.

Other boats had been painted with the same affection but with much less talent by their current owners. Their amateurish exuberance pleased all except the purist. Traditional and modern narrowboats mingled with the plastic riverboats constructed in the second half of the twentieth century. All had one thing in common: they appeared to be loved and cherished by their owners, a trait which distinguishes the canal and river enthusiast from the 'here to be seen' gin-and-tonic brigade.

In the middle of the activity on the far side of the canal lay *Genevieve*, a 40ft long Rugby-built steel narrowboat, with the owner standing at the blunt end. Both boat and owner were of traditional design.

Genevieve had a black steel hull and green superstructure surmounted by an open hatch at the rear. Square louvre windows gave glimpses of decorated pottery, flowers and woodwork. Terry, who resembled the chubby benevolent Dickensian character 'Pickwick', albeit not as rotund, wore dark-grey trousers and a brown polo-neck pullover that propped up a welcoming smile. He waved, and we all waved back.

Gathering wellies, coats and chocolates, our family tumbled from the car and chased rapidly across the road bridge in an expanding file, Michael at the front dropping things, and Ann at the rear picking them up. Experiences that would stand us in good stead in later years came thick and fast. On the other side of the road bridge, Mike overshot the narrow entrance to the towpath, letting Richard get there first; both fell over the low-slung moving ropes hanging between the boats and mooring pins and rings in the middle of the path; one rope stretched across the towpath from boat to fence by someone who could not be bothered to do the job properly, creating another potential hazard; the tap at the watering point had dripped incessantly to turn the immediately adjacent path into a bog; part of the concrete put down to reinforce the side of the canal had slid towards the water, leaving a hole to trap the unwary. Gathered at the side of *Genevieve* we made a quick count to assess the initial damage, and it revealed no significant casualties. One, two, three ... fifty yards and no child had got lost yet – good going, so far.

By this time Terry had got off the boat and was waiting on the towpath. He shepherded the kids on to the front of the boat into the warm custody of Jill, his wife. They disappeared inside, ignoring instructions to wait. My first reactions on entering the boat were those of surprise. Mahogany beams contrasted with knotty pine sides and gleaming white ceiling to give an olde-worlde half-timbered feeling. Space was everywhere: above heads; in lockers; under seats; around the table. Cookers, fridges and sinks were full size and not the cramped caravan-like equipment that we had visualised. Bunks were made for 6-footers and the table dropped down to make a respectable double bed. First round to Terry.

He had bought the hull, superstructure and engine, and then fully fitted it out at his intended mooring several miles away, the journey being accomplished in freezing conditions with no heating and no internal amenities – including an absence of floor. Happily the boat was now fully equipped.

After a leisurely cup of coffee while the two youngsters examined everything two or three times and reported back or called every few minutes, the engine was started up.

We cast off slowly to pass between the two lines of boats to the junction just beyond the pub. The two-cylinder long-stroke diesel thumped away under our feet as Terry and I stood at the back, one to steer and the other to absorb. At the pointed end the two women chatted about boat life and holidays afloat while the boys went everywhere they could and everywhere that they should not. At the junction of the Grand Union and North Oxford canals the boat was guided around to the left arm and headed into open country towards Napton-on-the-Hill. This section of the North Oxford countryside gives views across fertile farmland on both sides – and the views were magnificent.

There was a flash of metallic blue-green as a kingfisher darted low over the water from one concealed hiding place to another. Splashes turned into ever-widening rings on the canal's surface as some indeterminate underwater activity burst briefly into the above world before returning to its own and leaving the onlookers to wonder. Standing in an open space further along the bank, what appeared to be a length of light grey cloth hanging just behind a gnarled bush turned itself into a statuesque heron. The boat's slow but steady progress, accompanied by the muffled thump of the diesel, disturbed its mid-morning vigil and the long head and beak lowered slowly. With two downbeats of the low aspect ratio wings and a thrust forward on the long stalk of its landing gear, the heron was airborne. As the grey body settled into a more horizontal flying attitude the long neck retracted into the shape of an S to bring the centre of gravity within acceptable limits. The long legs tucked in behind to reduce the drag, the wings pulsed into a heavier beat to climb above the approaching hawthorns and the bird settled into an economical cruise mode.

Reaching a safe distance in front of the boat its wings stopped beating as the bird descended in a steady glide, the tip feathers automatically forming slots to maintain wing-tip control at low speed. Landing gear came down, body attitude increased, showing a flash of white breast as the neck extended. With two backward beats of the wing it touched down, the legs moving only a pace forward as the speed dropped to zero. It resumed a more wary meditation until the boat approached too close again, whereupon it repeated the process until, getting fed up with being repeatedly disturbed, it veered away from the track of the canal and was lost from sight.

By now we had reached the hill which props up the village of Napton. The windmill at the top had been in view for a long time as the canal kept to its level path around the bottom contour of the hill, but eventually the old engineers had given in to nature and had made the watercourse climb up the flanks of the slope by means of a series of seven locks. As the boat slid around the bend to approach the bottom lock it passed another craft coming out. The two gates of the lock were open, giving a view of a wet moss-lined stone chamber open to the sky but closed at the far end by a gate, past the sides of which small cascades of water escaped from the pressure built up behind.

Our boat went straight in with about 3in clearance on each side and was slowed to a stop by reversing the engine. The lock gates at the rear of the vessel were closed by spectators.

A face peering over the edge of the lock gave a grin of recognition, and then raised a quizzical eyebrow and a questioning thumb. Terry was well known on this stretch of the North Oxford canal. He nodded back to the lock-keeper that he was ready. As the gates behind closed, the echo of the engine became stronger. Within a few seconds there was the squeak and rattle of the rack-and-pinion gear at the upper end of the gate, raising a 'paddle' to admit a controlled cascade of water. The boat rocked slightly, first raising its front end as a result of the oncoming water. As the small wave passed underneath, the boat levelled out and then raised its rear end and tried to slide down the watery slope towards the far lock gate, but was restrained by a burst of throttle activity on the engine. We rose steadily towards the light; the strong eddies on the uneven surface of the water illustrating the powerful turbulence below. Several thousand gallons of water lifted the 9 tons of boat in the manner demanded by the laws of physics.

As our heads rose above the level of the lock sides the gloom disappeared from inside the cabin. We were able to see the lock-keeper leaning against the massive arm of the forward gate, waiting for the water to do its work.

Beyond the gate the canal stretched onwards towards the next lock. The echo of the engine within the lock walls died as the boat emerged out of the dim light and those at the back were able to converse at a normal level again. When the two water levels on each side of the gate were equal it shifted slightly on its hinge as the pressure was released and, without changing his stance, the keeper pushed it open.

From now on until we reached the top lock it would be our own muscle power which operated the other paddles and gates. With much shouting of 'Stay on', 'Stop that', 'No you can't' the lads were prevented from doing themselves a watery mischief, but towards the end of the climb they were allowed to wind the paddles up using a windlass key, but only with two other arms straddling theirs to prevent accidents.

'Are there always several locks together like that?' asked Ann.

'Not always like that,' said Jill, 'sometimes there are singles and sometimes there are thirty to forty!'

Before reaching the last lock we came to a longer stretch of water where the boat was to be moored. Here again there were boats on either side of the long pound with people apparently just fooling around.

'Well, was' fink of 'ee then?' said Terry in his best imitation of a Bristolian accent.

'Not bad,' came my guarded reply, 'but what is it like when it rains?'

'Wet outside, dry in – try it out soon.'

And so we did.

First of all we went for a long weekend and then a week. The children laughed from start to finish, even when soaked to the skin ascending the Oxford flight from the south side, rising towards Napton. This time the heavens opened and stayed open to such an extent that there was no point going inside until we got to the top. Here on the top-level pound, Ann and the children went inside to change as there was about an hour to go before descending two locks to the moorings. The wind became stronger and stronger as each tight bend was navigated with great care. Too slow and the wind would blow the boat onto the bank, needing the efforts of everyone to get it off; too fast and it would ram the bank anyway.

One open stretch was particularly memorable. The day had become darker and here the wind came from the left, making it necessary to steer towards that side so as to go straight down the centre of the canal. Rain accompanied the wind, reminiscent of the horizontal monsoon encountered in Tangier, but two topcoats colder. As the rain struck the flat side of the boat, the wind took it over the top in a strong looping curve. By squatting slightly in the hole for the rear access hatch it was possible to look down an almost rainless tunnel to the front of the boat 35ft away.

Happily there was a lull in the weather as we reached the top lock on the Napton flight, so it was possible to moor without the rest of the family getting soaked again.

The next few days were filled with talk of narrowboats, canals and locks, and words such as nice, fun, quiet and happy. There was nothing for it but to have, hire or share a narrowboat. 'Hire' or 'Share' gave us no freedom so 'Have one' it was.

Following a painstaking perusal of adverts large and small in the *Waterways* magazines, a route was plotted through fifteen boat-building yards from Hertfordshire to Cheshire on and off the Grand Union, Trent and Mersey canals. In company with Terry I lined up a dozen or so boatyards to see in one weekend with several different types of boat in each. The constructor would build the hull and 'they' would do the rest – easy!

A fascinating weekend it was, looking at boats, boatyards, boat builders and boat enthusiasts. Some of these people were businessmen and produced a boat for a price; some produced a boat that they themselves had loved and appeared unwilling to part with it when it was finished; and there were others who would only build and sell a boat if they thought that the prospective owner was worthy of it. The idea was to have Terry on tow for sound advice when required, but in practice it was a case of 'leading from behind' as his enthusiasm tended to become even warmer when confronted with panoramas of canal scenery on all sides.

On the second day, after staying overnight at my mother's, whose home was situated about halfway along the route, we motored on. Somewhere around Stone in Staffordshire Terry's enthusiasm knew no bounds. Searching for the premises of a certain builder it was necessary to navigate down old side streets, over narrow bridges, past disused railway lines, and finally come to a stop on a stone quayside where twitch, ragwort and foxglove were attempting to beautify the otherwise dull corners of this man-made industrial wasteland.

On one side of the canal stood an iron foundry, the glow of the smelt surging and waning in the smut-streaked windows; from the other side a large brewery exuded the strong odour of malting hops. Terry's Pickwickian features expanded into a smile of well-being and satisfaction.

'What more could a man want?' said he. 'A coal fire on one side and an unlimited supply of ale on the other!'

Pleasant as my short experience of boating had been, it was at this point that I realised that with a little bit of artistic licence it could be made even better.

As our budget was limited, we could not afford those boats built with great attention to detail by the man-and-boy teams. So it was that after much consideration and comparison, doubt and indecision, our choice was limited to having a hull without superstructure, and we asked Messrs Hancock and

Lane of Daventry to make one. The process of ordering was simple. We selected standard designs of bow and stern, then we simply specified the distance in between which was required for accommodation. The sitting room, dining area, kitchen, loo, bunkroom and engine room were drawn on a piece of squared paper, added together, and heigh ho, there was a boat! – Or nearly so.

However, two other factors had to be taken into account. One was the cost assessed in pounds sterling per foot of boat; the other was the area available for completing the building. To put it more simply, this was the distance between the garage and the rockery in the garden at the end of the cul-de-sac, or, as the French say with their non-conformist attitude, *voie sans issue*.

Our choice was to buy a hull only, as immediate funds would not stretch to superstructure or fitting out. The length requirement was overriding – 50-footers were definitely out. Forty-six feet it had to be, assuming that the overhanging bough of the chestnut tree in the wood next door was cut off.

Delivery dates were quickly arranged and then re-arranged. A cancellation had occurred and, as one of the directors was a Concorde 'fan', we agreed that if he could have a look at the aeroplane at close quarters he could save himself a lot of work by not advising those in the queue ahead of us that their delivery dates would change. So instead of being last in the queue of thirteen our delivery date was quickly moved up to second. Thus the director was introduced to a totally different world of engineering and the boat was delivered early.

The engine was ordered after a recommendation by a colleague from a local pair of enthusiasts who 'marinised' conventional engines. The boat builders did not have a 1.5-litre engine, which was the standard, but they did have a 2.2-litre BMC ex-taxi engine, whose provenance was unknown, but was pronounced to be 'First Class'. With it went a brand new American 'Paragon' gearbox. We obviously had some reservations about ordering a taxi engine whose history was unknown, but after nearly thirty years of continuous use within a taxi the engine has had just one core plug and one water pump replaced. The new gearbox was sent back to the agents three times, costing up to £520 on each occasion.

The arrangement to deliver the boat thirteen weeks early would have been fine had it not been for the Russians. It was in the mid-seventies and the Cold War was still on. In an attempt to encourage *détente* and to prove to the world that the leading nations in supersonic civil aircraft design were the Russians and the French, in the reverse order, the latter had arranged conferences at widely spaced intervals between the two civil supersonic powers. Occasionally the British were allowed to have their say, and it was to this end that one of the conferences had been arranged at Filton. These conferences were very formal, since they took place at the height of the Cold War. They were usually held across large tables with plenty of microphones and headphones in use. In cabinets hidden from the gaze of the participants were translators, armed with copies of the papers scheduled to be read by their authors, giving simultaneous translations in Russian and French. In Filton the translations were to be in Russian and English. Of all this protocol the British engineers knew nothing.

And so it was late one evening when the office door opened and Eric Hyde, who never knocked first, popped his head into the room.

'We are talking to the Russians tomorrow about power plants, 9.30 a.m. in Filton House Conference Room,' he announced.

'What is the form?' I asked.

'Don't know, boy. Nobody tells me anything.' His head disappeared.

Eric Hyde had many dislikes.

He disliked the navy and anyone associated with it. During the war he was coaxing a damaged Spitfire back from a sortie over France when, passing over Portsmouth, the navy opened up at him with their anti-aircraft guns.

Another of Eric's dislikes? *Weybridge*. At that time our Masters were located there.

Then there was his antipathy towards communists: his politics were to the right of Genghis Khan.

Finally he disliked anyone who did not speak English.

Maybe this was the reason that he was a bit perfunctory with me. He'd be thinking *Foreign Commies who probably didn't speak English! What next?*

It was not much use trying to coax any more information from him. In preparation I decided it would be politic to brief Dave, Ivor and whoever else was around, just in case. As usual the team were due to be scattered across Europe, or were already scattered across Europe, so it looked as though I would have to give a solo performance as far as power plant representation was concerned. 'What's next?' I fretted, thinking what a relief it was that the boat was not due until … When? I struggled to remember. Then I did remember: 'My God,' I thought. 'It's due tomorrow lunchtime!'

Next day the groups were assembled at Filton House at 9.30 a.m. with me explaining to everyone that I would have to miss lunch, whatever the arrangements. Three of our French colleagues stood in the large conference room with five strangers who could have been French, German or what have you. They certainly didn't fit the conventional preconceptions of a collection of broad, Slovene-featured, top-coated men, amongst whom were some with faces with Mongolian-type features.

These were the people who had to be taken very seriously. In a very short time they were producing a flyable supersonic transport, the true performance of which was as yet unknown, whereas the Americans had so far produced only a wooden mock-up. Although there were similarities between the Russian Tupolev Tu-144 – the 'Concordski' as it had been christened by the British press – and the Concorde, there were significant design differences.

A TECHNIBIT

The original designs of Concorde were many and varied. After the flying wing era, with its Gothic plan form and engine intakes shaped like a row of Norman arches (the 'architectural period'), had passed the fuselage emerged, initially with a mid-wing position, then with a high wing position. In these versions there were six engines, grouped together, wherever possible. Eventually the wing descended to the common-sense position below the fuselage, with the six engines under the wing in the region of the lower Mach numbers. Following the decision to collaborate, the engines were then separated into two groups outside the landing gear and the number reduced to four as the aircraft was resized to meet the French Medium Range requirement.

The Russians, who were obviously aware of this changing scene, had decided to keep the engines in a single block of four installed under the wing. This gave them a problem with the location of the landing gear, which had to be squeezed outside the framework of elongated engine intakes. Thus the inner engines were aligned behind the nose wheels. This configuration, warts and all, was the first supersonic transport to get airborne. However, the power plant configuration was unsatisfactory and, in an admirably short time, they had separated the intakes into pairs and, again, in the production version, they had realigned the engines and intakes around the landing gear. To knowledgeable engineers these were feats of considerable technical and engineering brilliance, considering the datum from which they had started and the fact that the presence of the landing gear had obviously complicated the whole exercise, as each six-wheel main leg had now to be accommodated inside each nacelle. In addition they had later overcome some of the low-speed handling problems by designing, building, testing and installing retractable, flapped foreplanes above and behind the pilots' flight deck. These people were to be taken seriously.

In the Filton House Conference Room the tables had been arranged in a very large hollow rectangle, with microphones and earphones laid out at 3ft intervals all round – about twenty in all – for the eleven participants. A glass-visored booth for the translators stood in one corner with enough cabling to furnish the *Queen Mary*'s electrics running into it. The whole setup would have been more appropriate at a plenary session of the United Nations.

Introductions were made by the French.

Eric Hyde, as was his wont with strangers, had suppressed his far-right feelings and adopted his effusively polite 'number two' approach, but immediately took the initiative.

'What's all this for?' he demanded, indicating the arrangements in the room, making his point that the design office personnel, as the principal actors, had been left out of the loop as usual.

'Our Russian colleagues sit on one side of the room and we sit on the other,' said the leading Frenchman.

The thought of five people on one side of the room and a similar number sitting facing them 20ft away appeared not to be too ridiculous to those who thought that protocol was more important than technical content.

'And these?' questioned Eric, indicating the microphones.

'For simultaneous translations,' came the patient reply.

Eric the One addressed 'our Russian colleagues'.

'Do you all understand English?' he asked in a disarming manner.

'Yes,' said our Russian colleagues. (They had probably read more secret American reports than the Americans had.)

'Then we don't need simultaneous translation,' Eric decided. 'Take the microphones off, push four of the tables together and the translators can sit at one end and butt in if we get stuck on the tricky bits!'

Whilst our French colleagues were but-butting about the 'declared protocol', the rearrangement was accomplished very quickly.

'If you will be good enough to sit that side,' Eric said, addressing the Russians, 'we and our French colleagues will sit this side and the translators can sit at that end. Thank you.'

He smiled sweetly at them all and sat down, knowing that round one was his.

It was at this point that the best dressed of the Russians, whom we assumed to be a politico and immediately nicknamed 'Boris the Red', decided that he had better regain the initiative.

'It is the declared protocol that the visitors are to provide the chairman,' he announced. 'I will act as chairman. The first subject is power plants. Would you be good enough to read your paper first and then we will read ours?'

There was a moment of silence. First of all protocol, then translators and now technical papers. When were we going to be briefed properly about forthcoming meetings? We always went to meetings to discuss, whereas the Continentals went armed with the party line and were learning to play rugby and football (but not cricket!).

Eric looked at his sole representative of the Power Plant Group (me) in a manner which suggested that I ought to be prepared to give 'our' paper, and I looked back at him in a way which reminded him that he had only mentioned this meeting yesterday afternoon and had forgotten to mention any papers. To provide a paper at that short notice would exceed my normal daily ration of technical miracles.

Round two, game and first set to the Russians.

'I will not apologise for my colleague not producing a paper,' said Eric, turning back to the Russians without blinking an eyelid. 'We have decided in this context that they are f****** useless. Far better that my colleague here tells you what we have done and then you can ask any questions you like!'

'Good!' said the Little Russian Power plant (LRP) man before the politico (Boris the Red) could get up to phone Moscow for instructions. 'Good!'

The initiative was now with the home team again and for an hour I spoke of power plant achievement past and present without giving away anything of significant practical detail, making it sound good and in places better than good.

'Good!' said the LRP man again. 'I now have a question.'

In fact he had several, and they were precise and to the point. So many in fact that even the chairman had to call a halt to make the presentations even-handed. He called on the LRP man to speak.

'I have prepared a paper, but it is not as good as your presentation. As a courtesy I will therefore do the same as you,' said the LRP man. And before the chairman could veto him with a 'Niet' he had launched into an explanation of their techniques in perfect English. His opening sentence ensured that he would get unwavering attention.

'We did not have the courage to design so complex and accurate a closed loop control system as have you done on your aircraft.'

Boris' face (he was the politico) was bland but tight-lipped and his pale blue eyes spoke volumes. They were reminiscent of small lonely camps at the far end of a vast Siberian waste.

'But nevertheless we have an effective system for the role the aircraft is currently called to perform.'

The chairman's face softened slightly, the size of the camps (his eyes) grew larger and appeared to inhabit a less harsh area, and he relaxed a little. Later we would find that the 'role' he referred to had become a relatively short one because of inadequate performance. Indeed, there was a scurrilous rumour circulating that the aircraft was to be used as a mail plane limited to carrying verbal messages. When subsequently fitted with a military version of the engine it was much better, but did not venture beyond its home frontiers.

For the best part of an hour the Russian spoke, answering questions fully in English, replying to the Toulousians' questions in French, and correcting his colleagues' observations – or at least, from their expressions and his benign countenance, we assumed this was the case – in Russian.

Technical round to us. Overall – evens.

He sat down to nods of appreciation from our side of the table and a look that implied that we-will-check-if-you-have-given-state-secrets-away-and-woe-betide-you-if-you-have, hidden behind a terse nod from the chairman.

'And now we will have Aerospatiale's paper on Autopilots,' said Boris.

'That is formally not our field,' Eric the One butted in. 'Hugh, we will leave you to monitor this one.'

'Come,' he said to the LRP man. 'You don't want to listen to papers on Autopilots do you?' – It was said more as an instruction than as a question – 'Let us go and look at intake control systems and talk power plants in the laboratories.'

The last bit was said with a winner's smile and a gracious nod towards Boris.

'Good!' said the LRP man. 'Let us go!'

Boris had the air of a man who had lost both his man and game, set and match to a counter-revolutionary, and before anyone could get out a 'Niet' they were away.

At a pace any proud farmer would set if he were taking a prospective purchaser to view his prize sow, Eric the One strode down the corridor between rows of electronic equipment. The two power plant men followed several strides behind, the Russian with a thoughtful look on his face. Before they reached the Test Equipment Bay he turned, poked a finger upward in an interrogatory manner as though testing the temperature of the air and said, 'There is one observation of your chief that I have not heard before and I do like to comprehend as much as possible.'

Based on his questions and technical exposition of the last hour or so the other waited for a blinder.

'What was that then?'

'Tell me.' There was a moment's hesitation before the Russian proceeded. 'What means f★★★ing useless?'

Rather, it seemed as if he had bowled the technical blinder.

'Well…' Explanations were slightly confused, but he got the point.

'Ah, thank you. I think we have similar expressions in Russian!'

'I'm sure you have!'

He did tell me their version, and I have wished many times that I could remember it. What a wonderful, personal, puzzling, under-the-breath weapon it would have been in any boring meeting.

The impending arrival of the boat resulted in apologies to all for missing lunch, but I agreed to meet them all at the Dragonara for dinner that evening. They showed much interest in the boat, asking if it was an approved communal project and would the commune have the use of it? Their response to the 'not Pygmalion likely!' answer showed that they were well read.

This delay resulted in my journey home being one that broke several records. Near the end of the road in front of the house stood a large low-loader with a gleaming black hull standing high above the crowd of children (it was half term) and adults around it. Mike and Richard had spread the word well and there were long, short, thin and fat children in all combinations in, over, and under the lorry. The picture would have suited any Giles cartoon. The driver, an artist of the road, had driven up the steep zig-zag road which climbs the hill overlooking the Severn and had then backed for about 100yd down the cul-de-sac. He had no trouble in avoiding the two parked motors belonging to a difficult neighbour who had 'forgotten' my request of the previous evening for everyone to park in their driveways so as to avoid any damage. The driver now stood at the door sipping tea, wearing a very relieved smile. So would anyone who had completed that journey.

There appeared to have been some tension.

'What's up?' I asked Ann.

'Oh, nothing now,' she said. 'This gentleman knocked on the door and presented me with an invoice for one narrowboat hull. I had told him he would have to take it back if you didn't arrive as I had no idea what to do with it.'

They all laughed.

'Where's the crane?' I asked.

'It hasn't come yet,' she said.

'Then I don't know why we are all laughing then. He may have to take it back after all!'

Hardly had the words been uttered than the worried look that had swept anew over the driver's face was banished by the sound of a heavy diesel engine in compound low gear, grinding slowly up the first of the S-bends at the bottom of the hill. As it breasted the hill at the corner of the cul-de-sac there was a cheer from the assembled crowd, which died rapidly when the massive contraption stopped and reversed to have a second bite at the sharp bend. Slowly it growled its way up the road and stopped behind the lorry carrying the boat. The gaggle of children and adults moved to absorb both in their midst.

'Are we ready then?' I asked.

'No,' said the crane driver from the cab. 'We have to wait for the foreman.'

'I'll put the kettle on again,' said Ann.

Fortunately there was no time for a pre-lift cup as the foreman drove up almost immediately. He gave Ann a curious look, no doubt thinking of the occasion a day or so previously when he had visited the site to see what kind of crane was required.

On that day Ann had just returned from a night's duty as a staff nurse, as she then was, supervising a seventy-six bed maternity hospital that was suffering from a chronic shortage of staff, trained or otherwise. She had seen the children off to school and had prepared herself for bed when the foreman rang the doorbell. He had been unprepared for a vision in a nightgown and robe, and was even more unprepared when she invited him in. As he started to go downstairs she corrected him by giving him a smile and saying, 'No, up here,' and leading the way up the stairs. To his surprise, dismay, or relief, it led to the living room, not to the bedroom. No wonder he was a little bit shaky during the talk they had afterwards.

Now, however, he was composed and in command of the situation. The lorry and crane were shuffled alongside one another. The steady-booms of the crane extended sideways to give it the appearance of a large red crab. The tall jib of the crane extended and then another length appeared, and yet another. As the jib extended to its full 50ft, this signal of unusual activity brought all those children who had not yet responded to the call running towards it from all directions. Some were now sitting on garage roofs, walls, fences, in windows and doorways; others were trampling across gardens, flowers, as well as each other. While this was happening, there was a rush to finish laying the stones and planking on which the boat was to rest for the next year or so.

'That branch is in the way,' said the foreman, pointing to a branch in the higher reaches of the horse chestnut tree, which leant over the fence in a friendly manner. Ladders were produced and a frantic bout of sawing removed another offending branch. All was set.

The boat hull was cheered all the way up and all the way down to its resting place under the chestnut tree (quite a feat) between the rockery and the garage. On the steep hillside, with its stern dug into a hole in the lawn near the rockery and its bow standing high on a wall of old kerbstones level with the garage, it had the proud air of a Viking longboat on its way to Valhalla.

Coffee was served to all the adults. Lemonade and orange squash was gulped down small necks that were relieved from the strain of looking up at 4½ tons of steel dangling high over the garage. It was possible amongst all the excitement to detect a tinge of regret that no vital cable had snapped and the ensuing crash had not taken the house and all tumbling down the hillside.

Still, they couldn't have everything.

Refreshments had been quaffed and with nothing more in the offing some small voice shouted 'Football', and there was a cascade of small bodies running down the road to the recreation field. Having thanked the drivers with beer money and cups of tea all round and having settled the ship it was now back to the Comrades.

A livelier than anticipated presentation in the morning, followed by lunch and the reading of more papers would have slowed down any meeting.

This one was no exception, resulting in general relief all round as it broke up for the day. A dinner at the Dragonara was scheduled for the evening, which meant a quick dash home, a hello, wash, shave, pat the boat hull, a goodbye all round and a return journey to Bristol.

What marvellous eaters and drinkers the Russians turned out to be. Even Boris was smiling, which they all took to mean that no state secrets had been spilled in the impromptu presentations, and no one had defected. Toasts flowed like wine:

'To International friendship!'

We all drank to that.

'To the Concorde in the hope that we may see it land in Moscow.'

Again, we all drank. (Now they have seen it.)

'To the Tupolev 144 in the hope that we may see it land in London one day.'

We all drank. (We haven't seen that.)

'To engineers.'

Everyone drank. Boris smiled.

'Confound all politicians.'

Everyone drank, Boris stopped smiling.

Perhaps that might have contracted détente by a smidgeon so we changed tack.

'Have you yet seen Bristol?' someone asked them.

'Is permitted?'

'Is permitted!'

So saying, one Englishman poured four well-lubricated Russians into a Renault 12 without crushing anyone's enthusiasm.

First stop was next door to St Mary Redcliffe to look at the architecture from the outside (being 11.30 p.m. it was most unreasonably closed). Words like 'beautiful', 'magnificent' were used as well as Russian phrases, which probably meant 'Not a patch on the Kremlin'.

We moved on again to the quay opposite the SS *Great Britain*.

'The first iron screw merchant ship in the world,' someone explained. 'Unfortunately it is shut up for the night but you can visit it tomorrow.' There were more Russian phrases in hot discussion. Would they accept the invitation, we wondered?

'We think that the first iron screw ship was Russian but we cannot remember its name,' said one. There were English phrases muttered under the breath saying, 'Screw that one' and out loud saying: 'I wonder how we could have been so misled for so many years?'

We arrived at the Clifton Gorge Suspension Bridge.

'The Clifton Suspension Bridge,' an English voice announced. 'It may not be the first suspension bridge in the world but its setting is magnificent.'

There was no contradicting either of these two statements. If there had been any wine about at this hour we would all have drunk to that. Under a star-studded sky, lit only by its street lamps and the lights of the city far below, the beautifully proportioned white bridge had a sobering effect. As they peered upwards, downwards and around, a veneer of political difference could not mask the fact that engineers, whatever their creed, admire good sound engineering produced by masters of the breed.

Back at the door of the hotel, amidst profuse thanks for the driver, the presents of Bristol Blue glassware, and the trip round Brunel country, the Russians apologised for having no presents in return, but promised to send pictures from Tupolev.

Visions of details of Badgers, Bisons, Tupolev Tu-144 (Concordski) and magnificent aircraft were dissipated weeks later when the slides arrived. They had been true to their word and had sent pictures of Tupolev – their people making speeches, receiving medals and generally being a heroic company, but very few views, even distant views, of current aircraft!

Sometime later, following the Russians' visit, I found a large brown package lying in the middle of my desk at work. No one could be found to say how it had got there. It contained a complete specification of the control philosophy for the engines of the Russian aircraft, including a very sophisticated reheat system. The control philosophy was based on a complex hydro/mechanical system and our suspicions were that the visitors, having left us, had then gone to visit the firm who supplied the controls for the Olympus. However, enquiries in that direction got us nowhere.

It was intriguing to learn that the engines for the Russian SST were similar to those for one of their new fighters. This gave us a clue as to why they were over here, as our control technology was entirely new and would enhance the performance of both aircraft. It also gave us a clue as to why the aircraft with the latest engines had not yet been allowed to fly beyond the Iron Curtain. The game was given away by a sentence, which a Russian translator had faithfully translated into English. In parentheses it read: (These Control Laws must be capable of being adapted to other engines, but this must not be told to the British engineers.) The specification eventually disappeared from the office just as mysteriously as it had appeared.

Work started on the superstructure and fitting out of our boat. It proceeded in spasms, being interrupted by work panics, visits to the Continent, Africa and the USA, and normal family life. The activity immediately attracted attention, sometimes from unexpected quarters.

When told of the proposal to build a boat on the land at the end of the cul-de-sac our neighbour on the other side of the road said that he 'supposed that some people had to do that kind of thing' but when he saw the size of the hull he moved house, saying that he did not want to live in a shipyard, considering that there was already a second do-it-yourself enthusiast directly opposite and a car under permanent maintenance next door. The neighbours suspected that his departure was more probably associated with the total of six children in those three houses, coupled with their other friends in the road. It turned out that he was the local Environment Officer.

The lady who delivered the parish magazine didn't quite assess the preparations correctly.

'The Talbots are certainly preparing for the winter,' she reported to her husband. 'You should see the size of the oil tank that they are installing! And they are putting a balcony on it!'

While he was bed-and-breakfast touring in Scotland, a neighbouring colleague, Tom Madgwick and his wife Chris, met up with two strangers in a bed-and-breakfast near Gretna Green.

'Where are you from?' they asked him.

'Portishead,' he said, expecting the 'where's that?' response.

'Ah, that's where that chap has that bloody great boat in his garden!' they said.

While I was working in the boat one weekend there was a knock on the side and I heard a gruff 'allo' as a head pushed itself over the front end.

''Allo, excuse me, I am Egve from 'olland and I 'ave 'eard of your boat and vish to see it please!'

It transpired that my boat's fame was not as widespread as it at first appeared. Someone a few streets away had seen the boat and was in correspondence with this fellow who owned a Dutch sailing barge and was in England on holiday.

However, work progressed over the next three years, despite interruptions to Morocco, America, and work at Filton. The thirty internal beams were curved Utile – a beautiful wood similar to mahogany – cut from 6in by 2in lengths. Even with Granddad's old ripping saw the task was impossible so the wood was loaded onto the roof rack of my Renault 12 and taken to the foreman of the firm's packing shed.

'Look, I've got two different shaped formers here,' I said. 'Could you cut out the beams to match if I left the wood here for, say, a week?'

'Christ, man! You can't leave stuff like that lying around here,' they told me. 'We'll do it at lunchtime. Come back this afternoon and pick the job up!'

The following are some boat-relevant conversation pieces from work.

Me: 'Don, the engine marinisation done by a local firm includes some heavy rigid curved cooling pipes. Have we got anything lighter?'

Don: 'What size are they?'

'Dunno, didn't expect a technical question. I'll bring them in.'

Two days later:

Don: 'We haven't got any light alloy pipes of the right size. The only material we have in this size is some titanium scrap. Will that do?'

And on another occasion I was asked:

'Ted, I need your authorisation to scrap the redundant prototype engine bay heat shields.'

'I'll ease your problem. Four of the larger ones should fit the engine bay of my boat!'

And another time:

'There is a lot of fireproof wiring waiting to be scrapped in the electrical shop, Ted. I thought you would like to know.'

'Why? What's wrong with it?'

'Nothing, except that it has the wrong indent numbers stamped on it.'

Thus it became the only boat on the canals with redundant Concorde prototype heat shields and titanium cooling pipes in the engine bay and CAA-approved fire resistant wire in the cabin.

'Ted, Rolls-Royce is breaking up the early Olympus test engines. Shall I reserve one for you?'

Things were getting ridiculous.

After the naming party where Ann swung a bottle of Somerset cider at the bows, we had hoped for a quiet slide into obscurity in order to get on with the difficult bit – the launch. It was not to be. One of the neighbours told the *Evening News,* the *Western Daily Press*, the local BBC, and HTV. The Press people arrived in the evening before and on the day of the 'Great Lift' the BBC arrived in time for it. HTV did not.

For this exercise the crane was even bigger than last time to cope with the extra tons that had been added. In consequence the low-loader transporter had to be parked on the sloping forecourt of the garages opposite. This also necessitated the finished boat being lifted over the lamp post and the silver birch, which also called for a larger crane. As the necessary grunting and heaving to line up a horizontally slung boat onto a skewed and sloping 'trombone' low-loader was under way there was a shout from the crane driver.

'It's toppling! I'll have to lower it quickly!'

The boat was quickly lowered, somewhat skewed, onto the extended low-loader and the crane moved forwards to achieve a straighter final lift. The photographers were having a field day. This larger crane, with its larger load, had outriggers to counter the sideways forces. The loads on these outriggers re-contoured the surface of the path beside the road, despite having large baulks of timber placed underneath to spread the effort. After a second lift and more grunting the boat rested squarely on the lorry, the crowd of watchers gave a round of applause and the owner of the Peppermill, one of the local restaurants, produced a bottle of champagne to lubricate the strained throats of well-wishers.

'You're wanted on the phone,' Ann called from the house. 'It's HTV.'

'Oh, Hallooo!' said a voice that could only belong to a producer. 'We understand that you are moving your boat and we would like to record it. What time will it be done?'

'We have just done it.'

'OH!' There were a few seconds of hand-held-over-the-telephone noises following this observation. Then it was clear a solution had been suggested.

'I don't suppose that you could put it back again, as that would make a better picture!' he asked.

'You are correct in your supposition! This is costing £20 an hour and after four hours they charge a premium. Why don't you send the cameraman to Gloucester Docks to see it going into the water?'

Later my suggestion was found to be fraught with problems. The convoy started to move out, down the steep, twisting road to the main road by the Severn and thence through the village to the M5, towards Gloucester. First the low-loader, with the boat on the back and with Richard and Michael in the cab, backed carefully down the road. The boys, glowing with a stern warning about behaviour and bubbling with excitement, watched the crane, now folded up and stowed, as it followed them to the junction. After cleaning up and locking up, Ann, Terry and I followed in the car and caught them up at Gloucester Docks.

'Any problems?' I asked.

'Only when we turned off the Bristol Road here. We disrupted the traffic for five minutes trying to turn and knocked a bit off a building. But the boat's all right!'

Which was all that mattered at the time.

'We're ready to lift, so smile for the cameras!' said the HTV man who was standing by the crane and, in common with most of his breed when there is no producer, director, focus puller, etc., present, he took charge.

'I want you to lower it into the water and drive it off to the lift bridge. I've arranged for them to lift the bridge as you approach!'

'Hold on a bit, I don't even know if it floats yet!' I said.

'Oh, come on, I've got a deadline to meet!'

The crane and the low-loader were arranged in position and the narrowboat was lowered into its element.

Fact one – it floated.

Fact two – it was fairly level.

Fact three – the exhaust was well above the water line, so the protective tape put over the hole in case of a gross miscalculation could be removed.

We compromised on a quick look round, took the family and Terry (the real expert) on board, started the engine, waved to the camera, and cast off for the first time. As the boat passed under the lift bridge, the ensuing silence told all present that the quick look round had been too quick. The engine had stopped. The fuel had not been switched on. The boat glided into the pool of Gloucester Docks in total silence. There was just enough way on, combined with a helpful wind, to get it to the dockside, accompanied by a frantic attempt to bleed the injectors. The dockside and the restored engine note arrived at the same time. We were therefore able to manoeuvre the boat to the spot indicated by a very helpful harbourmaster and batten down preparatory to leaving for home.

The crew got back just in time to see a picture of the boat being raised over the trees and the lamp post on BBC local TV in a neighbour's house. There was no picture on HTV of it getting its bottom wet. Instead they had a more newsworthy picture of a farmhouse where the farmer had just shot his wife with a double-barrelled shotgun.

Back at work Mick Wilde was worried about future communications with me at weekends. Mobiles had not been invented at that time. The obvious replies of 'anticipation' or 'wait until Monday' would have added to my growing list of career-limiting statements. Why not be helpful, I thought?

'You can always send someone down the towpath,' I suggested.

There was no reply, so it appeared that my main objective was likely to be achieved.

As expected, Concorde cooling pipes, engine bay heat shields and fireproof electrical wiring were still doing yeoman service forty years later.

12

THE NORTH AFRICAN CAMPAIGN – PART I

The design of the Concorde, as it was now known, had been under way for several years. The problems caused by lack of appropriate research in the years prior to the start date were being brought to a sharp focus. Without putting too fine a point on it, the period of flight testing called Tangier One had been chaotic, with the flying and test teams in Tangier and the design teams at Fairford and Filton. Tangier had been chosen because there was not much air traffic, it was close to the Atlantic Ocean and the aircraft could go for supersonic flight straight after take-off.

A TECHNIBIT

In addition, it was under the very cold atmospheres high above the tropics where the engines could demand more air than the intakes could supply and the most critical power plant conditions manifested themselves. It was here that the intake control systems had to take control and limit the air mass flow demands of the engines – a very sensitive area when dealing with engine people!

This was not the era of satellite communications, mobile phones and high-speed data transmission via the Internet. All data and messages were passed verbally by authorised aircraft control representatives on high frequency radio late at night, so that the results could be worked on through the night and transmitted back early next morning. Messages had to be relayed to the Fairford tech office from the HF transmission cabin by someone who may have understood imperfectly what the technical question meant and, by the rules of radio transmission, the answer to the wrong question had to go back via the same route. Thus it was demonstrated conclusively that this contact via a third person was no substitute for face-to-face discussions.

However, the rules of radiotelephony were reasonably well obeyed and the new nametags created at that time became the standard for a very long time afterwards. Messages such as 'Ask Tango Whisky Bravo if he and Juliet Echo Tango can confirm Juliet Mike Lima's findings…' used frequently, night and day, ensured that the labels stuck.

Tangier Two was to be different. All concerned were to be on site on the airfield at Tangier – pilots, flight observers, ground support crew, data analysts, design office representatives, et al. This meant that, in theory, there would be no need to keep continuous contact with Filton. However, this theory, like many others, tripped over itself somewhere in practice.

Also, on second thoughts, why not Tangier? Sun, sand and a few days of recreation! The Flight Test and Support teams had gone by Concorde, of course, so there was no room for the small group who had to do most of the brainstorming work and take the responsibility for failure. Success, as usual, would be credited eventually to the non-participants.

Terry Brown, John Legg and I left for Gibraltar by British European Airways in a De Havilland Trident Three. The Trident was so called because of the installation of three engines in the tail section. The Trident Three had differed from the original design in that it had yet another engine at the back. If it had been re-christened the Quadrant it would have been thought to have been a new aircraft by the accountants and lawyers on the board and no self-respecting board would have voted the development money to get the project off the ground.

From the air the small, wartime runway at Gibraltar looked little larger than the Trident itself. There was a rumour that, in wartime, no pilot could land there unless he had been there before – which made emergencies rather difficult to envisage from a respectable distance, such as behind a desk in Whitehall. If anything went wrong they could always blame the first-time pilot for being unreasonable by breaking the rules rather than wanting to become a wartime statistic.

Our approach was low over the sea, passing yacht masts to left and right and the touchdown was bang on the threshold. The engine thrust reversers were already in action, having been deployed in the air over the sea, just beforehand. The brakes were applied immediately on touchdown. Much to the small group's surprise everything that should have worked did work, even though the aircraft wasn't one of ours. As we came to a stop and turned to backtrack to the terminal we saw the sea at the opposite end of the runway to where the aircraft had touched down. It was just underneath the wing on the outside of the turn.

With a couple of hours to kill, the three of us took the obligatory taxi ride to the top of the Rock, conducted by the most polite taxi driver that we had met anywhere in the world. Like our policemen, Gibraltar's taxi drivers are wonderful. In the hazy distance, across the Straits we could see our objective – Morocco – quiet and peaceful, and looking surprisingly green. We pondered on this as the taxi turned to go down from the apex of the Rock. Why was it green? Why was there no sand?

Back at the airport no one could avoid noticing that several fellow passengers who were boarding the Gibair Vickers Viscount were showing signs of close encounters with the grape. Having been released from the surveillance of the more orthodox followers of their creed they had for some time over-indulged themselves and most were trying to drown the effects with copious draughts of coffee. A few, past caring, were lubricating the slipway into oblivion.

Once on the aircraft it was clear that Gibair's profits were enhanced by the extraordinary quantities of spirits, wines and cigarettes changing hands. To serve all passengers during the twenty-minute journey, the exchange of bottles, cigarettes and scent continued even after the aircraft had completed the short flight and the passengers were descending (or in some cases falling down) the steps. Panicked by the thought that Morocco might be dry, the group joined in the 'Easter Sales at Debenhams' game and, with a mixture of relief and disbelief, bought gin at 75p a bottle, whisky at 80p and cigarettes at 95p for 200. Worries about what the customs men would say were dismissed as we were waved through to a waiting Flight Test reception committee. On the other hand the locals were stripped of bottles, dirty books, and anything which could loosely be described as suspicious, or more correctly confiscatable and suitable for further study by the duty officers.

It was at this point that I realised that the contents of the side pocket of my briefcase – wallet and money – had gone into confiscation between moving from the plane to the arrival lounge. Yet more forms to fill in when we returned.

The car journey to the city was uneventful, a miracle worth commenting upon by the hardened travellers who had been there for more than a day. There was no sand and not a camel in sight, but there were several overloaded donkeys with their owners sitting on top. As a rule the owner's wife, who had probably sown, tended, harvested and loaded the crop on the beast's back, whilst pregnant, was allowed to walk behind. During the last war, in consideration for the animal's welfare, the situation was probably reversed and the wife was allowed to walk in front, in case of land mines.

In the countryside, colour was everywhere, with carpets of flowers amongst the grasses. In the towns there was no colour except in the markets, a khaki and concrete maze broken only by shops selling kaftans and brassware, as well as fruit stalls.

Off the main street in a side street leading from the Modern to the Old Quarter, sandwiched between two kaftan shops, stood the hotel. If there was one thing that the Flight Test people could do correctly it was to organise themselves into good hotels and then, and only then, if there was room, the design office could go too. Hotel El Minzah was on the edge of the old part of the town. It was built on a modern version of traditional lines, with dark wood, white walls and tiled floors, with a restaurant somewhat along the lines of a Hollywood interpretation of an Arabic scene. The concierge in fez, tunic and black baggy trousers booked us in and less ornate bellhops were there to conduct us to our rooms. On the way we passed a silent procession of two, an elderly woman in white followed by Eddie Mac, a Flight Test pilot.

'They've lost my washing!'

This cry and the ensuing procession to the laundry were to become regular occurrences.

At 7.30 a.m. next morning a special bus was due to leave for the airport with mechanics, plebs and design office personnel. The Flight Test Department went by hired cars. However, the Flight Test planners had not made allowance for John Legg's lackadaisical morning routine, and from then on the bus left at 7.40ish with John still arguing about having to leave behind a small part of a large breakfast. At first it was thought that the speeding Moroccan driver was trying to make up for lost time, but we were to find out that all of them drove this way, especially if it was close to knocking-off time. The skill of the driver on the horn and accelerator was seldom matched by his skill on the gear change and brake. Roads were narrow and had no visible speed limit. *Priorité-a-droite* gave way to *Priorité-aux-poids-lourds*. Donkeys and women came at the bottom of the priority list. This was the land of the quick and the dead.

One dent and several cardiac arrests later we arrived at the airport. There was just one hangar, occupied by the fire brigade, and no office buildings for the use of the team. Experimental aircraft valued at £20 million stood in the open on the dispersal area. Aircraft 101 never looked better. During this phase of flying she was destined to become the fastest of all, reaching a Mach number of 2.24, or approximately 1 mile every two and a half seconds.

This speed became a target for the boys at Warton who were designing the Panavia Tornado. Every few months Terry would receive a call asking what speed had been achieved. In the early stages of the Tornado design Filton had been instructed to give the Concorde intake design and control philosophy to Warton, it being government property. However, in conjunction with the government research establishment they had messed about with it, reducing its potential in certain areas. At a later date the German branch of Panavia had been given the supersonic intake system control responsibility whilst Warton retained the supersonic aerodynamic responsibility. They then patented the control system design and tried to sue Filton for infringing their patent. Of that business, more anon.

Once Aircraft 101 reached Mach 2.24 the calls stopped coming.

The Queen Bee stood there in all her beauty and was tended by an army of workers and a few drones. On the grass beside it were two large army-style tents, one holding the spares and the other being the 'Technical Office' complete with canvas carpet, wobbly table and copying machine. Outside stood a large articulated pantechnicon equipped with computers and read-out machines capable of interpreting the magnetic tapes carrying the data from the Concorde instrumentation. At one side, with cables running across the grass to the technical tent, stood a petrol engine-powered electrical generator (the Genny). A short distance away the aircrew tent, an orange contraption about half the size of a canvas home for a modern family's camping holiday, contained the flight crews' orange-and-green survival suits and coveralls, masks and headsets.

In complete isolation, about 50yd from this collection of test and research paraphernalia, stood a type of bell tent, in white, but decorated in the manner of Genghis Khan's headquarters as seen in an MGM spectacular. Within this was a detachment of the Moroccan Army, which had been sent to look after our well-being. Beside it stood a small knee-high pup tent for the officer. Money must have been tight, or perhaps the officer had had to pay for it himself.

In theory the business of the morning would start with a discussion of the previous day's results, then a briefing with the flight crew, followed in the afternoon by a flight to around Mach 2 and back again. Whilst the pilots were trying to do what was asked, the engineers would be re-running checks to confirm that they had made the correct requests and then John Legg would go to the airport restaurant to complete his breakfast. At the debriefing after the day's flight they would listen to the crew's report, usually with utter disbelief, ask for the Observer's Logs (ObsLogs) of the flight and annotate to the nearest minute or second the section of test data which was required for analysis. In everyone's interest these requests were accurate and covered only a few seconds of flight. They were kept to a minimum to avoid the feeling of mental indigestion that goes with a surfeit of printed data, surge traces (see below) and black coffee.

The Flight Test technicians would then run their computers to analyse the raw data from the aircraft at the selected flight points which had been indicated to the nearest second. The others would go back to the hotel for an evening meal. For the majority of the participants the day was done, but for the three members of the design office team and a select pair from the Flight Test Technical Office, the work would start again in one or other of the bedrooms. Here the results were vetted, scoffed at as being impossible, rechecked, calculated and plotted.

Surge traces were graphs of pressures measured at various places inside the intake and engine and drawn at very high speed (these would be laughed at these days) by specialised instrumentation (which would also be laughed at nowadays). They were inspected and assessed, looking for trends in compatibility between intake and engine. After a couple of hours of grinding work, the below is a typical conversation piece.

Terry: 'With pressures as high as these the intake should have been blown off the wing.'

Brian: 'Oh, I forgot to tell you that on that particular read-out the decimal point is in the wrong place.'

John lit a cigarette before he would allow himself to speak.

With complete equanimity Terry got in first: 'That's a pint you owe me.'

Brian: 'Have a gin and tonic instead. As much gin as you like, but go easy on the tonic, it costs fifty pence for a small bottle!'

Me: 'Hang on! This is my room and that's my bottle you are offering him!'

Brian: 'Oh! It's late and I thought it was mine. Have as much as you like!'

It was time to put a stop to this before the bottle emptied.

'There are too many people in this room and it's late,' I said. 'It does not need a genius to plot graphs. We can do it in the morning, as I'm going to bed.'

These plots were essentially pictures of the airflow patterns and pressures in the intakes, at the engine face, as the aircraft achieved zero 'g'. It was necessary to review them before defining the next test in to see if they were compatible with the requirements of the engines. True to form Terry Brown produced the complex pictures from his briefcase on the bus the next morning. He had spent most of the remainder of the previous night hand-plotting them. His excuse was that he couldn't sleep. The real excuse was that he couldn't wait to see them. Not for nothing was he nicknamed 'Compatibility Brown'.

Generally, in the morning, some conclusion would have been reached. The intent of the next day's flying was agreed with the Flight Test manager at the airfield and his technicians got to work to translate it into a formal flying programme. The complete flight procedure would then be explained to and agreed by the pilots when they turned up. Special precautions had to be observed when operating close to, at, or beyond the currently cleared aircraft limits – which was most of the time.

The graphs of operating limits at these maximum speeds were in terms of sideslip and incidence (i.e. aircraft attitude) and were in the shape of a coffin. Hence the technicians referred to it in the briefings as 'Coffin Corner'. The aircrew, who were flying this 180-ton aircraft up steeply, down steeply and sometimes sideways, always without parachutes, towards its ultimate structural limit speeds around the periphery of its limitations, were not amused.

In the middle of one evening session, at about ten o'clock on the third night, my telephone rang.

'Who's that?' said the voice.

'It's me,' I replied, wary of giving too much away as the Russians or the Americans could be listening in.

'Collect as many people as you can and come to the airfield. We've been struck by a horizontal monsoon – the equipment tent is down, the Genny is inundated. *As many people as possible.*'

This appeared at first sight to be a reasonable request until it was realised that, by now, those not actually reducing results or being soothed by drink in the bar, would be out on the town – especially the aircrew who had been looking after the welfare of the British Consul's niece and her cortège – or was it corsets – over the past few days.

Those who could drive and had cars were rounded up. Messages were pushed under the doors of those out on the town. Away the small group ventured to the airfield in whatever wet-weather gear we could muster – which wasn't much, since in Morocco we had expected sun, sand and sandstorms, not mud and monsoons.

The journey was a nightmare of lashing rain, wandering animals and kamikaze lorries. By the time the cars arrived at the test site the generator was functioning and soggy figures were wandering around by the fitful light of the aircraft inspectors' torches. These torches were used by the inspectors when looking into various holes in the aircraft to see if the job had been done as specified, or to see if anything had been left inside by mistake before the lids were screwed down.

At first the newcomers shouted instructions to one another, but then, realising the futility of this, all hands helped to re-erect the equipment tent. The rain had raised the underground water table to within an inch of the surface and every blow on a tent peg brought a spray of watery mud over shoes, up arms and into eyes. Thus the hammer swinger's eyes were half closed when striking the pegs. Volunteers to hold pegs became fewer and fewer.

The side of the tent, which had fallen down, was re-erected several times until only the unwary could be tricked into standing inside the tent to hold the large tent poles. Not until they had a man on each guy rope did a semblance of success emerge. Within half an hour of this manoeuvre the tent was erect and the walking wounded were being given the last of John Legg's Coca-Cola. Thumbs were bound and toes massaged.

The equipment in the tent was recovered from the rain-soaked floor. A pint of muddy goo poured out of the precious spare Air Intake Control

Unit (AICU). Looking for advice in the maintenance manual was pointless as there would be no reference to such an eventuality. No spare AICU meant limiting testing.

The unit was labelled 'Death by Drowning' and prepared for an urgent flight back to Filton next morning in the bomb bay of the Canberra support aircraft. When it arrived at Filton the next day it was discovered that the residual water had frozen at high altitude in the unheated bomb bay when in transit. The unit was thawed out, cleaned and tested, and it was later found to have had the best serviceability of all those used in the several years of trial. Not all engineering is logical. However, in later years no argument would ever get 'Freeze in a solution of Moroccan mud' adopted as an accepted preservative treatment. Traditional resistance to change would keep it out of the manual.

Once the equipment had been restored to as near original condition as possible, a tour was made around the other tents. The Moroccan guards appeared to be having a discussion session, but the officer, who could only crawl on elbows and knees into his small tent and was therefore at water surface level, was huddled wet and morose in his sleeping bag.

At the edge of the site the small aircrew tent was still valiantly resisting the blast, but on further inspection it was found that, since it didn't have a storm sheet, the thin sides had filtered the horizontal rain into a mist, which had passed through the tent, soaking anything that stood in its way, before passing through the opposite wall. Inside the tent, on a long, mobile hanger more suited to *haute couture* than *haute vitesse*, hung the first item which had borne the brunt of the gale. It was an orange flying suit labelled John Cochrane, Deputy Chief Test Pilot. It was sodden.

No flying suit meant no flying, so we draped plastic covers over the remainder and took John Cochrane's suit back to the hotel. By now the hour was very late and the night porter was asleep on the floor behind the desk. Nevertheless, on awakening, he appeared (outwardly at least) to be a bright young fellow, so he was charged with getting the uniform dry before 10.30 a.m., or whatever time the aircrew had breakfast. And so to bed, after reviewing the next day's flight-test programme once again.

Half an hour later, since the casino was closed, the aircrew entered the foyer of the El Minzah hotel and re-awakened the concierge to get their keys. This man had been lying on what appeared to be an orange carpet behind the desk. As he moved to retrieve the aircrew party's keys, one of them, John Cochrane (who came from Scotland), noticed as he leant on the desk to prop himself up, that the orange 'carpet' behind the desk had a name sewn onto it. As he re-focussed his gaze he realised that it was his own name. Instant recognition brought all his latent highland anger to the surface.

'That's ma bluidy flying suit!' he shouted.

So saying, he dived over, grabbed the suit that the concierge had been lying on as a method of trying to dry it out, paralysed the poor chap with a blast of charged invective and stormed off to find the ground crewman who had the responsibility of tending the aircrew kit. From all reports the Campbells of Glencoe (Highland Scots who famously resisted English subjugation) would have crumbled in the face of the ensuing verbal attack on the crewman. This poor wretch had been asleep throughout the storm and consequently knew nothing of the rain, the wetting of the suit, or why it had been used as the concierge's mattress, supposedly flying there on its own. Whenever the salvage team met this character thereafter they were followed by a haunted, accusing look, since he knew they were the instigators of his misfortune.

The next day was spent moving the equipment tent to 'higher ground' (all of 6in higher) and digging trenches around it. These trenches immediately filled with water. In the 'Technical Office' the edges of the carpet were floating by now and another such move became necessary if they were to avoid trench foot.

Outside, Aircraft 101 dripped majestically. Inside the wing, above the engines, there were so-called 'dry bays' containing equipment but no fuel. This was a precautionary measure against the possibility of fire. Today the water, which had entered whilst the engines were being changed, was being mopped out.

As no one was prepared for this type of weather it was decided that me and Skillen, a bright young Northern Irelander of acid wit, would go into Tangier to obtain rainwear. Several hundred dirhams were peeled off the petty cash wad and off we went to the city, debating all the while what the Arabic for gumboots might be. For some time the two of us wandered into and out of shoe shops, waving away offers of leather shoes, slippers and, occasionally, sisters. We stood somewhat dejectedly in the town square and were about to call it a day when another bright young urchin asked us if we wanted a sheepskin jacket.

The answer 'No!' didn't put him off, nor did 'Nos!' to the rest of his list, and neither did a firm 'Bugger Off!' Eventually, more in hope than expectation, we told him: 'Gumboots, Wellingtons.' Then, remembering it was a French-speaking country, tried, 'Souliers Caoutchouc.'

This last gamble in fractured French suddenly paid off, as his eyes lit up. And within a couple of minutes we were standing in the 'Street-of a-thousand-gumboots' amid string-bound piles of wellies at the backs of a row of shops. The bargaining started at the standard one third of the asking price and stayed low, especially as the salesman's face cracked slightly when at the end we said that we wanted twelve pairs.

Whilst these were being packed together the three of us set off to find the 'Street-of-a-thousand-plastic-macs'. Apparently it did not exist, but after much searching we found one shop where the bargaining was done on a sheet of paper, with the shopkeeper writing down a figure which we crossed out and wrote down one third of this, which in turn he crossed out and so on. His price steps down were larger than our steps up and when we stopped crossing out and, with the urchin saying, 'Go' we walked out. We had completed the sale at our price, or so we thought, until our go-between salesman offered us the wrong change.

We looked at the urchin, who had thoughtfully picked up the piece of paper, and we wrote 'Police?' This encouraged him to give us the correct amount of change.

As we gave the young lad a good tip, mainly for appearing to be on our side in all matters, we asked him why he had helped us bargain. He showed us the tip and said 'I am not Moroccan!' I suppose he was an apprentice bandit so we gave him bit more money.

By this time the tents were rearranged and secure, and the design team sat at the table in the 'technical tent' drinking the first vintage of John Legg's new stock of Coca-Cola. However, our self-congratulations were cut short by the abrupt appearance of the stocky, dripping figure of a fitter in the doorway of the tent, dressed in one of the plastic macs and a pair of gumboots. It was fairly obvious that he was about to blow a gasket as he extended his arms forward, palms upward.

'Look at 'ee!' he declared.

The plastic mac barely covered his forearms and he slowly brought his arms up forward to shoulder level and silently turned to show that it had split down his back.

'And that's not all,' he shouted over his shoulder in a Bristolian burr. 'I casn't get they gumboots off, they'm too small!' and then he hobbled off into the mud.

The Moroccans had won this round. The plastic macs were all made for females and the boot sizes were of the slower-selling diminutive ranges, with nothing larger than an eight.

Laugh? There wasn't a dry seat in the tent.

The tests were not going well and there was a large depression centred over the 'Technical Office', which no amount of late nights could dispel. It appeared as though we had crossed to the far side of the frontiers of science and had to knock on the frontier gate to get back into friendly territory.

1 Bristol Type 188. A supersonic research aircraft aimed at Mach 2 and later Mach 3. The engines were de Havilland Gyron Juniors with reheat. The value of this aircraft was that it showed us what not to do. It can be seen at the RAF Museum at Cosford. (BAC)

2 Concorde power plant. The power plants were affected by almost everything – the one next door, landing gear, slush and debris from the wheels, atmospheric transients and crew actions. (BAe)

3 Bristol Type 221. The Type 221 (top) was a much-modified second model of the Fairey Delta 2. The first model is flying alongside. The fuselage was extended, and a new Ogee wing and lowered engine air intakes were added. The landing gear was from the English Electric Lightning (mains) and Fairey Gannet (nose wheel). (BAC)

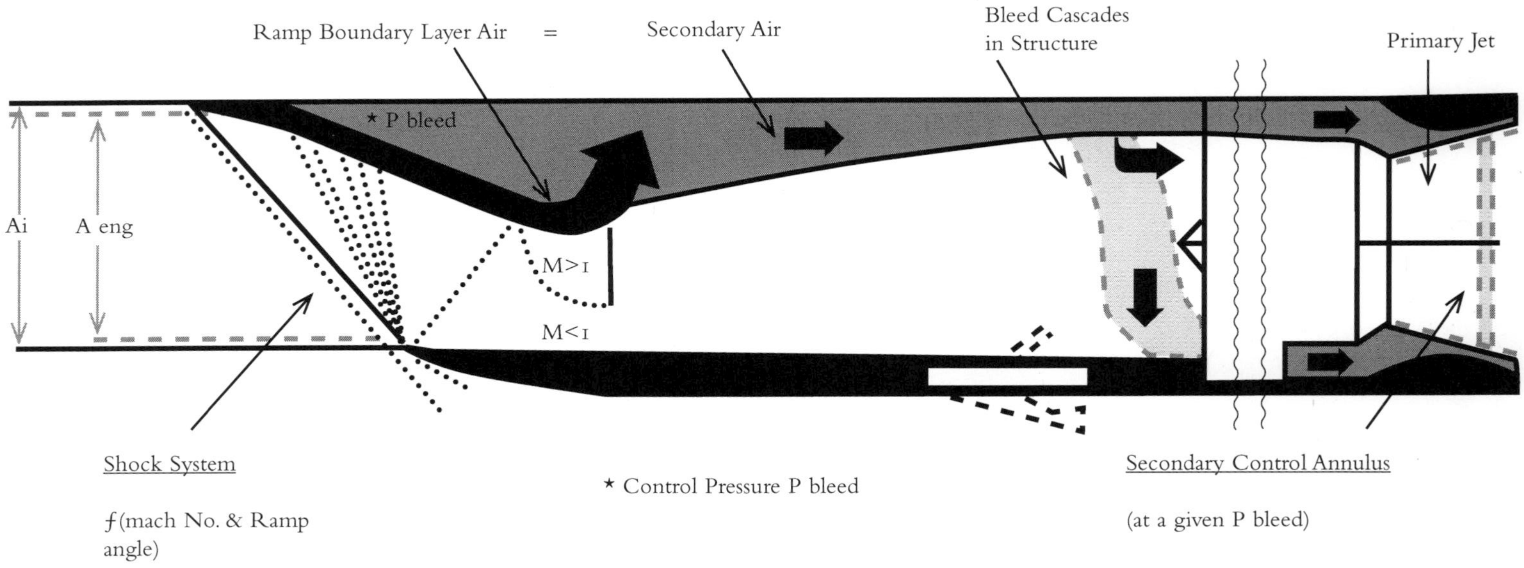

4 Power plant airflows. The ramp positions were controlled by the ramp bleed pressure to keep the oblique shocks just forward of the lower cowl lip. The ramp boundary layer was removed and passed around the engine. In the secondary nozzle the flow rate was controlled by the engine exhaust flow and the ramp boundary bleed pressure. (Author)

5 Avro Vulcan. Five Bristol Siddeley Olympus engines in one aircraft. The thrust differences between the two standards may be judged from the relative sizes of the exhaust nozzles. (Rolls-Royce)

6 Tupolev 144. This later version incorporated drastic modifications, carried out in a relatively short timescale. Engines and intakes were moved outboard around the landing gear and a retractable foreplane added. (moninoaviation.com)

7 *Josephine Ann*. After being christened with a bottle of Somerset cider, the boat is raised over the trees to be settled on a low loader for a 'maiden voyage' to Gloucester Docks. (Bristol United Press)

8 Topical update. The traditional red arrowheads were remodelled to show two Concordes, waiting to have one painted as top view, and one as viewed from underneath. (Author)

9 Celebration. Terry Brown, Michael, Richard, Ann and I put the donation by the Peppermill, a local restaurant, of a bottle of champagne to a different use. (Bristol United Press)

10 Tangier 2. Aircraft 101 being serviced beside the Equipment Tent with the small blue 'Crew Room' in the foreground. The Technical Tent was off to the right. (John Allan)

11 Design discussion. Terry and myself waiting for the flight data to be printed out. Hotel El Minzah, Tangier. (John Allan)

12 The Black Machs. Eric Ruff, Cliff Richards, Ivor Rye, John Legg, Terry Brown, Mick Wilde (Project Director), Derek Morriss and myself wearing a 'carefully crafted' decoration and carrying a diploma with an individual citation and a communal one 'For Incontinence in the face of a Bleeding Impossibility'. (BAe)

13 Edwards AFB. Bill Schweikart, Ann and I in front of an F-111 Stability Research aircraft. (Hugh Dryden Research Center)

14 The B-1. The B-1A prototypes were designed for Mach 2+. The in-service aircraft are flying as the B-1B, capable of up to Mach 1.2. (aviastar.org)

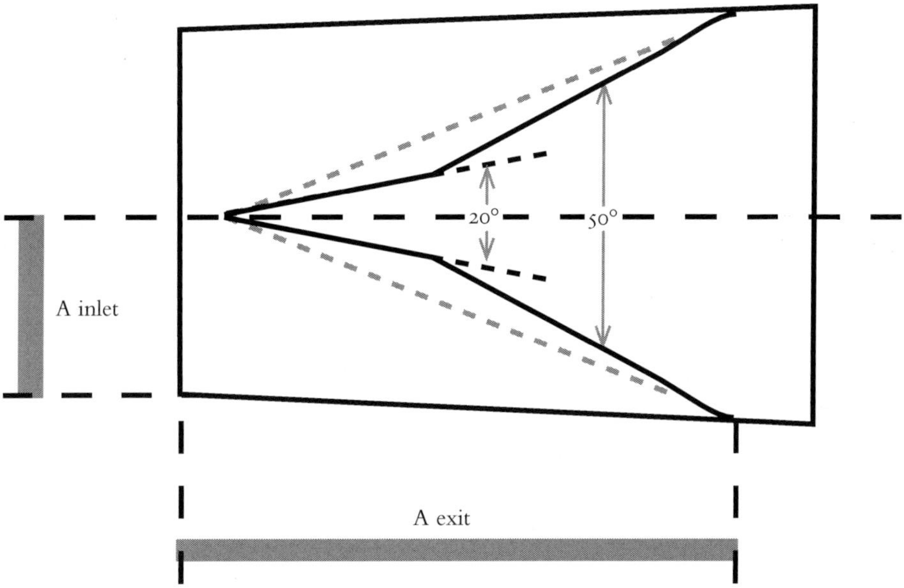

15 Concorde boundary layer diverter. The initial shape of the diverter between the wing and the nacelle on the prototypes was too 'blunt' to accommodate the oncoming wing boundary layer and, therefore, later aircraft had the included angle reduced to give satisfactory results. (Author)

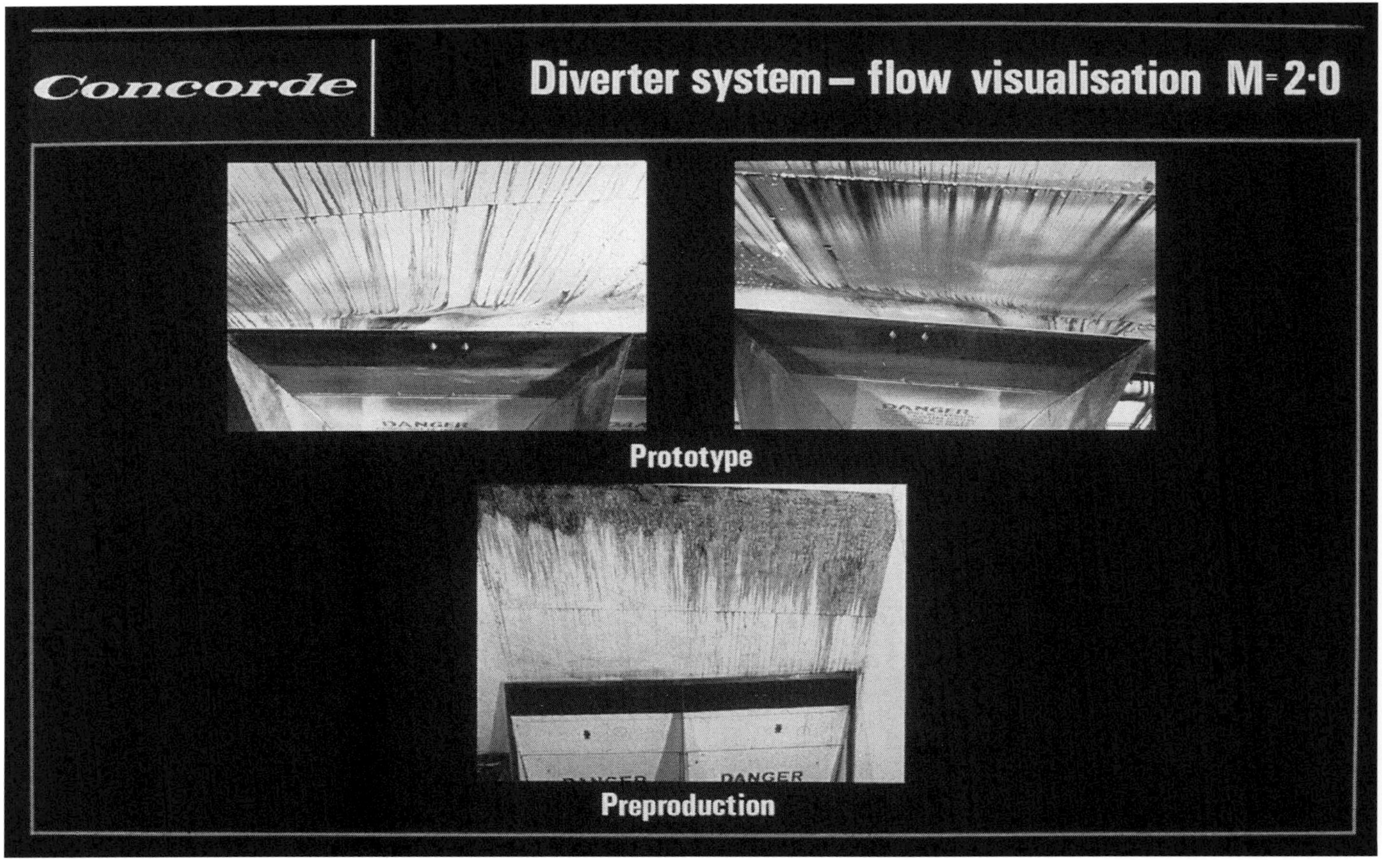

16 A bucket, castor oil and oil lamps. Prototype inboard and outboard surface flows show the presence of a shock which slows the flow and diverts it sharply left and right, interfering with the main intake flow. The two bright spots on the ramps are small cones containing the 'magic holes'. The new diverter showed a much cleaner flow pattern. (BAe)

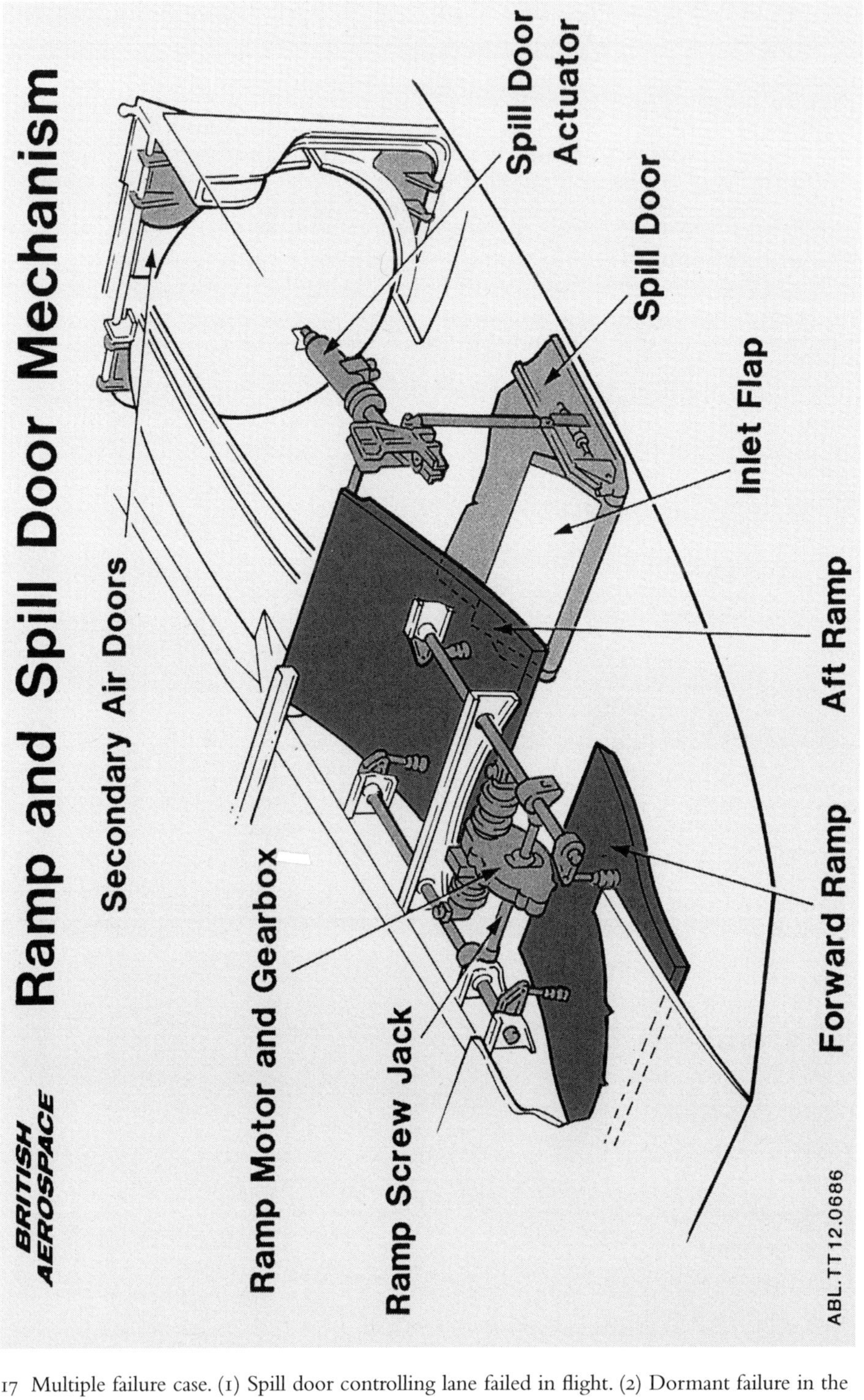

17 Multiple failure case. (1) Spill door controlling lane failed in flight. (2) Dormant failure in the alternative lane. (3) Wrong crew drill. (4) Engine surged due to consequent ramp movements. (5) Interactive surge in adjacent engine. (6) Maintenance error in replacing this intakes ramp actuator before flight allowed the surges to break the actuator/ramp drive. (BAe)

18 Effect of multiple failure. Following the multiple failure incident, the front ramp was blown forward and out of the intake at Mach 2. (Author's collection)

19 The rear ramp was present but incorrect, as it hangs on its hinges, hiding the engine. (Author's collection)

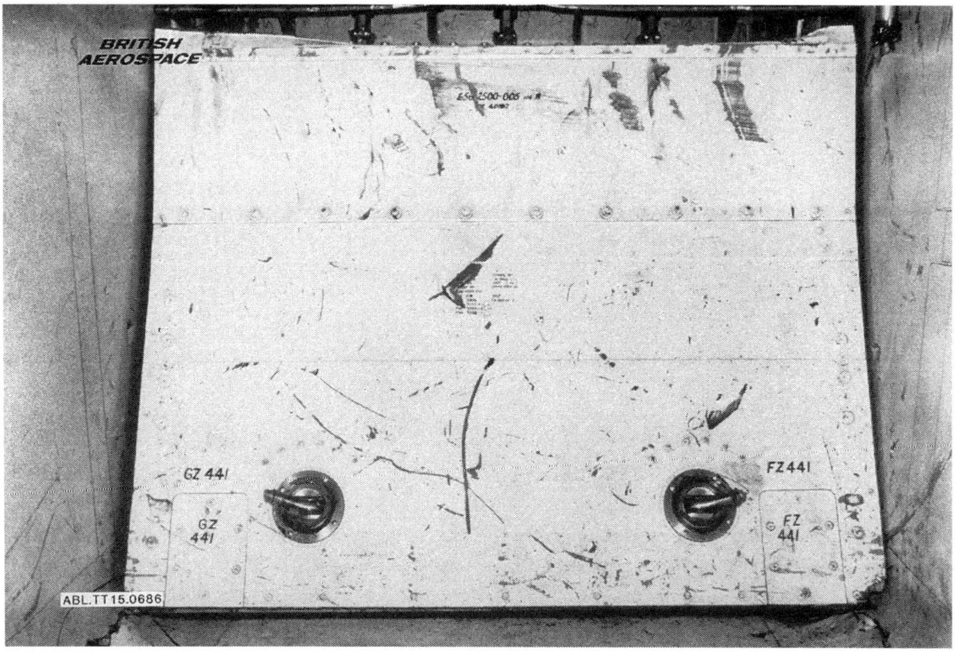

20 Effect of blade failure 1. The fractured low pressure compressor blade lies behind the front row. The support for the front bearing has disappeared, as has the bearing itself. Consequential damage further down the compressor caused mayhem amongst the smaller blades and a titanium fire. (Peter Bashford)

21 Effect of blade failure 2. In the high pressure section the blades are titanium, which when fractured and rubbed against the titanium casing cause intense 3,000°C fires. In this particular case, a section of the casing was burnt through. A row of stators was also burnt through and pushed through the gap. The rotor blades were reduced to stubs. The two sections of the engine rested on the nacelle doors. (Peter Bashford)

22 Rudder failure. There would have been less publicity if the aircraft had not been full of Americans stranded in Australia. (BA)

23 Fire test rig investigation of the Paris crash. Air from the circular exhaust of the blow-down tunnel enters the fire rig where a full scale mock-up of the side of the nacelle and the landing gear can be discerned. On top of the rig there are representations of the landing gear bay in the wing and fuel injection points. At the rear there is a flame simulation of the engine reheat exhaust. The construction beyond the rig deflects flame and/or unburnt fuel upward. (BAe)

A TECHNIBIT

Airworthiness officialdom in its wisdom had agreed that the firm should demonstrate that the aircraft could reach near zero 'g' (g-force) at all flying speeds without any surges (i.e. big bangs) from the engines. In practice zero 'g' is astronaut country, the point at which people leave the cabin floor and start to float towards the ceiling, but they should do this without any surges.

To achieve this laudable objective the control surfaces in the intake (three surfaces each as big as a modern kitchen table) had to be moved in the correct sequence and fast enough and accurately enough as, in less than one hundredth of a second, they slowed down the air approaching the intake from around 1,350mph to 350mph at the engine face. They then had to feed it in an even distribution to the engines at each instant of the manoeuvre, no matter what the aircraft, the engines, the pilots, (or Granny), happened to be doing at the time.

Each of the four intakes was controlled by a digital electronic control system, the first digital system for a civil aircraft, with a second one to take over at lightning speed if the first one failed, even in the middle of fast transient incidents, such as identifying engine failure. Only the Control Laws and functions are generated digitally on Aircraft 101 *et seq.* as programme pressures would not permit the servo loops to be brought into line along with the necessary rewiring of the aircraft already on the production line. These black boxes, specified and built at Bristol, had laws that were about three times as complex as the analogue units controlling the engines, and even the latter gave Bristol Siddeley grey hairs. Within these digital boxes the complex 'laws' – meaning relationships between pressures, aircraft speeds and surface positions – all interrelated so that if anyone was changed it affected the others.

The 'laws' were encapsulated in PROMS, small programmable electronic chips, and had to be defined in a way which would guide the intake/engine combination safely through a minefield of surges, no matter how turbulent the atmosphere turned out to be or what the pilot was trying to do with his engines.

It seemed that at this stage the design team had now got themselves to the position where they appeared to have each foot in a different minefield of surges and could not sit down for fear of a third. No one was going to clear operation at zero 'g' this way. There was no other alternative but to adopt the philosophy, beloved of yokels, that: 'if you would wish to get to where you want to get, it is best not to start from where you are'.

Swallowing our pride we put in a call to Filton to send the dynamics software specialists who had programmed the control boxes, together with a suitable set of spares and a PROM-blowing machine. The latter was a device, which, in a controlled manner, punctured webs of electronic circuits within the chip to give the desired effect.

What to us appeared as a sane request appeared to the upper echelons at Filton as mighty suspicious and a HS125 executive jet arrived forthwith, happily containing the ideal combination of talents: Technical Director, Bill Strang, and the Chief Power Plant Engineer, Jim Wallin.

Jim had been transferred from Weybridge to Filton to bring his wide experience of civil and military subsonic power plants on Viscounts, VC 10, BAC1-11, Valiants, and Vanguards onto the Concorde. This experience was welcomed by all at Filton, much, he admitted, to his surprise. On engines his background was unimpeachable; however, supersonic intakes were a new field and he was learning (as was everyone else!). He arrived, twirling his military moustache, not knowing whether to look critical or conciliatory.

Bill, on the other hand, had the power to grasp any technical question, however complex, and, within a few minutes, would be leading the discussion into areas not even conceived by those who had had days to think about it. He walked into the technical tent wearing his usual bemused expression, which had misled so many of the unwary.

'Would you please give me a brief on where we are so far?' Bill began.

The fun was about to start. The 'technical tent' was full of people analysing the last day's testing, so I, together with Terry, John and the two newcomers, retired to the empty restaurant at the airport, to look for somewhere where an uninterrupted technical discussion could be held.

Jim Wallin was asked by Bill, 'that in order to save their limited time here he should go and investigate whether there were any more practical problems that had come to light'. Jim looked a bit peeved but had no option but to do so.

Terry started to go through the problem from the beginning. Soon the questioning began.

'What happens if ...?'

Terry, the boat-building aerodynamic genius, and his colleague John Legg, had developed a computing double act which, for sheer speed and comprehensive coverage, left other participants on the starting blocks. The instant that a problem was defined the number crunchers would be produced from side pockets whilst the brains were already assembling the data. One of the pair would do the first part of the calculation whilst the other was preparing the basic input data for the next:

'Free stream Mach number?'

'Two point Oh three one on ADC1.'

A TECHNIBIT

Each aircraft had its own idiosyncrasies due to slight build differences. The three Air Data Computers (ADC) which calculated the aircraft speed derived their basic data from different sides of the aircraft and the nose probe, giving the impression, due to small imperfections in the build, that one side of the aircraft was travelling slightly faster than the other, so all calculations were based on one side's output.

'Ambient temperature is minus 51.'

'N1 on Number Four is 101.5.'

'That makes N1 over Root Theta…'

'What's going on?' Bill asked.

I tried to explain as best I could whilst trying to keep up with the number crunching.

Very soon we reached a stage where the three were lagging a bit behind in response to observations such as: 'I see that, but what happens if…?' The perpetually bewildered expression on Bill's face was still there, but it took another turn when, in response to a question, the two partners went into their double act to derive yet another answer. For some time the question-and-look-up session continued, but now there was a fourth participant slightly ahead of the rest.

However, having agreed eventually that the proposed way forward was a reasonable one, likely to lead eventually to a satisfactory solution, the visitors left for Filton.

Within a day of their departure, faith had been restored within the upper crust at Filton and a group from the Dynamics team who had engineered the Control Unit arrived on the airfield.

As the design team sat in front of the technical tent, the monsoon having departed, the slim figure of long-haired Liz, the programmer, was seen picking her way across the roughly cut grass, accompanied by two male companions.

'Bless me!' said one of the fitters (an approximation); 'A bint' (another approximation); 'What the hell is she doing in this hole?'

'She has come to blow our PROMS,' I said, not thinking.

The fitter looked up and down with renewed respect, thinking that he had learnt a new word for it and walked away muttering something about the design office fixing themselves up with the best of everything, even in the field of personal services.

The small digital computer that the dynamics team had designed, based on a new enlarged specification written by the aircraft men, was the first in its field and was brilliantly conceived, but because of shortcuts taken to cram in as much capacity as possible, was fiendishly difficult to re-programme correctly first time. The Tangier phase of testing was no exception. After one abortive attempt Liz sat outside the tent staring at sheets of paper, frowning in concentration. An offer of help was cut short when I found that the sheets were in a Binary notation and, in consequence, were scientifically covered completely with a scattering of ones and noughts. Somewhere on these sheets there were a few ones and noughts in the wrong place. I excused myself rather quickly.

After a short time her face lit up with the same light that Archimedes must have generated before leaping out of his bath shouting 'Eureka'.

'It's obvious!!' Liz announced.

Ones and noughts were rapidly reshuffled and they were ready to blow again.

A TECHNIBIT

Back at base, 'blowing' was always carried out under carefully controlled conditions in the laboratory, using carefully stabilised electrical supplies; and from start to finish the exercise of definition, execution, installation and checking, took about a week.

Here at Tangier, using the sometimes-random output from a donkey engine driving a generator, the exercise lasted only until the next day to do the necessary standby boxes for the selected intakes and install them in the aircraft and fly the whole system. The philosophy was simple. Two full sets were to be blown, one after the other. If the test box showed that they were different, one set was probably wrong and, not knowing which, they were both to be thrown away. If they were shown to be the same, the odds that some random spike from the generator had occurred at the same millisecond in the blowing sequence of both sets were so small that they could be ignored. Strangely enough, even with the uncertain supply from the generator, no PROMS were ever thrown away. What eased the exercise was the fact that, in moving from analogue in the prototypes to digital in the following aircraft, only the command law generation was altered, the servo loops, sensors and most of the aircraft wiring remaining the same.

This approach gave some of the more theoretical of government officials who were trying to follow all these moves a severe attack of 'telexitis' (these were the days of telexes and unreliable telephones) but, other than delaying an expensive programme, there appeared to be no alternative. In any case, in the initial tests the new laws were only put in the standby control lanes and the crew had the other lanes, still in the previous configuration, to fall back on for any emergencies.

Once blown and OK first time, the testing carried on apace, the sun appeared to be brighter and smiles reappeared all around, except possibly on the faces of the mechanics who had to get back to work. Pushovers (climbs and dives) to zero 'g' and beyond were carried out many times on each flight. For any onlooker at the debriefing sessions who had not already known which was which, the pilots could be recognised with red faces from their exertions and the observers, who sat facing their instruments across the width of the fuselage, had pale faces, after going many times sideways over to zero 'g'.

Eddie MacNamara, the polite, quietly spoken Scottish pilot, had mastered the art of the pulling exactly the 'g' that was called for at each manoeuvre.

'How do you manage to hit zero "g" so precisely?' he was asked at one debriefing.

'It's the sweeties,' he explained, in his precise Scots speech, keeping a perfectly straight face.

'The what?'

'The sweeties on the window. When the packet of mints start to move upwards I know I'm there!'

So much for developing the sophisticated flying instruments that were fitted to the instrumentation panels to indicate the value of 'g'!

The mentally exhausting daily round was by now beginning to tell on all concerned. The original five days had stretched to ten and then through Easter to the third week. Repeated messages to home about delays had got through to the Flight Test wives, but for some reason not to the design office wives and both they and the children were a bit fraught. Telephone calls were at best uncertain and at worst were cancelled, as they usually came through in the middle of the night. Letters reached home after the team had arrived back.

Each day we would depart for the airport at about 7.40 a.m., John Legg permitting, and would return at about 6 p.m. Then followed the daily ritual of the visit to the kaftan shop next door to the hotel to beat the proprietor down to the one-third level before anyone would buy. The process met with little success in the early and middle stages of the test programme.

Afterwards we ate and settled down to analyse and re-analyse the day's results until one or two in the morning. However, after about a fortnight of this non-stop intense brain work, the group became noticeably stale and took a day off.

The ground crew had to do an engine check and consequently there was no flying on this particular day. We had offered to help, but then thought of the previous week's incident, when Number Two engine had succumbed to the dreaded 'FOD', and withdrew the offer.

Foreign Object Damage, so called because the 'Objects' causing the 'Damage' were 'Foreign' to the engine, and were not items that might have been sucked up from the foreign soil of Morocco. This had been an all-too frequent problem with the most powerful vacuum cleaners on earth installed under Concorde's protective wings. One small bolt could result in thousands of pounds outlay to refurbish the engine. Tangier had been no exception to such a catastrophe, and amateur and professional teams were formed to change the unit as quickly as possible. The amateurs were those in the design office who had designed the installation, defined the test programme and written the instructions on how to assemble, disassemble and install the engine. However, in the eyes of the authorities they had not passed the proper examinations to be aircraft fitters and were therefore not qualified to touch these engines. The only solution to being able to allocate adequate manpower to the job was to keep the authorities occupied elsewhere.

Everyone who could be spared helped to remove pipes and other items from the damaged engine and install them on the new one as they stood side by side on their cradles in the open, beside the aircraft. Thus the new engine would have the correct 'dressing' to fit the appropriate nacelle.

As I lay under one engine trying to see which way a pipe should be removed, one of the fitters joined in and started to remove another component. The fitter's spanner slipped and he took the skin off his knuckles on an adjacent hunk of the engine. The confined space under the engine turned a dark shade of blue as the fitter's agony was expressed in positive Bristolian invective. An edited version of his comments went like this:

'If I could find the crazy bastard who designed this f★★★★★★ installation, I'd stick this f★★★★★ pipe up his f★★★★★ arse!'

The person working beside him tried to make himself look small, but to no avail.

A Flight Test Observer working higher up the engine bent down and, with a grin, said: 'Bert, may I introduce you to the technical manager from the power plant design office. Perhaps he would do?'

And so it was that discretion overcame any thought of valour and the design personnel decided that they should take a day off and let the development team get on with the installation and test of the new engine. These specialist fitters were quite competent and could look after the job themselves, having done it fifty times before without 'expert' help. Anyway, in an emergency they could break from tradition and read the instructions in the maintenance manuals if all else failed, even if at times they professed that the instructions were incorrect.

13

EXCURSION IN A FOREIGN LAND

We had been working flat out at Tangier for nearly three weeks from 7.30 a.m. to 2 a.m. the next day, non-stop, apart from an hour or so for the evening meal. Even during the meal the talk was of technical matters. This method of working was beginning to produce a staleness, which was not good when working at, or on the other side of, the frontiers of science. What was needed was a relaxing day off. Perhaps a tour around this part of North Africa would do the trick.

'Especially if we could have a look at the Mediterranean,' said John.

All that was required was a map, money and a car. If one lesson had been learnt on the many trips to foreign parts, it was that no journey should be started without a map – a recent map.

Foraging expeditions to the bazaar and shops produced only regards of deep suspicion when a map of the town had been requested. Cartes Touristiques were quite obviously regarded as the essential equipment for a foreign spy. The shortage was caused either by tourist demand or the *mañana* system of business. Like the Irish, the Moroccans did not have a word that carried the urgency of the Spanish *mañana*.

In the end we realised that the solution had been staring us in the face in the foyer of the hotel for at least two weeks. A large Michelin map of the country was pinned to the wall. All that was required was a requisitioned piece of tracing paper to hold over the map of Morocco and for someone to carefully trace the proposed route from Tangier, down the coast and then across to the Mediterranean. This procedure was carried out under the suspicious gaze of doormen, bellboys, visitors and, most probably, spy catchers.

In keeping our heads down over the past weeks of working there was sufficient money for the trip, but the next task was the most difficult of the lot. To make the journey the Flight Test manager had to be persuaded that at least one of the many cars booked out to Flight Test could be spared for the day. The subsequent investigation into the number of people regularly using each car led to the conclusion that, apart from the various cars for the pilots, his own was the least likely to be utilised on official business that day. The bargain was eventually struck, and we arranged for him to be taken to the airport at his normal starting time so as to free the car for the day.

Next morning being bright and sunny, Terry, John, Skillen and I drove the Flight Test manager to Tangier Airport and then set off on our expedition. On leaving the airport we encountered our first snag. The map had been copied before we'd decided to start from the airport, and Tangier, where our map began, was several miles to the south. The thought of asking an Arab in French for directions and then getting the Moroccan version of 'If I were you I wouldn't start from here' was off-putting and encouraged our reasoning that if we went west we would hit either the coast road running to the south or the Atlantic. Just in case it might be the Atlantic our brakes were tested, with a success rate of about three out of four. Roads in this area were narrow and it was essential to have plenty of brake power. In any case we imagined that the lack of a speed limit would lend spice to the drive. So, we discovered later, would the existence of a speed limit.

At red traffic lights, those drivers who refused to play 'chicken' against the stream of cross-traffic came to a stop. As soon as the lights changed in their favour, all those behind pressed their hands on their horns. The din was shattering and unending as groups on the cross-streets picked up the challenge as soon as the lights changed again in their favour. Once we hit the main road the locals came past at a high rate of knots, blasting their horns from the time that they first came into sight to the time that they disappeared into the distance.

Heavy lorries kept to the middle of the road until they met another heavier one. Losers in this game of Moroccan 'Big Chicken' roulette could be seen rusting by the roadside in recumbent postures. By the time we had reached the main road running south I had had enough of being on the wrong side of the road on the proper side of the car but without a steering wheel, and had swapped seats with the driver. No one in the design office liked to be driven by any of the others as 'they all drove too fast'. Usually seniority counted and the senior one would be found either at the wheel, or rolled up asleep in a defensive position on the back seat.

We encountered a lot of police activity at irregular intervals, with cars being stopped and searched, presumably for drugs. For some reason we did not arouse any attention from the *gendarmerie* until about 9 miles inland from the coast on the southernmost leg of the journey. Up until that point things had been going reasonably well, and the daily threat of pan-blasting anal discharge had worn off and the dreaded Tangier Tummy Bugs were sleeping off their daily exertions. (Experiencing 'Tangier Tummy' and 'Casablanca Crap' were the low points of the Concorde's North African campaigns.)

However, the gods had obviously ordained that no day in this particular phase of the North African campaign should go smoothly. From a well-camouflaged position around a fairly tight bend, a young policeman stepped out into the road and raised the strong arm of the law.

The three brakes that were working that day brought the car to a curving stop under his outstretched hand. Despite strenuous corrective efforts, car and *gendarme* finished up on the grass verge. The car was where the brakes had taken it, and the policeman, in his efforts to avoid it, was taken elsewhere. He centralised his *kepi* (cap) and smoothed down his uniform. He seemed unruffled by the erratic manoeuvres made by the car. As has been said before, in this country there were only two states of motion – the quick and the dead.

'Papiers!' he demanded.

We produced our passports.

'Non, pour le voiture!'

Clearly any fool could tell that we were foreigners, but had we stolen the car?

No one had any idea at all where the car's licence, ownership and insurance papers were to be found. Visible pockets were searched but to no avail. The boot and, in a last desperate act, the engine compartment were examined minutely. Had Flight Test fouled it up yet again? The ensuing exchange in French accompanied by well-practised Gallic shrugs on our part and native Arabic gestures on his, got us nowhere. It was made clear that without the car's papers we would be arrested if we went 'that way' (up the road) and also if we went 'that way' (down the road).

Each time we dissented we were persuaded of the justice of his argument by the way he hitched his revolver case one more notch around his belt. We tried the beautiful country ploy: 'We are tourists here enjoying your beautiful country and wish to see more of it.'

The hitch of the gun holster on his belt indicated that if we didn't shut up and produce the papers we would see much less than had been planned. We tried the Concorde ploy – it had never failed in any country in the past.

'We are British engineers working at the Airport of Tangier on the Concorde.'

'What is that?'

Not only had it failed, but also it had crashed, and now we were shaken to the core to find that here was someone who had never heard of it!

'Perhaps we could go back to the last town and telephone Hertz to send the papers in another car?' someone suggested.

Surprisingly this idea succeeded, as by now the police officer was getting a bit fed up with people who were obviously clowns and not convicts on the run. What is more the gun had done a quarter circuit of his waist and was resting against the buckle of his belt.

Thankfully we set off back down the road in the direction whence we had come, but round the next bend we stopped the car.

'Let's have one last look before we go any further,' I said. 'It would be a pity to report failure of the mission to Flight Test!'

If there had been a set of spanners in the car, we would have had the *engine* to pieces in our efforts to find the errant papers. Happily that was unnecessary. The car, a Renault 16, had what appeared to be a bench seat at the front. The driver and passenger seats were joined in the middle by a similar small squab that could be raised to expose a deep pocket. Inside here was a plastic folder containing the car's papers.

Apologies to Flight Test. The paperwork was correct this time. Turning round we backtracked and approached the spot where our friend had hidden again. This time he came out cautiously, ready to take avoiding action if needed. On seeing who it was again his gun came round several notches, but stayed in its holster when the documents were produced with an explanation of where they had cunningly hidden themselves. His patience appeared to be wearing thin. How could anyone, even if they *were* British, drive a car around his country without knowing where its documents were located? With a beautifully choreographed 'gerroff!' arm gesture he indicated the exit route. Putting on suitably chastened looks we drove gingerly away.

This episode had taken John Legg's thoughts away from food and by now two foodless hours had passed – not even a Coca-Cola was consumed. From the back seats the pressure to find sustenance mounted at every corner and it was a very thankful driver who pulled into a parking space on the pavement in front of what looked like an Arab 'transport caff'. The green frontage appeared to have changed over many years from drab to tatty. The ubiquitous Coca-Cola sign, whilst still legible, now hung close to the vertical from one nail. Nevertheless, the doors stood wide open, revealing tables, chairs and a good-looking waitress. That, and the need for food, eliminated any lingering doubts. We went in. Whereas conversation in the brush with the law had been possible but difficult, it was in the café that the language barrier became a brick wall. The menu was written in scribble on one side and in what seemed to be French phonetics of the Arabic sounds on the other. Ten crazy minutes of using the Coco-Cola, Agfa and Total advertisements as the Morocco equivalent of the Rosetta Stone language school got us nowhere, or to be more correct gave some letters in words that could not be identified due to the large gaps between them. If it had been possible to fill the gaps, the results would have been words which no one would have understood any better, as they were still in Arabic. So the game of Arabic scrabble was ended with no points awarded and the waitress was summoned.

She was a small, pleasant but shy girl who had been watching with some amusement. At this stage in a novel she would have walked over to the table and asked what was wanted in a Liverpudlian accent. It was not to be; she could speak some French, but could not describe the dishes. A suggestion that she should draw them was not understood by her and was hooted down by those sitting around the table, by remarks such as: 'You try to draw a rice pudding yourself and see how far you get!'

We thought that she had been offended by the guffaws as, at that moment, she turned and walked towards an old battleaxe of a woman sitting in the shadows behind a cash desk. They exchanged a few words in low voices and then she pointed an index finger at our table. What unwitting sin had we committed this time? The finger crooked and beckoned and she walked towards the stairs leading below. No one moved. Had she misunderstood? Were we wanted all at once or one at a time? This was a restaurant wasn't it? Had the menu been for food or for other pleasures? The expressions on the faces around the table were a sight to behold. At the top of the stairs she stopped, looked back and gave a winsome smile, crooking a finger again and walking downwards.

'Geronimo!' someone said.

'But before lunch?'

'She wants us to look at the food, you fool.'

'Ahh.' There was disappointment – or was it relief? – all round.

Down below in the kitchens fires burned and cauldrons bubbled. On the sides of the kitchen, set into the walls, were blazing fires on which were a whole sheep, several chickens and a large cauldron.

Our waitress lifted a lid from a covered tray and said something incomprehensible. There were blank looks, although what was on the tray seemed to be palatable. Out of the darkness beside one of the fires a voice said 'Baaa'. We said 'Yes' and a man who appeared to be the cook stepped forwards into the light and smiled. The next dish had us all wondering – something's 'sitting on their severed stumps of neck', as T.E. Lawrence would have it?

'Yuk!' one of us said.

The cook stopped smiling.

'Manners, everyone!' said another.

'Er, no thanks,' I muttered.

The cook scowled, using a look that implied that this dish was his favourite *plat du jour*.

So we moved on to the next vat, cauldron, grill and pot, slowly making a circuit of the kitchen under the watchful eyes of the staff. Flames leapt upwards to holes in the roof. Smells mingled and passed tantalisingly close to us without being recognised. Small bags containing spices lay to hand to provide a pinch here and a camouflage handful there. Chickens which had offered their all hung from hooks beside meat carcasses which had been persuaded to do likewise. No one mentioned eggs and bacon.

And so our kitchen tour went on, with the cook and staff recovering from a collective sulk and gradually becoming overjoyed. We climbed the spiral staircase back to the dining room to await the meal. By this time all of us were ravenous and had consumed a goodly quantity of a red wine rejoicing under the name of Doumi – or as it was afterwards christened, *My Doom*. This wine, no doubt grown in the land of the Prophet for export and consumption by tourists, grew smoother and tastier as time passed. In due Moroccan time the meal arrived. No one could be sure what had been ordered so the dishes were taken in rotation. Three of the group eventually called a halt to the stuffing process and eventually even John did likewise.

Feeling replete we paid a remarkably small bill to the dragon lady sitting in the gloom at the back of the restaurant, gave the waitress a large tip, and headed for the car. There had been no 'car minder' around when it was parked and there was no minder around now. Windscreen wipers, hubcaps and other detachables were still in their allotted positions, so that it was safe to assume that the car 'protection racket', which existed in the cities, had not reached the outlying settlements. There was no need to look at the map as the town had only one street in and out, and out we went. In the mirror a gentleman in a turban could be seen waving (or perhaps shaking his fist). It could have been the proprietor wishing us *bon voyage* or alternatively indicating that the wrong bill had been paid. On the other hand it could have been the car-minder awoken from his siesta, realising that the day's takings were leaving for the Mediterranean.

Feeling relaxed, replete and caring little, the open road beckoned. As the car climbed the foothills of the mountains the roads were deserted. There was no hidden policeman looking for cars carrying drugs and the suicidal pedestrians and kamikaze lorry drivers were conspicuous by their absence. Soon we were heading north to satisfy repeated demands to see the Med. It was with a carnival atmosphere that our car approached the next large town. The narrow roads where speeds were unlimited had been left behind and now the Renault was travelling down a road which widened to five lanes within the town's boundaries, assuming the boundary point to be that where the massive hoardings became end-to-end and the houses peeped from underneath.

Whilst following another car at a reasonable distance down this wide road, a figure leapt off the pavement, blowing a whistle. Not another one! The car driver in front had seen this many times before and he kept going, leaving us to confront the policeman (for such it was) and to listen to his questions. The portly figure that supported a round nutty red face strode importantly across the road. A black droopy moustache, followed by the face, peered in at the driver's window.

'*¿No ha vista el disco?*' he asked, pointing down the road.

Little bits of Spanish spittle accompanied each Spanish 's'.

This time we knew what he wanted, although none of us could understand a word he said.

On the right-hand side of Morocco, as you look up the map, was an enclave which the crafty Spanish do not mention when they are making aggressive noises about British possessions such as Gibraltar. This was Ceuta, where the Spanish sit looking north across the straits to Gibraltar in an attempt to find out what is going on over there. And around Ceuta the clever devils placed Spanish and Arabic speaking *gendarmerie* just to confuse unwary travellers such as us.

We knew what he wanted and produced the car's papers.

'*¡No quiere los …!*'

So we produced our passports. These were importantly waved aside. The nutty face became redder and the droopy moustache bristled.

'*¿No – ha – vista – el DISCO?*' he said, and his words were accompanied by a garlic-flavoured tsunami that blasted its way across the car's interior. The occupants leaned back in unison as the wave passed over them.

Skillen, sharp as ever, recognised the last two words.

'He wants you to buy a ticket for the policemen's ball.'

A blast of laughter from the occupants of the car was cut to ribbons as the revolver holster was hitched forward and the button holding the flap was released.

'*El disco … treinte kilometre!*'

Strains of long forgotten Italian came back to me as he said *triente kilometre*. We all strained as one to look rearwards, following the line of the fat, pointing digit. There was a 10ft high oversize concrete disc, which we had seen looming over the advertising hoardings, and this had, on one side, a '30' with a yellow slash through it. It was not advertising the North African equivalent of Heinz Varieties at all, but indicated that the speed limit on this five-lane road was 30km per hour – about 20mph – in contrast to the unlimited speeds in the narrow country roads.

Our expressions of sorrow and regret were punctuated by a distant succession of ascending screams from an open exhaust fitted to a powerful motorcycle, which was yet to appear at the far end of the road. From the noise, it appeared to be coming up fast through the gears towards the policeman. Blowing his whistle and flailing his arms, our porky friend scuttled across the intervening three lanes to intercept. However, this wasn't his day, as the motorcycle had no intention of stopping and neither had we. Whilst his attention was diverted we exceeded the speed limit again, this time intentionally. Anyway, if he had taken down the number of the car it was booked out in the name of the Flight Test manager.

By now it had started to rain; nevertheless, John's second objective, the Mediterranean, was near. On leaving the far side of the town, around a bend in the road, there it was – the Mediterranean: wet, windswept and miserable. For about two whole minutes, standing on the beach beside the car, half-closed eyes shaded against the return of the horizontal monsoon, we observed very little before giving it up as a bad job and setting out on the last, westerly, leg, back to Tangier. The tracing of the hotel wall map was consulted and a decision was made to skirt Ceuta and take to the hills again, but this time in a more or less direct line towards Tangier.

The road got narrower and narrower, but the speed limit was obviously infinity judging by the behaviour of some of the locals. As the car ground its way upwards it went into the low cloud that accompanied the rain. Even under these foggy conditions it was possible to perceive the way in which some enterprising civil engineer had solved the problem of cutting a road at right angles through the ridges of these mountains. Each ridge had a V notch cut through it and the resulting rubble had been used to form a route across the next valley. It was on one of these narrow infillings that we met what appeared to be a gaily lit block of flats racing towards us through the murk. Perhaps it would have been safer if it had been a block of flats on wheels, but it was worse – it was a Moroccan *camion* (lorry) with fairy lights all over the front, driven by another unregistered lunatic. Swerving, swearing and sweating we avoided the big vehicle and the precipice, and were in the process of offering up a prayer when what should come along but another block of flats driven in the same kamikaze manner by a competing idiot.

By the time the next such infill between mountain peaks had been reached and the road had broken through the cloud, we were rewarded by a view of more peaks jutting out of fog banks. Our nerves had added to the effects of gradually filling bladders and so a halt was called to get out, admire the view and attend to nature. Both front doors were opened at the same time, letting the crosswind in and the precious tracing of the map out. It skated across the road and over the man-made precipice on the far side. One at a time, each of us, who had all remembered not to pee into the strong wind, looked over the edge and followed its fluttering flight. There were no volunteers to go and retrieve it.

14

SUCCESS (OR NEARLY SO)

It was back again to the testing, flying carefully, or nearly so, at Mach 2-and-a-bit, happily surging away only where the aircraft went beyond zero 'g'. We invented corkscrew manoeuvres to give combinations pushover and sideslip, testing the piloting skills of those at the pointed end, pushing gingerly into 'Coffin Corner' (so-called because the limits of 'g' and sideslip combined looked coffin-shaped when plotted graphically). Finding no nasty surprises here, we followed up with manoeuvres that, considering that they were done on a sedate civil transport aircraft sideslipping to zero 'g' well above Mach 2 would have brought tears of joy to the eyes of a fighter pilot. In reality it nearly brought tears of nausea to the eyes of the Flight Test Observers, whose sideways-facing seats meant that they were still going into all these manoeuvres left shoulder first.

Within a few days the team knew that they had cracked the problem of flying safely when flying efficiently at the required supersonic cruise speed. If ever the aircraft encountered zero 'g' the hundred grannies on board were unlikely to be frightened by a noise like a train smash when they were floating towards the ceiling (provided that everything worked!).

What would happen if it didn't work? What could happen if some faults developed which stopped one or two intakes from controlling correctly, as indeed they might? Easy! It was in the book. Any pilot could do it – they hoped!

At the end of the campaign of testing, a team representing the Civil Airworthiness Authority (CAA), including Gordon Corps, the CAA test pilot, arrived to give the official verdict on the whole exercise – pushovers, sideslips, pull-ups, arbitrarily slamming the throttles in any direction, fixed intake drills on one and two engines – and the position of the pilots' coffee-cup holders. After a careful briefing the official team climbed aboard and assumed responsibility. The BAC test crew sat alongside, monitoring every action just in case they did anything that might bend our precious aircraft.

With frontal aspects exhuming confidence and fingers crossed behind their backs, the design team watched as the big bird taxied to the far end of the runway, disappearing from sight where the runway curved down to meet the sea. The dust cloud and heat haze rose, and moved rapidly rearwards as power was applied. Because of the distance the noise came moments later. Along the runway the fin appeared, moving fast, then we saw the whole aircraft. The nose rose in the air, a dust cloud vortex sprang from the wing tips very briefly as the aircraft lifted majestically, the sun flashing on the cockpit, then the wings. She turned and headed towards the Atlantic for the final assessment.

A TECHNIBIT

In the previous years there had quite regularly been long discussions between aerodynamicists, pilots, systems engineers and airworthiness authorities on the problem of intake control surfaces stuck in the wrong position. This type of failure would, within a short time, mean that the wrong amount and distribution of air would be supplied to the engines. Hence a surge.

Aircrew Operating Procedures for such an eventuality in the fixed intakes of subsonic aircraft had never been required before and, therefore, it was new ground for everyone. In consequence, there were many difficult ways of proceeding which, over the years of discussion, had been whittled down to a single set of rules.

In essence, once the failure had been diagnosed, the pilot was given the job of adjusting the engine speed to suit the immovable intake configuration by observing the position of a group of instruments called eta-B meters. In effect, these meters read the aerodynamic pressure above the front ramp, which gave a measure of the position of the shock-wave system in the narrowest part of the intake and gave the pilot a hint as to whether he should throttle up or throttle back. Unfortunately, because of the need to put the essential and more regularly used instruments directly in front of the pilots, the only recourse the pilot had to read the less-used eta-B meters was to look at them on the flight engineer's panel over his right shoulder.

Some three hours later, on a tip from those monitoring the progress of the tests over the HF radio, the designers gave up attempts to eat 'airport omelette', drank the last vintage of John's Coca-Cola and gathered outside. A speck over the ocean gradually developed into the familiar swan-necked appearance of Concorde on the approach path to the runway. The CAA pilot had simulated failures of the control systems at Mach 2 and was assessing his ability to bring the aircraft back from Mach 2-and-a-bit, 10 miles up, to a safe landing at sea level with two intakes fixed. The first and last stages of the exercise were the tricky bits, as the two affected engines were gradually starved of the air that they needed to develop full thrust. He had performed the first stage under the watchful eyes of the test crew. He was going to carry out the last stage under the critical eyes of the whole team.

Under normal circumstances we had been able to watch the whole of the approach and touchdown from a vantage point beside the tents. However, the approach we were watching now was very different, as the complete aircraft disappeared from sight below our field of vision. The sea was down there! Had the pilot completely misjudged it? Worse, with the intakes fixed in the supersonic position giving limited power, had our aircraft touched down in the sea? We offered up a quiet prayer – quiet, because we understood that sudden, loud prayers made God jump. It worked, as Concorde appeared a few long agonising seconds later, having touched down on the extreme limit of the runway.

We were told later that the Airworthiness Assessment pilot had been concentrating on running the engines within their limits and had arrived back at the airport a bit short of altitude.

Mindful of the old adage that in an aeroplane 'it doesn't matter what you do as long as you don't hit the ground (or the sea) whilst doing it', the firm's Deputy Chief Test Pilot in the co-pilot's seat had quietly and slowly moved his hands up to the reheat switches behind the throttles, fully prepared, if the position got any hairier, to bang the switches on, regardless of protest. Happily this action, which would have indicated the failure of the tests, was a few seconds short of being required. Nevertheless, both pilots were in a bit of a lather when they sat down in the debriefing tent.

While the formal process of debriefing got under way, one of the Flight Test Observers, who had been following the tests on the intercom, gave a wink and a quiet thumbs up to the technical team.

This small gesture told us all that was required. It had been a long and tortuous way from that first encounter with surges at supersonic speeds. Supersonic flight had today been shown to be both efficient and safe under adverse conditions. The team had got there – provided that the Production Aircraft, with different secondary nozzles, all behaved in the same way. Initially, they didn't. Hence Casablanca 1 and 2.

15

EXIT FROM TANGIER

Back at the hotel the panic set in. Most of us had had little time to look for presents to offer as an inadequate soothing balm for an overlong stay, a spoiled Easter, broken promises, and fewer and fewer telephone calls. Wives had had to cope with children, car breakdowns, broken fuses, and the normal patch-up-and-mend situations left behind by busy husbands.

One present that earned a lot of brownie points after Tangier I was a kaftan. To this end the whole team had been wearing down the resistance of the young lad in the kaftan shop next door to the Hotel El Minzeh by visiting it each evening as they got off the bus and offering one third of the asking price, without the option of negotiation. On this day we went in as usual, said: 'Sorry that we could not do business as we are off tomorrow,' thanked him, said goodbye and walked out. This manoeuvre produced the genie effect: he was standing in front of us before we had passed the window to leave. One more haggle and we had won, having agreed to sales at very reasonable prices.

Kaftans were produced in black, red, brown, white, green and orange, each decorated around the edges with gold thread designs. Some had buttons from neck to hem, others had sexy slits up the sides. All of us had wandered through this Aladdin's cave many times over the past weeks, but when the time came to make a choice the doubts set in. Our reasoning ran along the lines of: 'It's not what *I* like, it's what *she* likes. Or does she dress to please me? Or does she dress to please her friends? Or …'

Logic dictated that we should get ones that husband and wife both might like and make sure that it is not like any of the others. So we did.

On the basis that 'if that is the price I'll buy two', I bought a black one and a bright red one, identical in shape and design. Held up against a pretty assistant they looked magnificent. However, if we were setting out to make a splash at the next semi-formal or formal party, one or other of the dresses should be set off by the superb large capes provided for the daughters of the Prophet. These capes had a hood trimmed with golden thread and a long gold tassel at the apex. The decorative treatment followed the front lines of the cape to the ground and then the hem, to meet at the back. Bargaining was short and to the point.

'Can I have this at the same price as the kaftan?'

'Sorry, too little.'

'Would you wrap the dresses up as we have to go now?'

'OK, at the same price.'

Nowhere in the shop was a black one to be found.

However, the helpful assistant explained: 'But if you go up the road to the corner you will find our other shop. We have some black ones there.'

We paid and trooped out to tell the others where to shop for kaftans. Several took the advice and made a similar purchase that night. The shop took on the air of the first day of Debenhams' sales. The next morning I wandered up to the corner shop to confirm purchase of the cape before the rush started. Here again it was a bit like a colourful Marks and Spencers, but with all their stock in one small room. Kaftans and capes everywhere.

My opening gambit was simple and direct: 'Yesterday I bought two kaftans at your other shop down the road, but there were no capes in the colour I wanted.'

'I have capes of many colours!' was the reply.

'Can I have one at the same price as the kaftans?'

'Certainly, that is my shop, that was my young brother there, how much you pay?'

The bill was produced. He looked at it, then at me, then at the bill again. I smiled expectantly. The shopkeeper's brown face diffused red; his eyes took on a wild look, his expression changed from a smile to a grimace. (Obviously a valve had stuck.) With one leap he reached across to the telephone and dialled. The air became thick with Arabic and spittle. (Right! it must be the lubrication system.) For at least five minutes the lines burnt between the corner shop and the little kaftan shop next to the El Minzeh. The man had taken off with reheat going at full blast and was climbing like the clappers when he suddenly remembered that there was a customer present.

'No sell!' he screamed. 'No sell!'

Since the shopkeeper appeared to be beyond reasoning concerning what he and his younger brother thought was a reasonable price for the cape, I left. Walking glumly along the road I began to wonder whether two kaftans formed a reasonable recompense for Ann's forbearance, or should I look for something else?

Brass pots, pans, leather handbags, even people's sisters, all presented themselves as I pondered the contents of each cave. Fruit, beer, more brasswork – kaftans and capes! Standing in front of a small, dark shop there were a few of these hanging for show, but behind, yes *behind*, were row upon row of them, carefully packed, awaiting a sale! There was no need to bargain this time.

'The chap down the road is selling kaftans at this price,' I said, producing the bill. 'But he has no capes. Can I have a cape at the same price?'

This new shopkeeper looked at the bill, but was probably well oiled, as there was no explosion. Just a dark muttering under lowered lids as he walked to the door and looked morosely down the road.

'Is not tourist season but we must sell,' he said. 'Selling this price not stay in business long. Must talk to him.'

'I must go as I have a plane to catch at ten o'clock,' I replied. '*Avion depart a dix heures.*' This was just to reinforce the point that there was no time right now for him to discuss pricing policies with his fellow member of the Chamber of Commerce. (The time was actually correct, but it would have been a superfluous piece of information to tell him that the departure was set for the day after tomorrow. I knew that time meant nothing in this place.)

He looked at the bill, the date and the price.

'OK,' he agreed reluctantly. 'Once. No more.'

The hood, trimmed in gold, had a long golden tassel hanging from the apex. Gold needlework in repeated complex patterns ran down the edges at the front and met around the hem. Gold buttons joined the two at the neck. The specification was correct to the last detail.

Two days later Aircraft 101 sat on the hot runway being loaded to the eyebrows with ground equipment, spare wheels, large baskets of fruit, baggage, kaftans and test results. There was a problem with air traffic and, as a result, the take-off time had been delayed. The fruit was continuing to ripen.

Standing beside Aircraft 101 was a twin-engine Bulgarian Tupolev Tu-134 (suspiciously like the BAC 111) loaded with sweating passengers who were not allowed to get out to escape from the heat by standing under the wing in what breeze there was. Further away a four-engine Russian Illyushin Ill-62 (suspiciously like the Vickers VC 10) had just landed from Cuba in transit to Moscow. The passengers were being ushered in single file to the terminal building, stewardesses at the front and rear. Standing in front of the airstairs in an immaculate line, matched only by the sartorial perfection of their blue-grey uniforms, was the aircrew.

Somehow the members of the design team felt that they had to get inside the Russian aircraft to look at the standard of equipment, if only out of engineering interest. The Russians were obviously looking at Concorde and discussing it, so therein lay the answer. We walked across the baking tarmac and posed the question to the man with the thickest gold braid.

'Would you like to look around Concorde?'

'Is permitted?' Mr Gold Braid asked.

'Is permitted!'

In line astern and in step we moved across the tarmac to the steps up to the main entrance door to the Concorde.

'Where did you buy your VC 10?' asked a grinning Ground Crew Chief as we climbed into the aircraft. For a moment the Aeroflot captain looked puzzled, until he remembered that the West felt with some justification that a lot of their aircraft had been copied by the Russians. It was a joke! He laughed and turned to the next in line.

'Ruski, ruski VC 10!' he said.

The next man in line hesitated, saw the captain laughing, laughed himself and passed the joke down the line. Each person slapped the 'Chiefy' on the shoulder as they passed. The Chiefy was last seen walking away rubbing his shoulder as the Russians looked into Concorde's cockpit.

'Many instruments. Very small,' one of them said.

They looked at the passenger cabin with its many banks of test instruments and test positions for flight observers and relatively few passenger seats.

'Very impressive!' said another. 'Few passengers! Passengers are nuisance!'

Explanations started about the fact that this was only a test aircraft and there would be no room for many passengers with so many test instrument recorders.

'Russian joke!' the man said.

As they were escorted back he was asked about a tour of their aircraft. The answer was very short:

'Is not permitted!'

'Russian joke?'

'No! Russian Orders. Sorry!'

The 'Advanced Number One Ploy' had failed. Walking back towards Concorde 01 it was not clear whether the reason was Cold War policy or the joke about the VC 10. However, there was always the Bulgarian aircraft. A man with very little braid stood at the bottom of the short array of steps up to the open door of this aircraft as we walked by.

'Would you and the crew like to look at Concorde?' we asked.

Clearly this crew had been looking at the goings on with interest, as they were out of the aircraft before the minimal-braid man had finished repeating the question to those inside. The passengers were still strapped into their seats looking hot and miserable. On the other hand, the crew were a very cheerful lot as they boarded Concorde, looked around, probing into corners and making jokes about carrying spare tyres and equipment lashed inside the cabin.

'That is not required, even in Russian aircraft!' a Bulgarian said.

'This is a research aircraft and…'

'Sorry! Bulgarian joke! Would you like to see around ours?'

They were nearly trodden underfoot in the rush.

Our first impression of the cockpit on the left of the entrance was that this was where a Second World War Lancaster bomber pilot would have felt at home. At the centre of the cockpit, with just enough room for a man to pass between, two vertical 1in tubes of square cross section reached from floor to ceiling. From these two another three similar tubes on each side stretched horizontally above knee height to the side panels. Between these three sets of tubes the pilot's flying instruments were securely bolted.

There were three seats in a row, one for each pilot in front of the instruments and one in the middle for the captain. Hunched in front in the 'bomb aimer's' nose fitted to most Russian civil aircraft sat the navigator. With that amount of glass in front where was the weather radar, we wondered?

'What is the procedure in bad weather when approaching an airfield?' someone asked.

'Quite simple,' said the captain, 'I tell him move out,' here he indicated the navigator, 'and then I lie down, I am looking through the flat glass panel and tell the pilot on the left "up or down" and the one on the right "left or right".'

That was a conversation stopper if we were to remain polite. We were rescued by the steward who lifted up passengers' legs – the passengers were still strapped in all this time! – to show them the dinghies under the seats, then he showed us around the galley and offered several bottles of wine which were in crates in the gangways. The British airworthiness authorities would have had a fit. It looked as though some of the passengers might do so fairly soon too as, suffering in the stifling cabin heat, they saw some of their booze going out of the door.

A couple of months later when we met the CAA pilot Gordon Corps again, we told him about the bad weather procedure.

'Rubbish! They were having you on!'

He was probably still feeling the strain of the Fixed Intake Emergency Procedures test. Sometime later we met him again in the course of the certification process.

'By the way, you were not far wrong with that description of bad weather procedure,' he said. 'I've just been to investigate a mid-air collision over the Balkans and guess what? Amazing!'

Going back to our tour of the Bulgarian aircraft, take-off clearance for Concorde came soon afterwards. Air traffic was being a little difficult that day and insisted that they flew under the local airlane if they could not fly over it. Even though they knew that no aircraft were in the airlane at that time, they had set a task that they thought to be impossible. Brian Trubshaw, the Chief Test Pilot, never suffered fools lightly.

'Light the bangers!' was the gist of his comment when he heard the post take-off instruction. The reheat came on and stayed on longer than usual. The aircraft made it – and the Air Traffic Controllers were not to know with what accuracy. Of such incidents legends are made.

The passengers sat back and waited for the cabaret. They knew what was about to happen, because they had been told and had their cameras ready, concealed on their laps. The Star Performer didn't know that they knew. And thus the first 'supersonic streaker-to-be' undressed at the very back of the aircraft in the strictest secrecy (or so he thought) and ran up to the front of the aircraft followed by the cheers of the passengers as he passed. At the top he turned and raised his arms, which was a signal for all the concealed cameras to be raised and aimed. The flasher was flashed.

After that incident there was nothing to do except have the first 'supersonic cricket match'. This started a technical discussion on the fact that the ball (an orange) would have touched down about 2,000ft in space behind where the batsman had been standing when the ball was bowled. Brian Trubshaw's comments were even more basic when he was told that it was his turn to bat.

We arrived back home three weeks after setting out on a four-day trip. Little information had filtered back via Flight Test to the design-office wives about changes in programme. Their lives had been made all the more difficult by this omission.

Sequel I

About a month after the return to England the Arabian Nights Kaftan Party at Brian Gammon's house was a great success. Kaftans and contents were flaunted, examined and discussed. For some success also attended the Arabian Night immediately afterwards.

Sequel II

Several months later, Ann and I had occasion to go to a dinner dance over in Wales. Several of the works hierarchy were there, it being the annual bow-tie 'do' for the Bristol branch of the Royal Aeronautical Society. Having forgotten about it as usual, until reminded at the last minute by an over-efficient branch secretary who was drumming up business, I broached the subject and received Ann's 'nothing to wear' ploy in exchange. The usual reply: 'Go like that then and slay them all!' had been worn threadbare by now.

Having reviewed who might be there, and who might not, it was decided that Ann could get by with the red kaftan and black cape. The dinner went well, with Ann's outfit attracting many admiring glances. During the dancing we passed by one of the senior members who, with his wife, had been eyeing the dress for some time.

'I don't know how you can afford a dress like that, young fellow,' said the senior member, clearly working under instructions from the management. 'They must be paying these newfangled aerodynamicists too much these days.'

'I'm in the Power Plant Group these days – a systems man like you,' I said, hoping to head him off.

However, his wife was intent on trying to find out how we had managed to afford the dress, in the hope, presumably, of persuading her husband to buy such an item on one of his many sallies abroad.

'In Spain there were a few selling at £80 each,' said the senior manager's wife.

'Well,' I continued, 'after that extended episode at Tangier, we had to do something. Otherwise we would all have been grounded. You would agree that the wives have a rough time in this industry!'

The man's wife nodded enthusiastically, but as we were in the middle of the dance floor and causing a jam, we steered away rapidly before the conversation could get out of hand. It would have been cruel to point out that in Tangier similar kaftans could be bought for the equivalent of £12.

As the members left the club at the end of the evening, the couple I had been talking to stood on the steps waiting for their car. Ann came through the door, now wearing the cape as well. From the expression on the face of the senior member's wife, it was clear that she assumed that some other husbands were angels, regardless of possible financial problems. It would have been possibly career limiting to mention that there was a second kaftan in Ann's wardrobe at home.

Perhaps other people did not have three weeks in which to bargain.

16

THE NORTH AFRICAN CAMPAIGN – PART 2

> We are able to fly the aeroplane at Mach 2 ... and the engine sits there and runs perfectly happily. You can slam the throttles from one end of the quadrant to the other; you can do just what you like. We have done it all, all combinations of these things, and it just swallows the whole lot and goes on working. That in itself I think is the greatest single achievement on the aeroplane.
>
> Gordon Corps, Civil Aviation Authority Deputy Chief Test Pilot. (Quoted in *Concorde – Story of a Supersonic Pioneer*, K.T. Owen, Science Museum, 2001)

The final clearance tests were to be carried out on the French production standard Aircraft 201 from the airport at Casablanca. The aircraft was flown and serviced by the Aerospatiale Flight Test crews and maintenance team. In addition, a small technical team from Filton who specified the tests were to be flown out to monitor the results. Cliff Richards, another aerodynamicist, had now joined the party. He had been heavily involved for some time back at Filton and having his expertise close at hand was a significant advantage to the technical team and a balm to his wishes. He also had the advantage of looking like a young version of Omar Sharif and, once he had bought himself a *djellaba* (cloak), could walk anywhere in the town without being offered sheepskin coats, brass ornaments, or somebody's sister. He was even hailed by one person who claimed to have met him in Fez.

Unfortunately, at the beginning I was in a plaster cast from hips to armpit and had to stay behind and deal with phone calls which only spoke of trouble – deep trouble. The engines were surging when they should not have done so, even though they were being flown into the same flight regimes and with the same laws that had been cleared at Tangier.

This episode brought back the memory of an internal memo from Dr Russell, resisted by his secretary but nevertheless sent down to the design office accompanying a presentation textbook on the subject of supersonic air intakes to the engines. The memo said: 'This must be the second most complicated inlet known to man.' He had now appreciated that these inlets were not just holes in front of the engines.

Terry, John and Cliff had to define a series of investigatory in-flight tests in collaboration with the Aerospatiale Flight Test crew, and when these manually controlled tests had been completed, some confidence had returned as the aircraft behaved exactly as forecast.

A TECHNIBIT

In essence, the main problem of several which emerged was that at Mach numbers near to cruise the intake ramps on some intakes would drift away from their intended position and lead that particular engine into surge. The intake controlling pressure appeared to have insufficient gain in this area to prevent the drift.

Three different types of investigation were immediately undertaken.

Firstly to investigate the physical differences between Aircraft 101, from which the laws had been derived, and Aircraft 201. These would include such things as Flight Test and in-service engines, intake bleed levels, primary and secondary flow leakage paths, circular and TV-shaped secondary nozzles, and so on.

Secondly to investigate the problem flight regime, but this time with the intakes under manual control, probing carefully into the problem area.

Finally the intake control system standard had to be carefully defined as the control boxes were being modified continually. Assuring an adequate test standard for Aircraft 201, while not impairing Aircraft 202 which was due to arrive to do noise and overall aircraft performance assessment, kept the various teams working at full pressure.

The sarcastic comments from certain quarters had to be ignored.

However, the solution, once determined, involved not only the modification of the Control Laws, but a large 'no-no' in reducing the cruise Mach number from 2.05 to 2.02. This required a high-level meeting and the presence of our technical director, Bill Strang.

At the meeting Bill stood up to present the case, took his pipe out of his mouth and put it in his coat pocket. A short time into his comments it was quite clear that things were not as they should be. Smoke was beginning to issue from the jacket pocket: his pipe was still alight and was trying to bring the jacket into line. To the amusement of the audience Bill took emergency action, removing and disarming the pipe and patting the pocket into submission. He certainly got full attention from his audience thereafter.

Although there were several who disagreed with the proposal, there seemed to be no satisfactory alternative to that of reducing the target cruise speed. However, it had to be so if the programme was not to be unduly delayed and necessitated a return to base to carry out checks on the aircraft build standard and revise the intake Control Laws yet again.

The consequent phase of testing, so-called 'Casablanca 2', had already started before I was able to shed the plaster cast, so I arrived feeling lighter from the slimming effect and floppy from the removal of the physical support.

All was not well as I found that Terry was confined to bed having succumbed to 'Casablanca Crap' when he fell down into his soup at the evening meal. This trouble appeared to be more violent than the 'Tangier Tummy' experienced further up the coast when testing Aircraft 101, as on that occasion the local doctor had given him a spreadshot of liquid medicines, pills and capsules intended cover any contingency regarding top and bottom orifices, and any others that he might have forgotten. When we took him off the medicine he recovered.

The testing continued, but much more satisfactorily, and in the end André Turcat, the Aerospatiale Chief Test Pilot, expressed himself satisfied with the results so far, but of course there had to be reservations that there was more to clarify.

Following a check flight carried out by the French Official Services we made a presentation to the assembled company using some hastily prepared 6ft by 2ft (or metric equivalent) boards covered with sheets of A4(ish) paper displaying graphs of laws, surge margins and surges. The French test pilots seemed to enjoy the day by labelling us the 'Machs Brothers' (the Marx Brothers' comedy films were famous), which sparked the idea of having the presentation of the award at a later date titled 'The Black Machs Medal', to be made of a circular scrap of light alloy supporting the black Moroccan Star with a dirham at the centre. The citation was to have the motto: 'Issued for Incontinence in the face of a Bleeding Impossibility.'

However, it took a lot of persuasion to get the 'never-do-anything-without-another-meeting' British and French officials to signify their satisfaction by signing over a Moroccan postage stamp at the bottom of the last board, even though it was in jest.

It was ever thus.

17

PATENTLY OBVIOUS – TO US

'We have been instructed by the powers that reside in the upper strata of the Ministry to hand over the details of the Concorde intake and its control system to those designing the Tornado at British Aerospace, Warton!'

The voice on the telephone, from a character with a double-barrelled name that I did not catch, spoke with an air of authority imported from someone higher up the chain of command at the firm's headquarters.

'But,' I answered.

'All the buts have been butted by our top brass. However, as the ownership of the design lies separately with the British and French governments, we can't argue!'

'But, if Warton is collaborating with the Germans and the Italians, they will get the details.'

'Yes.' He would obviously stay in an office and not be sitting in an opposing cockpit.

'And whose side will they be on in the next war?' I asked. 'I suppose all that remains after the past years of hard work is to give it to the Americans and the Russians and everyone will have them! On second thoughts, knowing the security around here and knowing how they work, they probably have already had it in instalments as the development progressed.'

'I am sure that security here is adequate!'

'Have you seen the preliminary details of the Concordski and its power plants?'

The logic of the decision was obvious. An enormous amount of design and expensive testing had gone into the project and, although the details of the two aircraft would inevitably be different, the targets were similar.

And so it came to pass that our design was incorporated into the Tornado, albeit with changes that caused Terry to exclaim: 'What have you done with our beautiful intake?' Somehow the performance of the mutilated design was not as they expected, possibly because the engine designers and their Ministry counterparts exerted a stronger, more conservative influence on their side of the business than had been permitted by the power plant team at Filton.

We were led to understand that in the divisions of responsibility, the power plant supersonic aerodynamics responsibility appeared to lie with the Brits, whereas the supersonic intake control responsibility for the system which was to achieve that aerodynamic performance lay with the Germans!

Again it came to pass a few years later that we received another telephone call from HQ, but this time via the firm's Patents Office.

'The Germans have patented the intake control system and are suing us for an enormous sum for infringing their patent on the Concorde!'

'Tell them to get stuffed!'

'It appears that the designs are remarkably similar, so we *must not* take it that lightly!'

Guilty until proven innocent yet again.

'Did you know that we were told by the Ministry of Supply to give our design for both intake and its control system to them?'

There was hesitation at the other end of the line.

'How do you mean?'

The caller had to be a new boy.

'Our design was defined and working before the MoS gave the instruction to pass it on to them.'

'Oh!' said a relieved voice. 'So we did not copy it? Can we back that up with documents?'

'Possibly there are records from your department which told the design office that we could not patent things like this as they were jointly owned by Britain and France! Then again there would be the instructions from the MoS.'

'It would be very helpful if you could find such documents. Would you send them up to this office?' he asked. It was fairly obvious that he did not have a clue what was being talked about and would rapidly stand aside.

'No. We have aircraft to design. Perhaps you could put a man on to looking up your own records.'

Nevertheless, it was prudent to do a little probing into our records and memory banks as someone would be bound to fix a meeting with little or no notice, still expecting us to do all the work.

Which they did.

It transpired that most firms, with the exception of a few – like ours – would permit their employees to hold a patent and claim a substantial percentage of the dues. This particular claim, we were told, would net a total running into at least six figures if not defeated. Our minds went back to the mixed elevon/aileron control patented for the Type 221 mini Concorde where it was suggested by Russ that it would not be worth dividing the half-crown reward between four of our people.

We met Herr P, the 'inventor' and his lawyer in London. Three points became quite clear during the meeting: one was that our firm's patent hounds had not been following the field closely enough; the second was that neither the inventor nor his lawyer knew the background to the source of his 'invention'; the third was that the representative from BAe Warton, who was in design collaboration with the German firm, was very embarrassed.

Unfortunately for the 'inventor' his knowledge of the details of the design showed some deficiencies. However, his lawyer showed an ability to grasp the extent of these deficiencies when pointed out by our side. Even though this was a relatively new field in supersonic engineering he followed each cut and thrust and, from his glances at his client, seemed to want to prod him, or step in on technical points when the latter appeared to be at a loss.

Towards the end of the meeting he had obviously accepted the inevitable and was beginning to enjoy the discussion. Herr P had clearly not appreciated the finer points of our work, where, at extreme ambient temperatures (for example in Tangier) the aircraft intake had to take charge of the situation and exert a significant authority over the engine air mass flow control system – hitherto a heresy to engine manufacturers.

The question to be answered was: should we tell him, or not? After all, the Tornado was to be flown by British pilots, on our side in any war, and these servicemen should not be put at any disadvantage. It was also to be flown by Germans and Italians, but in a war, whose side would they be on?

'Since proposing and developing this system we have developed the control system further than you have indicated in your explanation of "your" patent. Several characteristics have been eliminated and significant ones have been added, for example, at low ambient temperatures.'

Herr P seemed to be at a loss at this point, much to our surprise and to that of his lawyer.

His lawyer looked at him expectantly.

Herr P cleared his throat. 'Perhaps I could borrow those reports and have my engineers study them?'

It was fairly clear why there had been a few gaps in the apparent understanding of the problem. It had to be brought to a rapid conclusion. Being already fully pissed off with the whole thing I must admit that I departed from the previous LegalSpeak decorum to say: 'Hell no! You might invent something else!'

The lawyer nearly choked behind the hand held in front of his face.

We, at Bristol, did not hear another word on the subject.

18

SMALL TALK IN SIMULATORS

Flight Simulation – Type 188

During the Second World War many pilots were given some basic training on the Link Trainer. This consisted of a cockpit surrounded by a foreshortened fuselage and stub wings to give some semblance of an aircraft. The trainer, mounted on a set of actuators, would respond in a limited manner to the pilot's inputs. Its main use was in teaching flying blind, such as in cloud or at night.

No satisfactory adaptation in the 1950s would represent the response rates required for the Type 188, so Godfrey, our pilot, was presented with a chair and a table on which there was a black-and-white television. The television presented a black screen, whereon a horizontal white line was projected with an inverted V in the middle. The idea was that the line, representing the horizon, would respond to the movement of a mini-stick. The inverted V would represent the aircraft.

As the stick was moved to the right, the horizon tilted correctly, but if the stick was pulled back at the same time, the horizon and the V travelled vertically up the screen instead of moving in unison to the right, as well as up. The basic equations were attached to the wrong axes.

Godfrey decided to wait for the real thing.

Flight Simulation – Concorde

One of the two Concorde flight deck simulators was at Filton, where the Training School originally instructed both aircrews and ground crews for the development as well as the in-service activities. As simulation techniques developed in parallel with the aircraft itself, so did the images of the environment seen through the aircraft windscreen. Originally, a screen picture showed the results of a camera shot from a camera being 'flown' over a countryside model of the approach to an airfield. Later, as technology improved, there were virtual images depicting the details of the layouts and environs of significant major airports worldwide. Within the flight deck the instruments, lights and controls are faithfully reproduced. Thus, in conjunction with the hydraulic actuators moving the complete unit up, down and sideways in response to the pilot's controls, the experience is very close to reality.

As in most occupations, those in an instructive capacity develop their own line of patter to alleviate their own feelings of irritation at the incompetence of their charges, as much as to amuse or impress those who seek knowledge. Those in charge of large aircraft simulators are no exception. Week in, week out they instruct their students, putting them into adverse hazardous situations in a safe environment to ensure that, in a real situation, they would carry out the correct procedures, instead of driving themselves and their passengers further into the mire.

During one early exercise the CAA Test Pilot allocated to Concorde arrived to give the stamp of approval for the simulator. The simulator team had checked and rechecked that it was working perfectly and had found no problem, so were full of confidence. All went well until he flew into the supersonic regime, when at a certain point everything appeared to seize up. He was not a happy man and expressed himself in no uncertain manner before departing.

The team tried several times to repeat the problem but could not do so, and therefore a second visit was organised, with the same result. The pilot was livid at having travelled so far just to have had his time wasted yet again. Once more the team could find no fault, so a third visit was planned with the *same* result of 'freezing up' at the *same* part of the flight. At this point one of the BAe team, Duncan Greenman, who had been following every move that the pilot made, leaned over and made an adjustment and everything returned to normal.

'What did you do then?' asked the pilot.

'I switched the reheat off,' said Duncan, 'which should have been done at Mach 1.6!'

These people know their systems and, equally, the systems knew the aircraft's true behaviour, even if expert pilots did not, as I was to find out.

For several years the yearning to have a go on the simulator had been building up inside my head, but pressures from more relevant areas had deflected a specific request. However, following a close encounter with the manager of the Training School, the question popped out. It was met with a 'why have you waited so long?' response.

My first attempt to 'land the Concorde' at a simulation of Kennedy Airport in New York hovered between bad and awful. It would have made world headlines if it had been for real.

'Bloody awful!' said the technician in charge. 'Try Kai Tak. It's horrendous! Past the hills, mind the skyscrapers, watch for the checker board, and stop before you hit the sea!'

There was something twisted with his logic here, especially as he had changed the picture to that for simulating landing in the opposite direction. After my first failed attempt on a relatively easy target, the simulator technician appeared to be enjoying himself. Kai Tak appeared on the virtual display and the flight deck settled itself comfortably at about 3,000ft on the approach path. From there on the approach went well and the touchdown was near perfect.

'Dunno why, but it seems to work out that way nearly every time!' said a very satisfied technician. 'Must be the shock of messing up the first one.'

'Can you do any better?' I asked the equally desk-bound sceptic.

Without a word the display was reverted to the approach to New York Kennedy airport.

Following a steady descent he broke off from the final flare and turned towards the skyscrapers. As they approached realistically close, the aircraft banked from side to side, weaving its way between the tops of larger buildings and finally climbing out. Throughout these manoeuvres I had been weaving in my seat in the opposite direction in an effort to miss the windows of the virtual buildings as they flashed past. The experience was so realistic that I had to take several deep breaths at each stage.

'I see that you can!' I said.

This non-pilot technician could probably fly the simulator better than any qualified one. The interesting adjunct to this display was the demonstration of the agility of this huge aircraft in its ability to perform such manoeuvres. Sometimes visitors from the outside would occasionally be accommodated, especially if they were important.

'Ted, there's a VIP visiting the simulator. Would you be on hand to fly with him and fend off the more technical questions?'

It was an instruction rather than a request and it came, as usual, at a very inconvenient time.

'I can't fly it. Can't we get a real pilot? My licence to fly swept-wing aircraft was limited to Tiger Moths and expired years ago!' I replied.

'British Airways will supply the pilot. You just look after the technical side!'

And so the next day a small group met in the boardroom at Filton House to deliberate on important matters like protocol. As no one had been briefed, all were experts. Conversation was cut short by the door being thrust wide open by a smartly dressed athletic person, closely followed by a second. The first one, the one with his right hand inside his jacket, fixed everyone with a short, sharp inspection and then looked quickly behind the door. At this point the second one overtook him and turned right into the dining room. Number Two then did a quick tour of the boardroom table, bending to look underneath to check for slumbering board members. Finding nothing suspicious they left, nodding to a figure standing in the corridor outside. The tall, erect, bearded figure of Prince Michael entered through the door and shook hands all round. Protocol disappeared with the detectives as the conversation restarted in new directions and continued throughout the lunch. However, it was soon time to go 'flying' in the simulator.

After settling him in the left-hand seat and running through the preliminaries, the BA pilot asked:

'From which airfield would you like to take off, Sir?'

After a silence the pilot explained that he could choose one of several.

'Oh, if that is the case, let us choose Heathrow,' Prince Michael told him.

...Which was the response that the BA pilot had hoped for. Within seconds the windows of the Heathrow Concorde Departure Lounge could be seen through the flight deck windows.

Following more preliminaries the engines were started and the sense of the aircraft being towed backwards and thence under its own power to the perimeter track was felt in the seats of our pants. The flight deck responded to a slightly uneven virtual surface activating the imaginary long nosewheel leg situated way behind the pilots' position. The cabin nodded up and down as the virtual remainder of the fuselage flexed under the input. With this VIP on board there was no delay to departure and the aircraft lined up for take-off. The take-off was straightforward with the aircraft (and hence the Prince) responding magnificently. However, as the aircraft continued in a noise reduction climb, heading towards the west, the BA pilot's voice registered a note of concern.

'A bit more to the right, Sir!'

And again, 'A bit more to the right, Sir!'

'Why all this "a bit more to the right" business?'

'Well, Sir, you are passing rather close to Windsor Castle and we would not like to receive another letter from Prince Philip!'

'Lord, no! One must not upset Philip!'

Flight Simulation – Lockheed C-130 Hercules

My son Michael, now in the RAF, invited the family to an open day at Lyneham, the base for the Hercules transport. Apart from a flight in one of the aircraft at low level, with us standing on the freight floor, looking through a safety net and the open rear loading door, the attraction was a flight in the Hercules simulator on approach down to the runway. The family took it in turns at the controls.

I, applying my Tiger Moth experience of forty years previously, tried to lose height by sideslipping the aircraft towards the runway threshold. I made the centre of the runway, on the centreline, but 6ft below it.

'We won't need a burial party!' said the instructor.

Ann, with one son at her side giving 'up or down' instructions, and the other behind her saying 'right or left', managed to touch down on the runway, but slightly across it. The instructor looked at her and said:

'I think we are in the NAAFI. Would you care for a cup of tea?'

Now it was Richard's turn. Like his mother he had never flown anything before. However, his landing was at runway level, on the runway centreline, but unfortunately a mile short of the threshold. The instructor looked at the virtual image and then at the sprog pilot.

'Shall we take a taxi from here?' he asked.

These experiences with just one family must have made his day, but no doubt he had only skimmed the surface of his vast repertoire of one-liners.

19

ENCOUNTERS IN TRANSIT

Transit 1

The Lockheed Constellation taxied up to the terminal at Toulouse with the two outer engines shut down. This was quite a common practice and produced no particular comments as we watched it from the terminal. The passengers filed through the departure lounge, walked across the tarmac, and boarded the aircraft by means of the airstairs. At the top of the steps stood two exotic examples of Arabian womanhood. Being lovers of beauty in all its forms, there were several complimentary comments as the group looked for their seats. Once the passengers were comfortably settled, the inner engines were started and the aircraft moved slowly away from the terminal towards the runway. At the run-up point the outer two motors were started, Number Four being somewhat reluctant, wheezing and hacking asthmatically. The pilot advanced the throttles on Number One and checked the magnetos. This procedure was repeated on Numbers Two and Three, but not on Number Four.

The group of engineers, including myself, sat back in their seats and surveyed the reactions of the few other passengers – there was no reaction at all. Perhaps they all reckoned that, as the aircraft had not refuelled and there were not many passengers on board, reduced power did not signify against the pilot's need to get to Paris quickly. Or perhaps they hadn't a clue what had happened.

The Toulouse–Paris leg of the flight was going to be interesting. After lining up for take-off, three engines ran up to maximum power with Number Four going as far as giving the impression of power without actually achieving it, with just enough speed to make the propellers invisible. We marvelled at the similarity between this approach and that of Concorde, where the Number Four engine is held down to a limited power level up until 60 knots, and then released to maximum.

The brakes were released and, happily, after an initial swerve due to asymmetric power and with no more power adjustment, we were airborne before reaching the end of the runway. Number Four was immediately shut down and the flight continued on the other three. At this point the stewardesses that we had noticed on entering the aircraft came round with drinks, food and more drinks. Their calming presence dismissed any further thoughts of faulty engines.

However, later on in the flight, when the stewardesses had stopped walking around, our misapprehensions returned and one of our party walked up to the galley 'to enquire' – or so he said. He came back with two half-bottles of champagne but no answers. 'Never got around to it!' was the excuse. Number Four engine was started up on the approach to Paris but never used in earnest. It was obvious that this particular airline employed only the best-looking cabin staff to deflect attention from the state of the aircraft.

Transit 2

During these early days of air transport for the masses, such a cavalier attitude was not uncommon.

Trips down to Toulouse involved negotiating the A4 from Bristol and all other towns in a hired VW beetle or some such vehicle, to Heathrow, Comet to Paris, crossing Paris by airport bus, and then Douglas DC-4, Viscount or Caravelle to Toulouse, followed by taxi to the hotel for an overnight stay. After the meeting on the following day the reverse journey would be undertaken that evening, fog, strikes, connections and serviceability permitting. The next day it might be cross-country to wherever. However, as the years passed, the firm introduced direct flights in both directions, progressing from a four-hour flight in a twin-prop eight-seat Percival President – with a thermos of coffee if you were lucky – through an HS 125 business jet with eight seats and a snifter of spirit if there was a director on board, to a BAC-111 and then a BAe 146 with a hostess to serve breakfast.

On the President those who could play bridge occupied the middle four seats, which were fitted with special clips to hold a temporary table, while those who could not play the game slept. Those who were not expert bridge players were press-ganged into playing if four enthusiasts were not on board. The rest served coffee between naps. On one such trip I was recruited to make up the four. The opposition was debating which calling method they would use. Not being a bridge player I did not understand a word and looked hopefully at Mick, my prospective partner.

'When I nod my head, you bid!' said Mick. We won hands down.

Headwinds occasionally lengthened the journey, causing the aircraft to land in Nantes or the Channel Islands to take on more fuel. Blown cylinder heads on the lowest cylinder, not uncommon with radial engines, called for emergency landings after a technical discussion with the passengers. Emergency lights were brought up deliberately to enliven the pilot's boredom and to see if the passengers would notice.

With so many people travelling to several destinations in Europe, the firm had set up its own Travel Bureau. The operators were kept on their toes by requests for travel to meetings which were on, off, and on again, with venues being swapped all too frequently. If the journey was not on the Bristol–Toulouse milk-run, then the route was on scheduled airlines. If the milk-run plane was full, as it often was, or the managing director wanted it, then the unfortunate extra people travelled by road, air, and road, air again, and taxi both ways, spending a lot more time travelling than in meetings. Aircraft designers who did not like flying were ordered to stop going by boat and train. Travel became the time to read the mail or write up reports.

After one of these on-off-and-on-again meetings no ticket was available for a trip to Paris, but, if I agreed, I could fly in the President to Southend with a director's party and would then be flown to Le Bourget on my own, the aircraft returning to Southend in time to pick up the top brass. All went well, and as we left England behind, my usual protection against boredom, the day's input of mail, had been read, annotated, and put away. With nothing in prospect for an hour, sleep overcame me, no doubt encouraged by the muted roar of the two Alvis Leonides engines and the miscellaneous rattles of the airframe.

This sleep must have been a deep one, as my awakening thoughts were not as clear as they should have been. From my seat amidships in the empty cabin one bleary eye noted that the left-hand pilot's seat was empty. The other eye confirmed that fact a split second later. By leaning into the gangway it was not possible to see anyone in the right-hand seat either.

Relax, lad, I thought, you are still dreaming.

But, I reasoned, if I was dreaming would I be telling myself to go to sleep?

By slowly turning round it was a relief to see that the cabin door was firmly shut. They don't carry parachutes on these aircraft, but did the crew hide a spare set for their own use, I wondered? Anyway the crew would not have shut the door after jumping out! By walking forward I calculated that the shifting weight might put the aircraft into a dive if the autopilot was not engaged. Would there be any chance of a prosecution if someone who only had a single-engine licence rescued the aircraft?

Stupid thoughts stumbled over one another as a fight for a logical answer gradually asserted itself. By tiptoeing (the Lord only knows why, as the load on the floor remained the same) up to the flight deck it was possible to see the co-pilot leaning on the side panel, looking out of the side window.

The question of whether he was still alive was answered, as he swung round.

'What's up?' he asked me. 'You look as though you have seen a ghost!'

'I, er … I've been to sleep and have just woken up. Where is the captain?'

'Gone for a pee. We will be landing in half an hour. I should have another nap if I were you.'

'No thank you, it's too exciting when you wake up!'

The co-pilot looked puzzled, but the return of the captain and the need to start descent procedures prevented any more questions.

Transit 3

A more interesting incident occurred on the twinjet HS 125 when I was returning from Toulouse one evening. There were two spare seats and it had been decided that it should divert to Paris to pick up another passenger who was needed urgently at Filton. As the new passenger had been there for more than the specified number of days, it was noted that he had claimed his full allowance of duty free drinks. The remainder had been on a day trip and, in consequence, in those days were allowed nothing, so they had to console themselves with coffee, as there were no directors on board with keys to the aircraft booze cupboard.

As the aircraft took off again from Le Bourget we were startled by a loud thump, thump, thump followed by an even louder bang under the left-hand side of the aircraft.

During the climb after take-off there was an earnest discussion between the original occupants of the passenger cabin on what the cause could be. The later arrival said nothing, although it was noted that he was rather pale. This was put down to French food.

When the aircraft settled into its climb to cruise altitude the cockpit door opened and one of the pilots walked nonchalantly down the cabin, casting rapid glances out of the cabin windows.

'Did you hear the bangs on take-off?' one of the passengers asked him.

'Oh! You heard it too? I did not mention it as we did not want to worry you!'

It was obvious that this man was by training a commercial pilot and had not really mixed with aircraft engineers before, but as he looked around at the expectant faces he must have thought that it would be safe to venture a piece of technical information, as it now appeared to him that these passengers were unlikely to panic.

'We think that the nosewheel has dropped off!' he said.

'Rubbish!' commented a chorus of voices 'It was something on the port side.'

He looked a little hurt. In any flying situation, unless you owned the aircraft it was bad form to contradict a pilot.

Suggestions flowed thick and fast. He was now pitched into the middle of a typical design office meeting with pilots present: those on one side wondering why they trust these machine managers with such precious creations, with the other side wondering how anyone who was not empowered to fly the aircraft could be so authoritative in their presence. One suggestion (more of an instruction than a suggestion) appeared to be the most practical of the lot:

'Go back, slow down and lower the undercarriage and see if you get three greens.'

This action would, if successful, show three green lights indicating that the two main wheels and the nosewheel were probably locked down safely.

'What if I don't get three?'

'We're in a bit more trouble than if you did!'

He turned towards the cockpit.

'And be prepared for any violent inadvertent longitudinal or lateral excursions as the gear comes up,' followed a voice as he made his retreat. 'There probably won't be any, as it felt OK when it came up after take-off, but it's better to be safe than sorry!'

By this time the pilot was probably wishing that he had never entered the cabin. However, the timescale was more pressing than usual and the trust that usually took months to break down the barriers between our professions was seemingly established in minutes.

The aircraft slowed down to its undercarriage-lowering speed. Gingerly the co-pilot fingered the lever that raised and lowered the gear and, with a nod from the captain, he pressed it down. With its customary whine and double thunk the gear descended.

Only two green lights glowed in the little round indicator – the ones that indicated that the nose and starboard wheels were locked down. In the cabin the seat belts, which had been donned automatically, were released and heads poked through the door into the cockpit.

'Thought so!' said one satisfied voice. 'Port side. What now?'

The pilots had not really lost the initiative, but they thought that they should reassert their authority in the air.

'Would you all please sit down as I have asked the Rolls-Royce 125, which is not far behind, to take a look.'

After a short time, from the rearward-facing seats it was possible to see a wing rising up underneath the aircraft and coming close – alarmingly close. This bit promised to be interesting. We passengers were to witness a bit of close-formation flying, but this time from within the aircraft itself instead of on the ground.

'Christ! He must have his head in the wheel bay!' announced one interested passenger on the other side of the gangway. 'I hope we don't meet any turbulence!'

The worry subsided as the wing slowly moved away.

'What did he report?' someone asked the captain.

'He says that all that he can see is a possible flat tyre,' the captain called back.

'Did you put on some sideslip to see if the gear swung in the breeze and was not locked down?'

No answer. The captain obviously wanted to do his own thinking and not to be hindered by the know-alls in the cabin who appeared to be planning the next step.

The design meeting resumed.

'We could ask Filton to foam the runway and land on the belly. We have never done that before!'

'Yes! The Rolls 125 did that successfully last year!' came the reply.

'I remember seeing it from the office window. Very spectacular it was too, that evening – sparks all over the place, made more spectacular by them being reflected from the underside of the wing!'

However, offers of more high-level suggestions were suspended as the aircraft descended and flew at very low level over Filton airfield. People on the ground were straining their eyes through binoculars to confirm or deny the observations of the Rolls-Royce pilot. As the Control Tower could not add anything positive to the total pool of knowledge, the pilot then announced that he would have to fly around the Severn Estuary, with landing gear down and airbrakes out to burn off excess fuel, thereby minimising any danger should there be any problem when trying to land.

Meanwhile, on the ground, other small scenarios were being enacted. Eric Ruff's wife had arrived with her children at the main gate to take Eric home. She was asking the security guard for the usual permission given to wives to meet their husbands outside the Rolls-Royce Customs Office. This was refused as an aircraft emergency had been declared. This method of clarifying the situation only threw oil onto a potentially inflammatory situation. Nevertheless, Mrs Ruff had to stay at the main gate until she and the very worried carload of small children were admitted after the 125 had landed. Unfortunately it was the Rolls-Royce 125 and not the BAe plane that had landed. The lady's husband and his colleagues were still aboard the stricken aircraft, which was buzzing the airfield and preparing for a sightseeing trip around South Wales.

By now the pilots appeared to have lost interest in suggestions from the design office – a traditional trait. During all this time the last passenger to come on board had been strangely silent. He appeared to be very withdrawn.

This was particularly true when Terry's goon-like sense of humour spilled over and he walked around the cabin shaking hands with all present, saying in a mock show of gloom, 'It has been a pleasure to know you.'

It was at this point that we realised that the quiet passenger in our midst was the one with the duty free booze.

'Come on, open it up! Then we can all take it with us when we go!' someone asked him.

Even this delightful thought in the hour of danger did not produce the desired effect of raising a smile. The comment that he couldn't be a power plant man, or he wouldn't be sitting at the back between the two engines, seemed to send him further into his cocoon. (An analysis of the effect of bursting turbine discs on the structure and systems of the Concorde had just begun.)

After what seemed to be a boring tour of the Severn, with wing-mounted spoilers and landing gear deployed to increase fuel flow, followed by a few interesting low-level circuits of the new Severn Suspension Bridge, the aircraft was lined up with the runway. There was no foam on the tarmac, so it looked as though the pilots were going to attempt a conventional approach, by landing on wheels. Well, in one life one can't experience everything.

'I suppose that if we come to a sudden stop I will be in a safer place than all of you,' said the plaintive voice of the man with the duty free, who was sitting at the back of the cabin, facing forwards. We looked up in surprise at the unexpected verbiage from that source. His face showed a spark of emotion – perhaps hope.

He was just trying to cheer himself up.

'Actually no!' was the response. 'We're facing rearwards and have the seats at our backs and you haven't, so if we come to a sudden stop you will pass us, clamped between the two engines.'

This load of nonsense had the reverse effect of that intended and any ray of hope that had appeared on our friend's face was extinguished immediately.

The aircraft lined up on the runway and started a slow let-down. The HS 125 is notorious for the difficulty the pilots have in producing a 'greaser' – meaning a landing without any significant bump. This landing, however, carried out on the starboard wheel only and then lowering the other two gently to the ground, was superb.

As the aircraft rolled to a stop, with the crash wagons looking very patriotic as they followed, their various lights flashing red, white and blue, the co-pilot stepped out of his seat, raised the door and let down the airstairs. With a flurry of energy the passenger with the duty free booze was un-belted and rushing straight down the gangway, knocking those rising from their seats back into them, dashing out of the aircraft, into the car park and he was gone.

The rest of the passengers got out in a more thankful manner, and refrained with some difficulty from kissing the ground in front of the ground crew. Bending down and looking under the wing it was clear that the tyre, while still inflated, had thrown its tread. With a high degree of accuracy, a piece of tread had been thrown at, and had smashed, the micro switch which would have told the pilot via the third green light that the undercarriage was down and locked in place. More worrying was the fact that another piece had hit the rigid part of the hydraulic braking system and put a very sharp kink in the pipe. It was on the point of fracture and, had severe braking been demanded, the landing might have resulted in a very different story.

One of those bending down to look at the damage surreptitiously kissed his own hand and palmed it on the ground.

'I'll fly with that pilot any time,' observed one of the passengers.

'Not here you won't,' said the mechanic by his side. 'Weybridge are taking over the Communications flying and he has been told that he is about to be made redundant!'

We deliberated on this piece of news as we filed into the Immigration and Customs room.

'We have one more passenger on the manifest. Where is he?' said a resigned Customs and Excise official who, by now, was on overtime – unpaid overtime, judging by the look on his face.

A grinning aircraft marshal popped his head round the door at that minute. 'I last saw him running away. He seemed to have had a bit of a scare.'

'Some people take these little difficulties too much to heart,' muttered a passenger.

The rest of us filed through and left the customs officers trying to contact the poor chap that we had unwittingly been so hard upon, in order to get him to come back.

Little difficulty or not, the man with the legal duty free still had to go through Immigration and Customs. Dammit, this wasn't France.

Transit 4

In France they probably would not have bothered. When I started one of my many impromptu trips on the milk-run I arrived at the departure lounge straight from the office on the other side of the Filton runway and, as usually was the case for a hastily arranged (twenty minutes' notice) day trip, without any money, English or French, but on this particular day, also without a passport. It was pointed out to a gloomy Immigration official that I did have my works pass with the original photograph restored. (The picture of Sophia Loren, which had been there for three years without comment, had been removed some time previously.) Crucially, the meeting in Toulouse was important so I had to go. The official became gloomier.

'You won't get into France,' he said. 'They will probably put you on the first plane out of the country – to anywhere!'

On our arrival in Toulouse we were met as usual on the tarmac by the local British Aerospace Rep whose function, amongst others, was meet the milk-run 125, and to guide visitors to their colleagues on the other side of the Customs and Immigration barrier. In addition, he had to collect mail and to accelerate the onwards despatch through customs of goods and spare parts, especially those for grounded aircraft. Today, as usual, there was a panic on and the new arrivals were the least of his problems. He led the eight passengers at a fast pace through immigration past the lounging officials, calling out 'Huit Anglais!' as he passed. The officials took one look at the eight English characters and returned to their lounging.

We were now in France.

After my meeting the procedure in the reverse direction was exactly the same. We boarded the 125, which had been to Bristol and back in the meantime with a load of French technicians and aircraft spares. The aircraft landed late in the evening at Filton and the passengers trooped into the Customs and Immigration office to be confronted with a different immigration officer.

'Passports please, gentlemen,' he said.

Now came the tricky bit – getting back into one's own country.

'I don't have mine with me,' I apologised.

'Where did you lose it?'

'I didn't lose it. It's at home.'

'Where in France is that?'

'It's not in France, I live in Portishead.'

Being a Bristolian he had heard of Portishead.

A long explanation followed, wherein the laxity of people letting others into and out of their respective countries was tut-tutted at every turn.

'We will have to fill in these two forms in the face of this irregularity,' said he. 'Name?'

I told him and he wrote it down.

'Place and date of birth?'

'Ashby-de-la-Zouch.'

He gave an exasperated sigh and threw the papers into the wastepaper basket. Going into the inner office he rummaged through his files and came out with a new set. It was going to be a long night.

'Ashby-de-la-Zouch is in Leicestershire, not France!' I explained, feeling every inch the criminal who was apparently trying to enter the country illegally.

The official bent down, picked the first set of papers out of the waste bin and handed them over the counter.

'YOU fill them in, or we'll be here all night! And don't forget your passport in future!'

With an effort of will, making a comment about the trouble being only over here was resisted and, after filling in the forms in duplicate, we all left before any more problems arose.

These were the people who had confiscated our colleague Earling's tray of apricots that he had bought by the wayside in France. They then re-read the regulations to find that those for private consumption were not prohibited imports so they remedied their error by telephoning him at home, asking him to collect his apricots in the morning. Unfortunately, the ground crew, who had been told to dispose of them, got the new message too late.

In the morning Earling was handed a bag of pips.

Following this one-day trip the expenses ogre struck again.

'Come and look at this scum on the top of the washing in the twin-tub. It's got numbers on it.'

These words were called up to me from the laundry room, a high sounding name for a small room off our kitchen.

The scene moves to Filton.

'Penny, those fifty-franc notes that I had last week,' I said into the phone that was 200yd away from my boss' secretary's office. 'I haven't used any of them.'

'But?' She was getting wary whenever expenses were mentioned.

'I left them in my shirt pocket when it was washed. I have them in a small plastic bag.'

'Well, iron them out and bring them over.'

'That's a little bit difficult. They were in the form of a scum with numbers on. The biggest pieces are where the number fifty is stamped back-to-back on each note. The number of fifties corresponds to the number of notes I was given!'

How this got past the accountants was never reported back, nor was that information requested, as it was not long after another wallet had been lost when disembarking from Gibair at Tangier.

One safe way to avoid such difficulties in the many ensuing sallies into Europe was to go with a colleague, but without any of my own cash – but of course, *with* a passport.

Transit 5

Apart from lack of passports, the most significant non-operational obstacle to travel was the paperwork associated with escorted equipment. If the paperwork was not impeccable, suspicious customs officers would take no chances. Take wind tunnel models, for instance. They were very complicated, very expensive and, in consequence, heavily insured, but of no use to anyone except the designer, or perhaps an industrial spy.

On the way back from a meeting in Paris between the British aircraft manufacturers and Ministry officials and their French counterparts, the President aircraft was carrying a large and expensive wind tunnel model used for power plant tests. In addition, it was giving a lift to two Ministry men to Gatwick, before departing for Filton. Always look after the officials! All customs clearance has to be carried out at the first port of entry and so, at Gatwick, the pilots left with the manifest to clear everything and everyone at one stroke. They came back with long faces.

'They can't understand the paperwork on the model and, in consequence, they are holding everyone on suspicion,' said one of the pilots. 'They need the input of someone in authority to clear it.'

The passengers questioned the pilots about the details of the queries.

'Well, the paperwork says that the value for insurance purposes is stated as £10,000.' (This was an enormous amount of money in those days.)

'It's a very complicated model, with engine simulation, taking many hours of highly skilled labour on expensive machinery,' someone explained to him.

'Right,' said the pilot. 'So why is the resale value given as £10?'

'Who in their right mind would want to buy such a model? Who has a wind tunnel large enough to take it?'

'The Americans and the Russians,' said the pilot, playing devil's advocate.

'No way would we sell them our secrets! They would have to steal it – and that's one reason that it is insured.'

Still somewhat sceptical, the pilots departed, taking with them the two Ministry officials who were looking a bit sheepish, as the aircraft had landed at Gatwick for their benefit. They would have to redeem themselves by vouching for the remainder of the passengers and their model.

About an hour passed and it was now dark. Across the floodlit tarmac the passengers saw the pilots approaching, accompanied by a man in customs uniform and two assistants, but no Ministry men.

'Customs have decided to impound the model pending further enquiries, but we can go,' said one of the pilots.

'What are they intending to do with the model?' he was asked.

'Take it to pieces, most likely,' announced the customs man.

'Over my dead body! That model has been tested in a French wind tunnel and must not be disturbed until it has been tested at Filton for tunnel comparison purposes. Otherwise it will have to go back to France for retest! This will put the programme back by several months.'

'Oh and by the way,' he added as an afterthought. 'The thing must only be moved when clamped into its box, and as those two together weigh three hundredweight, you will need at least one more man and a truck.'

This sledgehammer approach had little effect on the customs gentleman, who kept them all waiting until he had called up a truck and reinforcements. The model was removed with an agreement that two model makers from Filton would be sent on the following day, along with the necessary jigs, to remove any suspicious parts. The Ministry men had departed a lot later than if they had used scheduled airways, and the aircraft left for Filton.

Someone in high Ministry places had obviously been tackled in his club that evening by one of the Ministry passengers and had pulled strings the next day, as the model arrived at Filton the following evening, untouched as far as could be established.

Friends in high places can be very helpful at times, especially if they expect free lifts to continue.

Transit 6

Despite their fragility, birds have always posed a threat to aircraft when those two flying objects collide. The threat is usually close to the ground on take-off or landing, but there are reports of an aircraft hitting a condor as high as 20,000ft over the Andes. This particular bird must have been supercharged and frozen solid at the same time.

The firm had purchased an ageing DC-3, the ubiquitous Dakota, to be used as a communications aircraft between Filton and the Fairford test base. The first journey of the day was always from Filton to Fairford, carrying a full load of Bristol-based technicians. On this particular day the bird-scaring tactics of creating loud banging sounds, plus a tour of the aerodrome by a Land Rover playing a tape of a seagull in distress, had been only partially successful. As the DC-3 toiled off the runway with its load of semi-somnolent engineers, there was a loud bang as the remains of a seagull broke through the cockpit windscreen, passed between the two pilots, through the open cockpit door and into the cabin. Its momentum carried it about halfway down the aisle between the now fully awakened passengers. The bloody remains slid to a stop beside one man who had been reading his morning newspaper. He slowly lowered the page and looked down at the pile of blood, bones and feathers.

'What a disgusting way to serve breakfast!' he commented and resumed his reading.

Transit 7

The passenger smiled weakly as he lowered himself into the vacant seat in the tri-motored de Havilland Trident. He was obviously ill at ease with something or other. I nodded and resumed the interrogation of yesterday's mail together with some heavier but less urgent stuff left over from the previous week. Flights to Europe were an excellent time to get through the outstanding mailbag. During this reading session the next report in the batch turned out to be the Civil Aviation Authorities' report on recent accidents. To the designer these reports are essential reading as a means of picking up vital information on what might go wrong and so learning from unfortunate mistakes by others. This particular one contained a detailed description of the Trident crash at Staines a couple or so years before.

While reading this report there was a feeling of growing interest from the direction of the adjacent seat. Eventually there was a clearing of a throat and a voice said:

'Excuse me. I know it is awfully rude of me. I must confess to have been reading over your shoulder. And I find that now, being a nervous aeroplane passenger, I must ask you what kind of aeroplane was that one? If possible, I may try to avoid flying in one of that type!'

He looked hopefully at me.

'You are one flight too late for that! It was one of these!' I told him.

He turned pale, so there was obviously need for reassurance.

'But don't worry,' I tried to reassure him. 'It may not happen again, as they have revised their procedures.'

The worried passenger was quiet for a moment and then said:

'That may not have stopped me flying when I have to, but it has cured me of reading over someone's shoulder!'

He was the first out.

Transit 8

As with most new aircraft, testing of various less important aspects goes on well after entry into service. Concorde was no exception. During one 'let's do everything at once' test, Gordon Corps, the Airworthiness Test Pilot, was taking off in a test aircraft from Johannesburg, a 'hot and high' airfield. Here the engine power would be reduced by altitude and temperature, and the aircraft would have to attain a higher speed. He deliberately over-rotated, putting the aircraft at a disadvantage as far as drag was concerned. He then cut Number Three engine at a critical point on the take-off path.

Being already hot and high the engine thrust was lower than usual. Losing one engine made it much worse. Theoretically, however, it should have coped, since a safety system would automatically turn the wick up on the three remaining engines and their associated jetpipe reheat systems. Unfortunately, one of the remaining reheat systems (engine Number Four, of course!) chose to go out. Shades of the ghost of the Type 188! With just enough thrust to remain airborne the Concorde staggered across the scrubland until the fourth engine could be restarted.

For several days the atmosphere in the design office was at the same temperature as the jetpipe. Was it a design fault wherein altitude and/or temperature were involved, a handling problem, or what? There was no need for outside pressure to be exerted, although it came in spades. Yes! Of course the engineers knew the aircraft was now in service! No! We don't know whether it is the intake, the engine, the nozzle, the location, or if it is unique to that test aircraft with all its instrumentation.

Tests in Casablanca on a fully instrumented pre-production aircraft at sea level confirmed that the problem was one of ambient temperature and not of altitude. As there was no positive indication on the flight deck, it had been necessary to take cine pictures of the behaviour of the reheat from behind the aircraft. But what of the engine configuration? Would the effect of having no sturdy probes in vital places in non-instrumented engines be different? The obvious solution was to test an in-service aircraft belonging to British Airways flying into Bahrain, where the temperature is high enough for the purpose. However, as this aircraft was in service, and it would have to be built to a certain standard, a Special Category would have to be declared during the tests as it would also be necessary to test all engines in the emergency mode at the same time, due to limitations imposed by the British Airways operational schedule.

As this category would not permit the carrying of passengers, the tests would have to be done overnight between the scheduled passenger flights. And the whole exercise would have to be carried out before the temperature dropped too low and the aircraft restored to its in-service standard by the time it was due for its scheduled return to London next morning.

In preparation for the tests, I and three other Bristol engineers joined the Bahrain flight at Heathrow after having had a session with the BA engineers. The aircraft was to fly subsonic over Europe, then supersonic over the Adriatic, the Mediterranean and, in those more peaceful days, Syria.

As these aircraft had no quick access test instrumentation, the British Airways Chief Flight Engineer joined the party to sit in the cockpit during critical phases of flight. He was to note all the engine temperatures, pressures and compressor speeds shown on the pilot's and flight engineer's instruments during take-off, and again during the supersonic acceleration. Obviously he had to fly as an extra crew member as there were at least six or seven readings per engine to be taken in the thirty-odd seconds that the aircraft takes to get to 230mph. The BA engineer entered the cabin after take-off as the aircraft started its climb to subsonic operating altitude – the aircraft was now flying across Europe at subsonic speeds, before going supersonic over the Adriatic. All eyes were upon him. He stopped beside the group of engineers and proffered the results, apologising for the obvious signs of haste. They now had to look at these results to see if there were any signs of anomalies.

Whilst engrossed in this task two heads appeared from the seats behind.

'What's going on?' someone said in a North American accent. 'Do we have a problem?'

As this passenger and his colleague next to him had paid a very large amount of money for their tickets and the engineers were guests on the flight, it was thought politic to resist the urge to tell these two to bugger off, even though there was a lot to do.

'We are going to carry out some tests in Bahrain and we want to know if the engines are within a per cent or so of one another,' I replied.

'How will you know whether they are?'

'By using these temperatures and pressures and doing some long and difficult calculations before we get there.'

They took the point and the work proceeded as the aircraft crossed Europe at subsonic speed. Once the Adriatic coast had been reached the aircraft used reheat to accelerate to Mach Two-and-a-Bit and the Chief Flight Engineer came back into the passenger cabin with the new figures. The two heads belonging to the Canadian travellers reappeared, and they had been obviously having discussions with other passengers as two more joined them from across the aisle, together with another two more from in front. After a short silence an arm stretched across, followed by an apology:

'Excuse me, but that pressure is more than one per cent greater than the rest! What are you going to do about that?'

Again the urge to shut them up was resisted. They were obviously not idiots.

'We may find that the temperature and nozzle area will compensate for that when we have finished our calculations, Sir,' I answered.

Another arm came over the seat.

'May I offer you my calculator? It is one of the latest.'

'No thanks, we are used to ours,' was the reply.

But then the germ of an idea to get some peace took root.

'We have some proformas in which we have written the relevant numbers and they just need to be worked through according to the small formulae at the top of each column,' I said to them. 'And we are in a bit of a hurry.'

'I could offer to help as far as possible,' said one of the pair.

The proformas were handed out and a select band of what must be the most highly paid lot of non-technical junior technicians swung into action. Questions were heard passing between the new recruits to their neighbours, such as: 'I think I've slipped a decimal place. What have you got?' and 'Is the square root on the top or the bottom? Damn!'

We got down to a bit of thinking.

'Look, why are we bothering with all these calculations at this point?' I said. 'We're stuck with these engines anyway! We can see what we've got when we get back to Filton.'

'Agreed,' was the answer, 'but don't tell this lot as they're having a hell of a time!'

Talking to the two men behind it transpired that they were Canadians on holiday and had come on this flight 'just to experience the ride'.

One was an ex-wartime Canadian Spitfire pilot and the other had been catapulted off Canadian battlecruisers in a Vickers Walrus flying boat as his contribution to the war effort. He had taken a Walrus home with him afterwards and used it to take his friends duck shooting from his own personal lake in Canada.

Returning to the matter in hand, a message from the pilot told us that Eric Hyde had telexed Frank Crowfoot, our man now in Bahrain, to hire a photographer to take a cine film of the reheat in action, or not as the case might be. Taking a film of the happenings up the back end of Concorde in full reheat was an interesting exercise that had been done before in Casablanca. No problem.

As the passengers disembarked hands were shaken all round.

'Look me up in Montevideo when you get around to bringing the aircraft over!' said a Mr Grace, handing us his business card. 'I've never had such an interesting flight!'

'It's the first time I've been in an aircraft where everyone talks to everyone else,' said his friend.

'I may have slipped another decimal point,' he continued. 'And sorry about the Chateau Latour stain on the proforma!'

We engineers were beginning to glimpse another world, but matters of the moment intervened. The status of the aircraft had to be changed to permit it to carry out tests outside its normal cleared boundaries of flight and then the engine control amplifiers had to be replaced to enable it to carry out these tests with any or all engines in the emergency contingency rating, flown by qualified test pilots. The tests had then to be carried out, the aircraft restored to its original condition, reverted to a Civil Certificate standard, checked and refuelled before it could start the return journey at 8.30 the next morning. It was going to be a hell of a night!

When we arrived, Frank Crowfoot, known as 'the bearded wonder' due to his hairy head and whiskers, appeared to greet us.

'I've booked you into the large hotel over the road. But I don't think that you will get much sleep as the timescale is too tight and anyway the hotel was built on sand and they are drilling round the clock to reinforce it!'

Situation normal.

'And there's more,' Frank continued. 'Yesterday we had more rain in a couple of hours than usually falls in a year. Apart from the runway areas the airfield is a quagmire, mainly quicksand. All observations will have to be made from the end of the runway.'

'Well I suppose that we can…'

'No we can't. There is to be no engine running on the apron, nor halfway down the runway. Everything has to be done from the threshold at the end of the runway, even the photography!'

The thought of looking up the back end of the Concorde from 50ft with the engines at full blast, trying to see if the reheat was working properly had the makings of mission impossible. We would have to persuade the pilots to stretch a point or two.

'Has the photographer had any experience of this type of thing?' I asked.

'No. The only one that I could get in time was photographing the Bahraini top brass and I thought it best to give him only a sketchy outline of the job.'

By now the aircraft had been reverted to a test role and a black night had fallen. There had been no time to refuel and so the aircraft would be flying on its limited reserves of fuel with no passengers to weigh it down. In addition, all engines would be operating in the emergency mode. A quick mental calculation showed that the thrust would be almost the same as the weight.

'If we stuck the tail into the ground it would go straight up!' someone said.

'Then you would be given the job of lying underneath to look up the jet-pipes!' was the reply. 'Shut up and concentrate!'

We were now at the end of the runway with the aircraft in front of our group with its engines idling. The team were helping to set up the cameraman and the sound and battery men.

'I can't see the engines properly,' said the cameraman. 'It's too dark and I'm too close.'

The turbines were a dull red ring at the far end of the jetpipe. Even under these conditions the noise and heat were oppressive. At higher speeds they would get brighter until only a white ring of flame could be seen.

'Increase speed on Number One please,' said the man with the radio, following up with an explanation of the problem.

The pilot obliged and the engine note increased from a noisy roar to an ear-shattering roar – and it was only at half power, without the reheat. We all leant against the blast and looked towards where the cameraman had last been seen. He wasn't there, but perilously close to the edge of the runway, near the quicksand, there was a pile of clothes, tripods, cameras and batteries. If this was the effect of one engine without reheat, what chance was there with all four in emergency mode?

The pilots were persuaded, under any excuse that they could conjure up, to advance the aircraft further up the runway and the team behind retired to the extreme margin where the sandy bog began. The cameraman was reminded of his fee and persuaded to stay to finish the job. His pork-pie hat was firmly attached over his head by passing tape over the top and under his chin. Ear defenders were taped around his head and one of the local helpers, under instructions to provide help as required, sat under the camera with his back to the aircraft and steadied the tripod. Another man leant on the cameraman's back, happy with his role, as he was sheltered from the impending blast whilst making an effective contribution. The onlookers had disappeared.

I lay on the ground, binoculars at the ready, as the four engines were accelerated to take-off rating. The roar and the heat became indescribable. Then, with a bang, the reheat came on. A series of quick looks from behind protective arms showed that all four were operating perfectly before I put my face on the tarmac and covered my head with both arms to ease the heat problem. There was no escape from the noise, which rattled my head and vibrated my chest cavity. Anything, even digging the garden on a wet day, would have been more acceptable than this.

With its brakes released the aircraft had accelerated down the runway. In the darkness the sequence of pale blue, turquoise, and orange shock cones from each of the four exhausts could be seen quite clearly. In the cockpit the pilots were experiencing accelerations that were causing them to work at a frantic pace as the progressive speed checks occurred in unusually short intervals.

After brake release the 60-knot check on engine Number Four came up in no time, followed by the 100-knot OK check on the power plants' overall configurations shown by the four green CON (-figuration) lights. They were rapidly approaching rotation speed where the aircraft would be pulled up to an attitude of around thirteen and a half degrees before it lifted off the ground. Before the normal conditions of operation could be achieved the aircraft was airborne with the control column right back to keep the speed down, and was screaming towards the black, starlit heavens, the four brightly coloured shock cones trailing behind.

From the radio it appeared that the air traffic controllers in the control tower were having fits as they called up their friends to come and see the spectacle, shouting that they had never seen their own Air Force Phantom fighters take off like this.

And what of the cameraman? He was red-faced and looking like a man who had looked into the bowels of hell, and he was already packing up. To his credit he had managed to get a film of three of the four engines before the blast had pulled the power lead out of his battery.

'We would like you to take another from the other side,' I asked, but it was of no use, he had gone.

Our group followed him off the runway. While he went to recover and sort out his film, the rest of us went for a debriefing in the passenger lounge to await the pilots, who had completed a few more take-offs and circuits. When they arrived, they were not too enthusiastic about the situation, but were not specific.

'Were the nozzle areas correct and in line?' we asked them.

'As far as we could judge they were.'

'What about the compressor speeds, engine temperatures, and pressures and other parameters?'

'They seemed OK.'

'From what we could see, the thrust was there as there was nothing wrong with your acceleration times.'

This produced a wave of laughter, since the whole company knew how hard the flight crew had been working during the take-offs.

'Well, it's a design office decision,' said our pilot.

We realised that the problem was back around our necks as usual. A negative result would mean that the fleet would be grounded if the airworthiness officials were of the same opinion. From what we had seen and heard our minds had already been made up. Although nothing more had been said since having a short discussion with design colleagues we gave a nod, confirming current thoughts. We were engineers, not politicians.

'From what we have heard and seen the situation on in-service engines seems quite safe. Let's put the aircraft back into its in-service configuration,' was the verdict.

We never heard of the problem again after that.

At that our group broke up to go to the hotel for a wash, shave and breakfast, as the morning had almost arrived.

The drills were working intermittently across the road and sleep would have been difficult. There was time for a small, but leisurely, breakfast before returning to the airport for the return journey. At the airport we were now passengers and were ushered into the Concorde lounge and offered orange juice and/or Bucks Fizz, and a selection of cakes. On the aircraft we were shown to our seats and offered champagne again. It was now just after 9 a.m. The aircraft took off and accelerated to supersonic speeds after passing over Syria towards the Med.

'Could I offer you an aperitif, Sir?' asked the air hostess, continuing along the same lines:

'Would you care for any of these three wines with your meal, Sir?'

'May I offer you a brandy, Sir?'

The shuttle to Toulouse was never like this! But the journey home from the airport would have been much shorter. My god! The M4!

'Miss!' I asked our helpful attendant. 'Would you please call ahead and ask the firm to send a car to take four engineers to Bristol as it would be unsafe for us to drive, since we haven't had any sleep?"

'Certainly, Sir!' She smiled. 'A very sensible suggestion! Would you care for more brandy or a coffee?'

It seemed that the cabin crews were very well trained and the air hostess gave another knowing smile as she picked up the empty brandy glasses.

Many years later I received a card from Frank, now living in Australia, which had been sent to Tom King, an ex-Australian aircraft engineer who had done sterling work on the full scale power plant test rigs. The card mentioned the fact that, even though all requests for setting up the impromptu tests, cameramen etc. had been issued whilst the aircraft was on the way, no one ever said 'thank you!'

So, now I'm saying it Frank. 'THANK YOU!'

Transit 9

Compared to the British Isles, France is larger top-to-bottom and side-to-side and has larger lumps in the middle. Hence, when travelling diagonally, it is much quicker to fly. In the early days the internal airline Air Inter had difficulty in catching up with this growing requirement and pressed anything into service.

On this particularly windy day the chosen aircraft was an old Douglas DC-4, probably left behind by a US Army general on one of the many wartime airfields. The thought of scraping across the tops of the Midi on a dark night in the face of the Mistral in this aircraft occupied the minds of the seasoned passengers. However, Amy Johnson, Jim Mollison and others had done much more with much less, so there was hope.

Of the group of three, Etienne Fage was in front, and chose to sit in a seat next to a rather pretty girl who was in the window seat, looking at the activity on the tarmac. He had obviously spotted the two spare seats on the opposite side of the gangway, where we could sit and converse. Following him was the most senior man in the French design hierarchy at Toulouse. He chose the gangway seat and ushered me into the inside one, as he wished to talk with his colleague.

After she had eventually sorted out the seating, the stewardess stood at the front of the cabin and made her announcements in a loud voice. She then walked down to the back, turned round, and repeated everything. It was obvious that, amongst other things, the passenger address system was kaput. This did little to quell the general air of apprehension.

As the flight progressed the conversation across the gangway developed around power plants and the aircraft developed peculiar motions around its centre of gravity. Eventually I joined in and we began to monopolise the discussion. It petered out when it was noticed by all three of us that the pretty girl seated between the aerodynamicist and the window was becoming a victim of the plane's motion as it bounced across the rough airs above the Plateau de Mille Vaches. The cows must have been generating a lot of methane.

At first the one beside her got in a bit of close-quarter work as he tried to help, but it was not long before high seniority put gallantry before duty.

'Here, you obviously wish to continue the discussion with your colleague,' said the senior man.

From the look on Etienne's face, discussions with colleagues could not be further from his thoughts.

'Let us change places!'

It would have been career-limiting to argue.

The flight continued, but it became difficult to concentrate on technicalities, as on the other side of the gangway, with heads together, first aid and tender care were being administered very effectively.

20

ELECTRICIANS THEN AND NOW

As each day passed, the electrical and electronic controls to the power plant became more and more complex, and added more and more weight to the growing total. Several firms had submitted proposals for the many electronic boxes and one or two had fallen by the wayside. To give the required degrees of flexibility, Eric Hyde had taken a bold decision in the face of the more complex intake Control Laws needed to adopt the emerging new technology of digital computation. Had it had not been for this controversial decision, the Flight Test investigations would have been protracted to an unacceptable extent.

A TECHNIBIT

By now there were two intake control boxes per engine, each containing Control Laws that were three times as complex as those in the pair of boxes controlling each engine, to which had to be added an additional box for the reheat and another for the secondary nozzle. The last two were only there from political pressure to ensure that the French engine firm had a contribution. The whole lot, including wiring, weighed nearly a ton. The many changes required as the programme advanced could be judged from the identification letters for each new set of the intake laws, which advanced initially from AA, through AB and eventually to beyond TT.

Thus any discussion in these areas had to start with a check that all participants were up to date on the current definition. They became quite animated as the aerodynamicists pressed for yet more changes, almost aggressively as the electricians tried to slow the process down in order to meet their drawing and production targets. One of my job's responsibilities, being an ex-aerodynamicist, was to arbitrate at such times and defend the draughtsmen against the aerodynamicists.

However, my thoughts returned to my service in the RAF, where my previous experience of the care for colleagues' safety by my father's coalmine electricians had been severely tarnished in succeeding years by the gung-ho attitude of those conscripts of an electrical persuasion.

While I was still at grammar school towards the end of the war, I volunteered for the RAF College at Cranwell, to become a pilot and fly Spitfires. The tide of war had turned and the news of my volunteering was obviously the last straw for Hitler as, in May 1945, he shot himself. He decided to throw in the towel, presumably in a pre-emptive strike to reserve a poolside sunbed in Valhalla. Hitler's decision scotched any attempt for me to become a pilot, for, although I later passed all the examinations for an officer pilot's course at Cranwell, the war had now finished. In consequence, they (we always referred to the King as 'they', because the King always referred to himself as 'we') had 40,000 pilots that were not now wanted. A year later, a firm request from His Majesty King George VI to join him in the RAF (albeit at a somewhat lower rank) could not be ignored, even though the precise activity was not specified.

And so it came to pass after about twenty weeks' training as engine mechanics and another twenty as engine fitters, the prospective geologists, mathematicians, grocers and general layabouts who formed the intelligencia of the 26 September 1946 entry were allowed to sit in the cockpits of Hurricanes, Spitfires, Tempests, Vampires, Meteors, Lancasters, Ansons and Tiger Moths, and play with their engines. This was down to the luck of the draw.

The selection process for any particular trade was brilliantly simple. We all sat 'intelligence' tests. Those in the top bracket became Radar mechanics, the next group became engine mechanics, the next electricians and so on, down to jobs requiring minimal intellect. It so happened that this particular week there were no new courses for Radar mechanics opening up, so the top group became engine mechanics.

During the later engine fitters' course, a sub-group who tried to volunteer for the Glider Regiment (most of us, being ex-Air Training Corps Glider pilots, had been allowed to fly primary gliders in a straight line, and had been told that our turns would come naturally) were refused by a clever commissioned paper-pusher, who pointed out that the regiment's gliders did not have engines. Our answer was that we had been taught to use firearms and we would save manpower by being able to service the glider tug's engines and then jump into the glider and fly it. His response was a terse 'Bugger off!'

Subsequent postings to squadrons were selected in a not-quite-random manner. We were allowed to write down our preferences – usually as near to home as possible. The names were listed in random order. The RAF aircraft assessment station at Boscombe Down in Wiltshire had requirements for four fitters that particular week so, if he hadn't been posted elsewhere by an earlier selection, the first on the list to ask for Boscombe and the next three, regardless of their choice, were sent to that station. So Boscombe it was. We were paid 8*s* 6*d* per day for the sheer pleasure of sitting in the cockpits and listening to the crackle, bang and pop of these magnificent beasts whilst inhaling the bracing aroma of 110-octane petrol with a sprinkling of aviation kerosene.

Gloster Meteors and their jet engines had been introduced towards the end of the war and were still being developed. Like all new and current RAF aircraft, particularly the engines, they were over-inspected. On the Meteor the main fear was that the turbine blades would grow under the heat and centrifugal forces and cut their way out. These blades had to receive regular inspections.

Being compactly built, and therefore not a waste of prime body-building material like some of my more substantial colleagues, I could wriggle up the larger diameter experimental jetpipe of this test Meteor, clutching a short length of broom handle above my head to turn the engine and have a long Rolls-Royce special (and therefore expensive) feeler in the other hand to test the turbine tip clearances. This led to an increase in my popularity, as this procedure meant it was not necessary to remove the back end of the engine nacelle and disconnect the thermocouple leads and the jetpipe itself. Getting past the thermocouples was a tricky business, made more difficult by the fact that my arms had to be held above my head, wooden handle in one hand and feeler in the other.

On this occasion things were going reasonably well and the turbine was turning gently under the influence of my section of broom handle, albeit that I felt some discomfort because the point of the exhaust tail-cone was sticking into my forehead as I made attempts to get a better view of where the end of the long feeler was located.

Elsewhere on the aircraft there was a lot of activity by the other tradesmen carrying out their particular inspections, so the noise of a certain, later to be friendless, electrician climbing into the cockpit and removing the 'Don't Touch!' notice was not heard. All at once there was a familiar clunk, somewhat magnified by the cramped surroundings. My piece of broom handle became redundant. The turbine had started to go round on its own.

To the awe of the riggers working on the ailerons on the outboard wing, a body came out of the jetpipe, feet first, face up, and at escape velocity, in a straight line to land flat on its back behind them on the tarmac. This happened well before they heard the thunk of the second relay, which took the shaft up to engine ignition speed. Although the piece of wood and the feeler were still in my hand, there was an addition of two thermocouples, one caught in my belt at the back of my overalls and the other forced through the bottom of one of my breast pockets. The fact that the engine igniter plugs had been removed as a precaution only penetrated my mind after a hard horizontal landing on the tarmac. However, on mature reflection it was still a risk not worth taking.

Thanks to the electrician, may God rot his socks, it was now necessary to remove not only the back of the nacelle and the jetpipe, but also to replace the thermocouples and their wiring. This character complained bitterly when he was given the job 'as it wasn't him who removed the damned things!'

Some weeks after that encounter with a 'sparks' (as electricians were known), the job of installing a Gipsy engine into a Tiger Moth came out of the bag. Jobs were nothing if not varied at Boscombe Down in that era.

One of the few bits of streamlining on the Moth was a small pointed cone at the root of the propeller, and this was held in place by a small castellated nut on a threaded spike sticking out from the hub.

It was necessary to tighten the nut and to line up an opposing pair of castellations on the nut with the hole in the spike in order to insert a split-pin through the two and lock the nut in place. That done, it was the end of the job, and it was possible to look forward to an engine run, if someone could be persuaded to swing the prop.

To fix the nut, it was necessary to re-check that the magneto switches were off, thereby ensuring that the engine would not start due to any residue remaining in the cylinders after a bench check. Standing on a box it was possible to grasp the prop in one hand and put a spanner on the nut with the other. By holding the spanner firmly and pulling on the propeller, one could look at the nut through one eye to gauge the alignment of the hole with the castellations. At the precise minute I was doing this an electrician had arrived on the scene, with the objective of testing one of the few pieces of electrical wiring on the aircraft – from the magneto switches to the magnetos themselves. Regardless of the man in front of him (me) moving the prop around, he switched them on. The last man in the cockpit had been a rigger getting in and out quite frequently whilst fiddling with adjustment of the flying controls, and who had been warned to keep his hands off the switches. Thus, since I was concentrating on the castellations, I didn't notice the newly arrived electrician's activity.

A TECHNIBIT

As an aid to getting a fat spark when swinging the propeller for starting the engine, the makers, de Havilland, had one of the two magnetos fitted with an impulse starter – a short spring which wound up as the engine was turned through a small arc. It then flicked the magneto over sufficiently quickly to discharge a healthy spark to the appropriate cylinder.

The switches were now on and the magnetos were alive. The prop was continuing to be rotated slowly. The impulse starter flicked over and the engine coughed weakly. Even a weak cough from this type of engine was sufficient to jerk the prop into such motion that it connected with vital areas, sufficient to ensure that I was lifted bodily off the box and dumped backwards onto the concrete floor.

A startled, white-faced electrician looked out of the cockpit. An agonised red-faced fitter lay doubled up on the floor and glared back. Then the dam broke. Since leaving the cloistered surrounds of the grammar school nestling under the castle walls at Ashby-de-la-Zouch and joining the air force, my vocabulary had expanded with a lot of new words and phrases. The shock of realisation of what-might-have-been brought these all out in a controlled stream of forceful invective.

'What's all this f★★★★★ swearing about?'

The Chiefy, who had witnessed the last act of the incident as he walked across the hangar floor, was never backward in choosing an appropriate expression. More shaken and bruised than incapacitated, it was explained to him what had been going on and that it was OK now.

'You had better go to the sick bay for a check-up anyway – King's Regulations say that anyone hit by a propeller – whether alive or dead – must see a medical officer – so no argument!' he said. 'We don't want any loose balls dropping on the hangar floor! They might hazard aircraft safety!'

After interrogating the electrician and putting him on a charge, the senior man wandered off to his office chuckling to himself at his own witticisms. Deciding that I might as well have an hour or so off as instructed, I walked, with legs rather wide apart, the quarter of a mile to the sick bay where the limp-handed clerk told me to sit down even before I had time to speak.

'There's a panic on!' he said, and shot out of the door with no more explanation.

A short time later an ambulance drew up outside. The driver and medic came through the door quickly, followed by a clerk.

'Well?' said the clerk.

'Can't understand it,' said the driver. 'No signs anywhere!'

'Oh, my God!' the clerk shrieked 'All that blood! It must have been awful!'

'There wasn't any blood! Just no one – nothing!'

I put two and two together and got the wrong answer.

'What's crashed?' I asked.

At that time aircraft crashes at this research base were all too frequent. Earlier that month a recent crop of disasters had stood on the apron between the hangars of R & I (Light) and R & I (Heavy) on a fleet of Queen Mary trailers. Two of these contained the remains of a Linconia – a streamlined version of a Lincoln bomber which had been flying round the Poles doing magnetic field research.

Another pair contained a Miles Marathon, a new medium-sized, four-engine passenger aircraft which suffered from inadequate fire precaution design. When one engine caught fire, it spread inside the leading edge of the wing to the other engines, killing all the crew.

On the next trailer lay an Army Air Observation Post (AOP) slow-flying Auster which had demonstrated its slow speed approach over the hedge on its delivery (and last) flight and had unfortunately stopped dead in the boggy bit on the lower end of the field before nosing over onto its back. From the footprints through the canvas of the bottom side of the wing and the dried-up drops of blood between them we concluded that, as the aircraft lay on its back, the dazed pilot had righted himself to walk the length of the wing nursing a bleeding nose. It had been delivered by air and returned by road.

Next was a pile of rubble which was all that was left of a prototype single-engined jet with a full belly tank that had done too tight a roll at too low a level as it passed between the hangars.

The three new Vampires which had managed to take off, but not to land in a very straight line, were just being recovered. The fault lay with the bolts on the undercarriage retraction fittings which had bottomed before tightening sufficiently, allowing the legs to wobble and send the aircraft on an uncertain path off and on the runway.

'Nothing to do with you!' snapped the clerk, interrupting my morbid thoughts. 'We had a call – mischievous as usual, no doubt – about an erk being hit by a prop!'

'Ah! Perhaps this erk can help you there!'

The Chiefy, unknown to me, had obviously gone to the office to telephone for an ambulance and then had walked around looking for the injured party, thereby missing the ambulance crew.

After having had a kit inspection by a very amused medical officer, who let his imagination run riot in suggesting that there would not be many to join such an elite club of those who had survived being hit by a propeller, and whose appendage was now turning dark blue 'and would soon be black!' I limped back to the hangar. Dismay was added to agony when I saw that there was another fitter sitting in the Tiger Moth running the engine. The Chiefy explained that he 'didn't think that you could raise your leg that far to climb into the cockpit, nor would you care to swing the prop!'

'I didn't intend to swing the prop! Electricians have no experience of swinging a prop and I was hoping to get that particular one on the other end of it!' was my response.

Yet a third encounter with predatory electricians occurred towards the uncertain end of a two-year service career. The time of demobilisation was in the lap of the gods in the Air Ministry. All recruits had been called up in to the forces for 'The Duration of the Present Emergency' – a very variable feast, but very valuable to those who survived, as they could continue their education with all expenses paid. The fixed two-year National Service was yet to come. However, much to our surprise, after a year and ten months a few of us were told that we had only two months to go. In the luck of the draw some of those who were not released were sent to Malaya.

As our education had been interrupted, the air force would pay up to five years' college and maintenance fees. For the remainder of our service no kit could be exchanged for new, unless paid for. As the charge would be deducted from our pay and this process took three months, this was a no-go too.

From past experience, standing there in front of the flight office with hands in my overalls pockets, watching aeroplanes, I realised that I should have shown more sense. The Flight Lieutenant i/c Repair & Inspection (Light), who had been doing the same, turned to answer the telephone. He then stuck his head out of the office window and shouted:

'There's a Mosquito coming in with the port engine on fire. Go and have a look at it, if it manages to get here, and see what the cause was!'

The aircraft landed safely, but the one good engine overheated in the attempt to breast the grass rise from the runway to the hard standing by the hangar. It now stood on the grass with a heat haze rising above it. Picking up a 'Ladder, Short, Engine Inspections and Window Painting for the use of', I walked down to the aircraft, climbed up to the port engine and opened the cowling. If the bottles containing the extinguishant had been fired then the extinguishant would have evaporated immediately, but it would have left behind a pink tell-tale dye. There was no sign of pink dye anywhere, ergo the bottle for this engine had either not been fired or not been filled properly.

An electrician who had entered the cockpit by the small door under the belly of the aircraft and had experimentally pressed the correct firing button, remedied this fact within a few seconds of lifting the cowling. (Presumably the pilot had made the wrong selection.) Dye and extinguishant exploded into the nacelle. The extinguishant was icy cold and the pink dye used to indicate that the bottle had been fired, was expelled with it under pressure and entered every nook and cranny. The shock of it disturbed both the physical and mental equilibrium of the one doing the investigation and a multi-coloured bundle came to earth in a welter of blue words and pink overalls, with hands, face, hair, and forage cap also of that colour.

Comments from colleagues about pink fairies, elephants and the like did not restore my disturbed equilibrium. My colourful figure staggered back to the hard standing, wiping pink dye from my eyes and from one side of my face. There was no help from those observers who were clinging to one another for support, laughing at the situation. Their laughter turned to howls when the owner of the pink and white tear-stained face had to cling to them for support too.

The laughter started to subside, but restarted again when the Flight Lieutenant i/c R & I Light, whose daily tussle with the paperwork was being disturbed by the hysterics, stuck his head out of the window to see what the noise was about. He blinked, shuddered, and said that he would take more water with it in future.

An evening of vigorous scrubbing restored my exposed bodily parts to near normal colour. Little could be done with the forage cap or the overalls which had protected my uniform.

On the next morning's working parade my overalls were rolled up inside out and held under my right arm. The forage cap was put on my head at a non-standard angle, pink side down. The man who was right marker (always the tallest airman around) was 'fell in' and, on the order, the remainder 'fell in' in three ranks on his left. I chose the middle rank. If all had gone well any orders would have been 'read' (a euphemism for bellowed) and the parade dismissed. The men would then be dismissed to their duties by the duty flight sergeant. However, something in the centre of the middle rank caught the flight sergeant's eye. He marched smartly down the line and came to a halt with a stamp of his military feet. With two more earth shuddering stamps he turned smartly to face the ranks.

His chest expanded against buttons and belt as he drew in an excess of breath.

'THAAT MAAN!!' he bellowed.

Everyone looked in the direction that he was staring. In my blue uniform and pink forage cap, hoping to appear invisible in the middle rank, I tried to look nonchalantly ahead over the flight sergeant's head.

'I told you that you wouldn't get away with it!' whispered a voice from the rear rank.

By now the flight sergeant was standing slightly in front of the front rank, looking at the object of his ire from between two of these airmen. These two were getting the full benefit of this blast of decibels.

'AIRMAAN, WHY AM YOU IN FANCY DRESS?'

'It was caused by a fire extinguisher when…' I answered.

'WHERE WAS THE FIRE?'

'It had gone out.'

'GONE OUT? THEN WHY WAS YOU PLAYING WITH A FIRE EXTINGUISHER THEN? MY OFFICE – NOW! YOU ARE ON A CHARGE! YOU STAND FAST! THE REMAINDAH, TO THE RIGHT … DIIIIISMISS!'

My smart and lonely one-arm-swinging (the overalls were under the other) march across a now deserted parade ground, followed by a two-arm-swinging march by the portly flight sergeant, preceded a long dissertation given whilst standing to attention in his office. With several interruptions and a couple of telephone calls I managed to convince him that he was charging the wrong man. Nevertheless, he had to have his pound of flesh, as his sense of humour appeared to be nonexistent, and ordered that the offending cap and overalls 'and them boots' should be changed immediately.

'But Flight Ser—'

'That's an order! Get out!'

For a couple of days the owner of the cap and boots became the meat in the sandwich between the man in charge of the working parade and the man in charge of the stores. One would not have a pink cap and dirty boots on parade and the other would not change the offending cap and boots, as the owner was being demobilised in the next six weeks. There was no chance of getting it changed by any colleague who was under no such restriction, as the cap was now notorious. The problem was solved by my R&I (Light) Flight C/O who signed a chit authorising the bearer to wear a 'non-standard-issue headdress', excusing me from working parade and, after some persuasion, signed another one for 'stained boots'. The latter had been soaked in aviation kerosene when filling the belly tank of a Meteor and defied all efforts to raise even a dull polish. The offer by experts to use the well-known technique of raising a polish with a fire-heated desert spoon had worsened the situation by setting fire to a residual patch of embedded kerosene around one toecap, giving the appearance of a miniature fairy ring. All this time there was another spare issue of cap, uniform and pair of boots, but these were 'Best Blue' and were not, repeat *not*, to be used for work – even for a few weeks.

In those remaining few weeks, the chits became very worn due to the demands of eagle-eyed RAF Military Police who had nothing else to do. At this time the forces were allowed to travel off duty in uniform, which many did, as it was an aid to thumbing a lift. Although the rules allowed Best Blue to be used in these circumstances, the pink forage cap was worn as cocking a snook to authority. Army Military Police took no notice of a strange headdress, because different sections of that organisation wore forage caps of many different colours to denote their special affiliations, and perhaps they assumed that the RAF were starting to do likewise. RAF police pounced every time, but the chitty ensured that their transport of delight was always short-lived. It was a joy to watch their faces.

'So what do you think, Ted?'

The question I was asked pulled my attention back to the meeting in hand. To me it was clear that the modification was essential, as I had pressed the aerodynamicists to specify it. Now, how to let the electricians down lightly without showing too much bias? Experience had shown that these were a reasonably safe bunch.

After all, Dad was one too.

21

LITTLE 'UNS WITH BIG BACKGROUNDS

Some were small in stature, but large in worldly experience. They went about quietly getting on with the job with good humour and with no chips on their shoulders about past problems or misfortunes. Very often they had seen more action and, in some cases, suffered more than those who were constantly moaning.

Take Little Jim, Ches and Mike for instance.

Little Jim was a Liverpudlian, who arrived in the Power Plant Group to prepare himself to test run the Concorde engines once the hoped-for production run had really got under way. His background of engine experience during and after the Second World War, especially on V bombers, was immense and fully qualified him for the job. Within a few days of arriving he had read the *Powerplant Flight Manual* from front to back, and his first meeting was spent correcting the writer's impression of what was actually written down in it.

In coffee breaks he would regale the group with what were thought to be tall stories of past escapades concerning his passion for motorcycles and aeroplanes. His bald head would bob up and down as he described his 'adventures'.

As a 15-year-old he had been stopped by the police whilst speeding on a motorcycle. The motorcycle he had built himself from his collection of bits and pieces. At that age it must have been as big as he was himself. He was summoned to court and, because of his age, was taken in hand by a youth counsellor. The lady appointed to look after Jim's case took the little fellow to heart.

'You are lucky! This magistrate is an old softy,' she said, 'so appear very contrite and you will probably get off as it's a first offence.'

In the court Jim stood on the box provided and looked over the top of the dock. He said and did all the right things and, as predicted, got off with a warning.

Some short time later he was approached by a group of amateurs who were building an ultra-light popular aircraft called a Flying Flea – a French design that was later banned because of a dangerous characteristic in certain altitudes. The builders needed an engine and had heard that, even at this early stage of his life, Jim had possibly got one that was suitable in his collection. He had: a Blackburn Twin, which would do very nicely. On the day of the trial, on the sands at West Kirby, the engine performed very well, but the propeller did not. The shape had been carved incorrectly and the thrust was inadequate to get it airborne. Following what then passed for a Design/Flight Test discussion, the builders decided that what was wanted was a smaller, lighter pilot and, of course, the choice fell upon Jim who had turned up in case his motorcycle engine misbehaved. Despite protests he was lifted into the cockpit and briefed:

'This, when you pull it back, makes the plane go up, and when pushed forward makes it go down,' he was told. 'Push those forward with your left foot to go to the left and with your right to go the other way. You know how to operate the engine. Don't bother about anything else!'

Oozing with under-confidence, Jim opened the throttle and headed off in an uncertain path across the beach. To his credit he did manage to get sufficiently airborne to scrape over the small wall into the ornamental gardens where his uncertain path had led, but no further. The power had been sufficient to miss the two old dears on the seat, affording him a grandstand view of the approaching menace, but not the ground behind them.

At court he had the same lady who took his previous case to look after him again and fortunately the same magistrate was presiding, so the advice was the same. And it worked.

His Worship looked at the worried face peering at him over the top of the dock:

'Young man you can go,' he said, 'but if ever you come in front of me again, accused of driving a ferry up the Mersey, you're for it!'

As Jim finished his story the audience laughed, some feeling no doubt a shred of disbelief. However, Ken, another Merseysider, spoke up.

'I've got an old copy of the local rag at home with that report in it. Kept it for another reason. What did it say? Something like: *Mad motorcyclist does it again*.'

Jim's stories gained greater respect, especially when he produced a copy of *The Motorcycle* to prove that, at a later date, he had actually crashed when putting up a good show racing his own motorcycle against sponsored opposition in the Isle of Man. Being stationed at RAF Jurby he was located within easy reach of the famous circuit and each morning, before breakfast, he would take his highly tuned, home-built bike out for a couple of high-speed laps come sunshine, rain, or fog. On the day of the race he crashed whilst leading, taking a buckle from a policeman's belt with him as he left the road. The magazine *The Motorcycle* said that as a private entrant he had been doing very well 'until he came off'.

Jim had not been at Filton long before he asked if there was any chance of hitching a lift on a spare seat to Toulouse to visit a family that he had met during the war. He said that they had sheltered him for some time in North Africa. As that was some distance from the south of France there was obviously a story as yet untold. And so he was pressed to tell it.

During the North African campaign he was maintaining the American twin-engine bombers flown by the RAF. Very often, after maintaining the aircraft, the person responsible flew on the test flight. This fostered better maintenance and pilot confidence. However, on this particular day the aircraft fell prone to a hazard that occurred infrequently but gave rise to serious consequences when it happened. An electrical fault, common to both propellers, would drive them both into coarse pitch. This was only inconvenient when travelling fast, but hazardous when travelling slowly, for instance when taking off and landing. On the occasion of Jim's story the fault occurred just after take-off, the worst possible time.

Mindful of the old pilots' adage that it does not matter what you do in an aeroplane, provided that you don't hit the ground whilst doing it, the pilot dared not throttle back with a load of fuel on board. Very slowly they gained height over the Mediterranean, away from any Germans, with the engines flat out at full-bore and slowly overheating. It took some time to get to any altitude where it was safe to think of bailing out. By the time such an altitude was reached it was dark and little could be made of the ground below, and even less of where they were.

However, the time had come and Jim went first, floating gently down, wondering what lay below. He need not have worried as he had a relatively soft landing in the water, whereupon he inflated his Mae West (inflatable life belt) and discarded his parachute. All was still, remarkably still. He knew that the Mediterranean was long East-to-West, and relatively short North-to-South, so he inspected the stars through the thin overcast night sky, selected north and set out to swim in the opposite direction towards North Africa. After the second stroke he hit his head on the side of the swimming pool.

From the house to which it was attached came the sound of voices – French voices. Several questions arose before any move could be made. Where were the Germans? Were the French sympathetic to Vichy or de Gaulle? Where was his parachute? Groping in the dark he found his parachute and hid it and himself in the nearby hut, which contained swimming pool equipment.

By daylight it became apparent that he was in German-occupied territory, but after two days there appeared no option but to throw himself on the mercy of the house owners. Luckily they were all on the same side and kept him from the Germans until the Americans arrived. This happy band of warriors, starting from the Casablanca end of Africa, knew that they had not yet met up with Montgomery, who was starting from the Egyptian end of the continent, and took Jim's story with a pinch of salt. As a precaution they put him in their nearest prisoner-of-war camp, which held a lot of Germans and a few Italians that they had captured. The Americans did not have a separate one for the Brits. Jim was not a happy airman.

However, here he was at Filton, having located the family who had hidden him. By now they had relocated to the south of France. He hitched a lift on the Hawker Siddeley 125, which did the Bristol–Toulouse trip twice each day, usually being oversubscribed but, happily this time, with a spare seat. However, its take-off was delayed by a Hawker Harrier, on test by Rolls-Royce, hanging around at 10ft above the runway.

The pilot was possibly thinking of the demonstrations of the Harrier's versatility and especially the one to the Japanese where, as usual after every display, the aircraft was brought to the hover in front of the top brass and lowered its nose in a stately bow. This time the sunlit faces of the crowd turned to a black mass as the Japanese crowd bowed in unison, returning the salutation.

The constant noise from the Harrier alerted someone in the design office who noted the likely delay. The grapevine swung into action and the BAe office in Toulouse was informed that, as timing was already tight, they should have the MG sports car ready to get Jim from the airport to the station. With the sports car owner driving like a Frenchman, Jim made the train with minutes to spare.

Apparently the reunion went very well, to such an extent that several of his colleagues in Toulouse received invitations to visit the family. Another story verified. And yet another story to be told in later years unfolded on the way back. At the end of his stay it snowed, and snowed heavily. The roads were useless and the only way to reach the train was on horseback. In such weather the French trains in this locality would stop to pick up wayside travellers. So Jim went by horse to the rail track to catch his train. As the train was slower than the current timetable advised, the arrival at Toulouse was much later than intended. This had ramifications on his return flight, where he had to hitch a lift in a different aircraft. The co-pilot of this aircraft had reported in that he was ill and, in consequence, the flight would have to be cancelled. That was until Jim mentioned that he had started to take flying lessons and had a valid pupil pilot's licence.

'That's OK then! You are seconded as a pupil under training! Let's go!' said the pilot.

He flew back in the co-pilot's seat.

Jim's job faded away as the airlines cancelled their orders for Concorde and he went to work as a technician in the test labs. By this time he had acquired a wig and a girlfriend. However, this mundane work was not to his taste. One day, some time later, he telephoned.

'Just to let you know that I am leaving,' he said. 'I've got a new job.'

'Doing what?' I asked. It was of no use trying to guess, knowing Jim's work record.

'As Director of the Power Support Center for Solar Turbines in France.'

'Good God! How did you land a job like that?'

'They wanted an experienced engineer who was fluent in English, French and Arabic!'

It had been clear to everyone that he was fluent in the first two, as he had met his partner in advanced French classes at night school. But Arabic?

'Where did you learn Arabic?' I asked him.

'Cairo University, of course!'

'Of course!'

This story would have to wait until another time. It was obvious that he had learned Arabic sometime after he had been directed during the war to cross North Africa to meet the Americans to help them to set up an engine maintenance base. If he'd known the language at that time he would have been able to read the signs in one of the villages on the way across the top of Africa and would not have mistakenly lodged his men in the local brothel instead of the hotel, while he slept in the wagon to guard all the equipment.

One story that may never be told is the reason for his baldness and his yearly requests for a day's release in order to pay a visit to a Ministry of Defence establishment for a medical check-up. Something to do with standing too close to atom bombs on test in the Pacific, we understood.

Jim's roots were those of a typical Merseysider, but those of Ches were totally different. Ches was a member of a Polish aristocratic family. His father had been a cavalry officer in the army. One uncle raced cars at Brooklands, notably a fearsome beast called Chitty-Bang-Bang, so-called because of the noise that it made when the engine was idling. The massive engine was very slow revving and appeared to fire at every lamp post. This was the original Chitty and bore no relation to the better known (near) namesake Chitty-Chitty-Bang-Bang of the film of that name. It only came near to flying as it hit the notorious bump on the Brooklands track.

Ches' father met his end at the hands of the Russians in the Katyn Forest massacre. As happened in many of the aristocratic families in that era, the children were separated by the Soviets and despatched to far-flung parts of the Soviet republics. Ches and his mother were sent to Siberia, but he escaped by walking or hiding in or under any means of transport that he could find. He made his way back through hostile territory to Palestine where he joined the army. He eventually flew in Mosquitos. It was a pity that he never wrote a book about his experiences.

Of such early trials he seldom spoke. He had absorbed the local Bristol life and was a pillar of his church. At work he went about the task of proposing repairs to bent and twisted aircraft with his usual 'Yes, but …' questioning approach. Occasionally signs of the spirit that had carried him from one side of Asia to the other as a teenager would rise to the surface and he would puff his ever-present pipe more vigorously. However, even the pipe was pushed into the past when he found himself smoking it in the shower.

Then there were the humourists, like Mike Smith, who had risen from being a pre-war apprentice to Assistant Chief Aerodynamicist. He always had a beautiful way of putting things, whether he was telling you off, or telling a story.

He described his first visit to the late Peter Scott's new bird sanctuary at Slimbridge, a few miles up the A38 from Bristol. The sanctuary lay beside the wetland banks of the River Severn. He walked around the ponds, marvelling at nature's ability to cope with complex aero/hydrodynamics without having to resort to extensive analysis containing any suspicion of the use of partial derivatives or second order differential equations. However, even Mother Nature came a cropper occasionally. In this incident it happened to a squadron of Canada geese.

Not being a twitcher, he deduced that they were Canadian by their rather flat, sharp accent. As the squadron arrived above the landing ground, their leader detached his Number 2 to go down and assess the designated area. The 'volunteer' broke away from the leading V formation and descended in a wide curve, turning his head frequently to examine the constantly changing pattern on the largest area of water.

There appeared to be no one in the control tower in charge of keeping the runway clear and it was probably the random movement in this large pond that made him break off his intended approach and head for a smaller side pond beyond the reeds. Here he realigned himself on a steady descent, feathered flaps fully down, leading edge slats in the landing configuration and undercarriage extended forward to plane over the surface of the water on touchdown. A perfect approach, or nearly so.

It must have dawned on him at the last minute that this pond was not big enough to take the might of the whole squadron, or possibly, at the very last second, of himself. The runway was too short.

Mike continued his story:

As he approached the short runway threshold you could sense the panic in the cockpit. He applied full take-off power, but too late. Frantic paddling of the webbed feet in the water did not produce sufficient thrust boost to avoid the reeds at the other end. The runway length was below Operational Limits and the Obstacles were above. With a derisive toot the leader, who had observed the pathfinder's cock-up, led the remainder of his squadron straight into the melee on and around the main stretch of water. This whole area was filled with flapping wings, fountains of water and quacking, hooting waterfowl. It had the air of a school rugby match on a very wet field.

22

AGONY INCORPORATED BY DESIGN

'If you insist on walking on two legs, then you can expect some back problems at some stage in your life.'

My doctor's wry comment hid some concern for her patient's agony. It had started in the early hours of the morning with an unbearable pain in my left leg. Getting up and walking around the house had alleviated it somewhat, but the extent of the prowling about was limited by the fact that our house is upside down, with the living rooms upstairs and the bedrooms downstairs. For this reason, any continuous pacing was eventually likely to wake the rest of the family. Sitting or lying down brought a few seconds of relief followed by a rapid rise to maximum leg pain. A slipped disc in my lower back had trapped the sciatic nerve, meaning that everything downstream of the disc was in agony. Outside it was raining.

Morning surgery opening time came at long, painful last. It was relatively easy to get into the car, but within a few yards the car had to be abandoned where it stood and my journey continued on foot. At the surgery I continued to walk around the room until my turn came to go into the consulting room. The net result was advice to go home, take the pills, and lie down on a board for two weeks in the hope that the disc in the vertebrae would mend. It didn't.

Nor did it help being told that the leg itself was not really experiencing pain, it was only the trapping effect of the disc on the relevant nerve giving that impression.

The pills did not work either and an appointment was made with a specialist. Again, the advice was to go home and take stronger pills, but this time I was wrapped in a plaster jacket from armpit to hip, which was constructed over a muslin vest substitute. This outfit resulted in an undignified exit from the hospital with a vastly expanded waistline. I could not fasten up my trousers, or zip up my flies. Hence there was an urgent need to visit the shopping centre to buy a larger pair. And in the interim I used a strategically placed works report to conceal the openings.

Over the next six weeks I developed elaborate techniques to change vests whilst wearing a jacket by pinning the bottom of the replacement to the top of the one under the plaster and pulling it through, slipping my arms out of the old armholes and remembering to catch the new ones before they disappeared. The vest was then pulled down into place. Other strategies were developed to scratch the un-washable parts. As a slimming aid the plaster jacket worked wonders, and it soon became possible to lie in bed and look down the tunnel towards the machinery at the other end. The net result was that the heavy plaster jacket and all my clothes except tie and socks rested upon two very sore hips. The only solution was to return to the hospital for a remould, to be followed by another two-day drying out session. The effects were beginning to tell on the whole family, as my temper became more and more frayed.

It was doubly unfortunate that this happened to be the hay fever season. Each sneeze caused agonising pain, coupled with a defensive kick of my left leg in an attempt to relieve the spasm. Migraines frequently compounded the problem, producing periods of gloom. One major problem centred around the pills. Having taken pethidine in an attempt to kill the pain in the leg, would it be safe to take migril (a medication for migraines) to fend off the approaching migraine? And what should I do about the hay fever?

All the family found that home life left a lot to be desired. It was discovered that our row of houses had a build deficiency, in that the oversite concrete had lost a lot of the supporting hardcore (rubble such as bricks and broken masonry to provide support). The large rocks, which had been removed to make way for the foundations, had been used as infill and the smaller pieces of hardcore had slipped down in between. In consequence, the oversite concrete had followed the hardcore and the bedroom floors had followed the concrete. All our furniture had to be removed from the bedrooms, and everyone had to, or tried to, sleep in the playroom, while 7 tons of liquid concrete were pumped under the oversite concrete and the floor supports were rebuilt to the correct level. We now had some of the strongest foundations in Christendom!

However, that period was not without its high points. The meetings at work still continued as usual, with me being ferried in and out by helpful colleagues. The journey to Fairford could be undertaken only if the Douglas DC-3 made special journeys. The plaster left its impression on car seats, beds and the tops of my thighs, and it cut dangerously close to the essentials. One particular meeting with Rolls-Royce left an impression in more ways than one. The table was narrow, to accommodate as many people as possible in the small office. Designers sat on both sides and at the ends. In the middle of a small technical disagreement, the pollen struck me unexpectedly. My sneeze resulted in the usual reaction and my leg shot forward. A look of shock, followed by agony appeared on the face of the Rolls man opposite. His chair shot backwards as the kick caught him under the kneecap and he clutched at his knee with both hands. After a short time he said through clenched teeth: 'You have a hell of a way of reinforcing your remarks!'

When the laughter subsided our meeting continued, the discussion stepped up, and exchanges became fast and furious. There came a point where my leg pain necessitated a standing position. The centre of discussion being across the other side of the table, my leaning position brought the plaster jacket in contact with the edge of the table, or nearly so. Unfortunately, the hand of another Rolls man was between the two. Reports from the Rolls-Royce office on the other side of the runway subsequently suggested that the aircraft manufacturers were getting 'too aggressive in putting across their arguments'.

Other incidents offered some compensation, particularly in the case of the technical rep from an accessory firm who frequently reinforced the end of an inevitable joke with a punch in the ribs, accompanied by a loud laugh. The next joke was not a particularly good one, the punch was, but the laugh was cut to a gasp as his mouth opened into a silent scream and his eyes opened even wider. He never did it again.

Stronger analgesic pills began to have a progressively diminishing effect. The next level of painkiller was addictive and so something had to be done soon. My nights began with two pills, followed by forty or so minutes of sleep bending face-down over a pile of pillows in the sitting room. The process would be repeated three or four times during the night, each period being preceded by a quarter of an hour's pacing, to walk off the awakening pain before taking the next pills. Waking up became a thing to dread. Despair was setting in. A leap from the Clifton Suspension Bridge looked almost inviting. How the family put up with it could never be fathomed.

During one walk around the roads in the dark, dressed in a coat over my pyjamas, a white car drew alongside me.

'Could I ask you what are you doing out at this time in the morning, sir?' said the policeman.

'Walking off a pain in my leg,' came the lame reply.

'Would you get into the car please?'

'I can't sit for long.'

There followed a long explanation of the problem, followed by a suggestion:

'I will accompany you home and get confirmation.'

'I warn you, we will probably get a dusty reception as the family has been disturbed about four times a night for the last two months.'

The production of my latchkey at the front door appeared to satisfy him and he drove off, avoiding any confrontation.

It came to a point where something had to be done, and my doctor wrote a firm letter to the specialist. A place was found and a bed was allocated. (The National Health Service was different in those days.) The nurse brought some pills of a lesser strength than I had been taking over the past weeks.

'Take these and get into bed,' she instructed.

These pills, being so much weaker than I was used to, had no effect whatsoever.

'Get back into bed,' commanded the nurse. 'You are not supposed to be on your feet with those pills inside you.'

Remonstrations were of no use, and she had to put up with me walking around the bed all night. The next day a pre-med was administered to render my senses into a state suitable for the operation and, after a time, the theatre porter arrived with his trolley. In the anteroom of the operating theatre I chatted with the anaesthetist on the ethics of removing things from the bodies of patients whilst they were unconscious. This was interrupted by him asking if the pre-med had been administered.

'And what medicines have you been taking prior to entering hospital?' he asked.

The frequency and quantity of my medications caused him to replace the tray that he had just taken down and to pull out another from a higher shelf.

'When you feel the small prick and I tell you to do so, start counting backwards from one hundred,' he told me.

'OK, Ouch! Ninety-nine, ninety-eight … ninety-six – I'm feeling a bit woozy!'

'A bit woozy?' He looked surprised. 'You should have bloody well gone at ninety-eight!'

Awakening through the fog of disappearing anaesthetic made it difficult to decide what was different, what was missing? It was the pain! The pain had gone! Hang on a bit, I thought, after a small shift of position it always comes back. But it didn't! Not for many years and not to the same extent.

When the pain did ultimately return it was because the old scar had grown and re-trapped the nerve as it passed through the fairlead. The surgeon was at first reluctant to go in for another hacking session, but things began to get difficult and so another appointment was made. This time, following several promotions at work, I had taken advantage of the perks, meaning the operation was to be done in a private hospital run by the Sisters of Mercy. I realised that this would certainly remove the problem of young motorcyclists with broken legs taking over the wards and shouting into the early hours of the morning, followed by morning swearing sessions at the nurses who were trying to wake people up for breakfast before the doctors started their rounds.

Unfortunately the evening of admission coincided with one of my weekly migraine sessions. Standing up brought on the sickness, and lying down made the unbearable headaches more unbearable. The most tolerable solution was always to kneel beside the bed, stark naked for some unknown reason, and bend face-down over it, being completely covered by the duvet. While I was in this position the sister poked her head into the room and misunderstood the jumble of bedclothes over the bed. A search of the rest of the wards revealed nothing of the 'missing' patient's whereabouts. Returning to the room, she noticed the open window. Putting two and two together she made five. She reasoned that the man had obviously been in great pain and had been behaving in an unworldly, introverted manner. Dashing downstairs and picking up a torch she searched the grounds under my open window and widened her search, as she found no inert body. Some few minutes later she rushed up to the room, panting in mind and body, just in case she had missed something. She looked under the bed. At the other side of the bed she saw a pair of knees and other things. Standing up quickly she grabbed the counterpane and whipped it off me.

'What in the ★★★★?' As her relief became evident, several words were used which did not figure in the Novices Revised Handbook. There would certainly have to be a cascade of penances at a later date.

'What in the name of the Saints are you doing like that?' she demanded.

'Making advances to a migraine. Please go away.'

'You can't go around dressed like that. Put your pyjamas on again!'

I had no intention to go around anywhere, dressed or not. But in deference to this religious fraternity, the pyjamas were donned, followed by the duvet, and the world was shut out again.

The depressive feeling brought on by migraines cannot be imagined or described. The whole concentration is on the pain on one side of the head interspersed by sickness, which on occasions becomes unbearable – as exemplified by a chance meeting with a fellow sufferer who decided that he had to sell his precious shotguns, *just in case*. If the house should catch fire my thought would be 'so what, just send me the ashes!'

At work my secretary would gently close the door and fend off all callers, whatever their status. Only once was a positive corrective found. This developed from an intense argument with a colleague who insisted in barging in and who would never shut up whether he was right or not! This time he was in the wrong but would not admit it, nor go away. When he was eventually ordered out of the office I noticed that the migraine had gone. He was very surprised to be called back and thanked for that service.

There is no guarantee that once the lowered feeling and dull start-up pain has been recognised and the ergotamine pills are taken, that the pain will disappear. If it does not go then there is nothing to look forward to for hours or days but abject misery and intense pain. It can be worked through with great concentration, but it cannot be slept through. Standing up brings the sickness, lying down intensifies the pain. Being propped up at a 45° angle by the corner of a room soon becomes exhausting. However, once the migraine has cleared, the abnormal feeling of well-being and *joie de vivre* transcends anything experienced at any other phase of life.

Some years previously the problem had been misdiagnosed by the local doctor we had at the time. He had pronounced that it was sinusitis and, as things became worse, a 'specialist' was consulted. This man put the problem down to a bent septum, requiring a minor operation to correct it. The minor operation went well until the time came to be discharged. The dragon in charge of the ward had pulled out the bung in the nasal passages, giving the last bit a final tug, as it had become attached to the scene of the operation. It came out with a bit of tissue attached. She had then gone to lunch with instructions not to be disturbed. Minutes after her ministrations the hydraulics system blew a gasket.

Blood poured out of my nose and mouth and stained everything. The nearby patients alerted the nearest nurse on duty, who dashed up with a pan, which started to fill up rapidly. A debate ensued as to whether they dare recall the dragon. With a bit of encouragement from me, while I was head down watching one of my essential parts clotting in a rapidly filling bowl, the braver one of the pair ran down the corridor to find the nearest doctor. By the time the sister in charge had arrived, berating the nurse in front of the doctor for not calling her first, more positive action was in hand. The solution adopted was another operation and another bung, this time tied through the nasal passage and mouth. Ann arrived to find that it would be a day or so before she could take her husband home. She was five months pregnant at the time. Two days later my system blew again.

This time it was late at night after a heavy day for the theatre staff that, with the exception of a registrar and a theatre nurse, had gone home. Taking into account the happenings and losses of the previous week, things had progressed beyond the serious. After a quick dash to the operating theatre the proceedings began with me holding a cyclic blood-pressure measuring device so that the surgeon could read its weakly flickering needle.

'When I nod my head you fill him full of that,' the surgeon said to the theatre nurse, indicating the hypodermic that he had inserted into my hand. 'And then catch the auto sphyg before he drops it!'

I became conscious upon hearing a voice asking if she could get me anything. I was not aware of my response – a request for a nice dry Chablis – until I was told afterwards. Nor did I realise that I had had to be resuscitated once, and that two veins in my neck and one in my left eyebrow had been tied up, and that thirteen pints of someone else's blood had been used to top up my system several times. On second thoughts, the additional blood *did* register, as it seemed that the donors must have been suffering from the effects of advanced alcoholic poisoning. My last memories upon waking from the operation were of three nightmares. I remembered all three, and somehow had the feeling that they would reoccur. They did, not within days, but within minutes, and continued repeatedly in the same sequence.

Several cycles of nightmares occurred before I was lying awake again. After remaining there for what seemed like hours, and not able to see the ward clock, I asked the ever-present nurse what the time was.

'You asked me that only a minute ago,' she replied. 'Have you forgotten?'

The operation must have caused a series of displacements in the space-time continuum.

At the maternity hospital where she worked, Ann was sitting down to lunch with a group of her colleagues. They were joined by someone else, a fellow nurse who was full of self-importance. With the superior air of one in possession of information not available to the others, the newcomer began to tell a story that had just been relayed to her. So much for doctor/patient confidentiality. As she developed the story about the overnight saga at the general hospital, a growing realisation swept over one of her audience.

'My God,' Ann said. 'That's my husband you're talking about!'

Ann put her coat over her uniform and drove down to the hospital to be shown a form on the bed which lay there with a black eye and a large sutured gash on each side of his throat.

The form stirred and asked, 'What time is it?'

After answering the question several times she left to drive back to the maternity hospital. There she was met by the matron who, far from giving her the afternoon off, gave her the biggest roasting that she ever had before or since, for leaving the hospital without permission and in uniform, even though it was her lunchtime.

Within a few hours the next migraine added to my misery. My 'bent septum' had not been the cause of my migraine.

In the enlightened atmosphere that exists nowadays, this improbable saga would have ended with the patient suing the consultant for a wrong diagnosis, and also taking legal action against the hospital for some form of negligence. The Ambulance Chasers would encourage the midwife (Ann) to sue the spreader of medical gossip for mental distress, as well as suing the source for lack of confidentiality, not to mention pursuing the Matron for harassment.

It was a surgeon at the dental hospital, of all places, who first diagnosed my classic migraines.

23

RELAXATION

In Cars

In the years BC (Before Children), not only was the work hectic, but so was the play. Many of the design staff held parties in their turn and many took part in the Bristol Aeroplane Company (BAC) Motor Club activities. The Mini, with its ability to go flat out everywhere, had barely arrived on the scene. Cowboy clubs, those not under Royal Automobile Club (RAC) auspices and which did not demand an RAC competitors' licence, had not yet caused almost every road on the map to be designated as a blackspot.

The firm still encouraged its staff to take an interest in aeroplanes and subsidised private flying to a small degree. Private flying was relatively unrestricted and done in real aeroplanes, such as the Tiger Moth, from the old wartime Air Transport Auxiliary field at Whitchurch, which had a real wooden clubhouse and real grass for take-off and landing. Gliding was done at the ex-RAF airfield at Lulsgate and the Long Mynd and Nymphsfield when Lulsgate took over from Whitchurch as the municipal airport.

In order to encourage the participation of novices in rallies, the BAC Motor Club had devised a scheme whereby the locations to be visited were categorised as 'easy' or, 'less easy' and 'difficult' according to starting and stopping points. The novices did the fewest numbers of points, those who had won a couple of novice trophies did additional points and the 'experts' did the lot. This scheme of A, B and C points was adopted later by the RAC and many other clubs. The cars varied from home-built specials – not the smoothies of today, but skimpy hand-beaten bodies with a wheel sticking out from each corner and no weather protection – through to Baby Austin Sevens, Morris Eights and Minors to large Wolseleys and Sunbeam Talbots.

Good navigators were at a premium and coveted by the drivers, who were even heard to buy them a drink at the end of the evening. Occasionally it was a matter of telephoning round if the usual one couldn't or wouldn't make it. Thus it happened that, after I'd made three such calls, there had been two refusals and one acceptance for a Friday evening excursion. However, as usual, nothing ever went smoothly after things became difficult and this was no exception. Two days before the rally, the two refusals had telephoned to say that they *could* come out to play. As one of them was always first choice and all three worked in the same office, the only solution that offered itself was to take all three.

Snow had fallen the day before and so the extra pushing power of three navigators would come in useful, but their extra weight might make things tricky on the icy roads of the Mendips. What I had not bargained for was three opinions. Well into the second stage, with things going reasonably well, the navigators' instructions became more and more delayed. There was a crossroads coming up, but there were no offers of help.

'Which way? Which way?' I asked with a degree of urgency.

'Left,' said the voice beside me.

'Right!!' said a voice from behind almost at the same time.

'NO, NO straight on!!' said the third.

There was no solution but to stop and sort things out. Map references were checked and rechecked. One member of the crew slid down the icy road to consult the signpost.

'It's in the opposite direction!' he announced. 'We should be going down the road that we have just come up!'

Not one of them had been correct. There was nothing more to do but retrace our steps. This was the point where three navigators could make themselves really useful. The country road was narrow, icy and the car was facing uphill. No driver would relish the thought of backing down the hill on the ice to the crossroads because of the ditches on either side.

'Get out and push on the side of the car at the back, while I spin the back wheels,' I said.

This was a well-recognised technique. Initially we got nowhere until the man on the far side realised that he should be pushing with the others. The car moved slowly round and eventually faced almost the right way, perilously close to the opposite ditch. There was still some unfrozen water in the ditch, as one of the navigators found out when getting in from that side. The other two piled in from the roadside and away we slid. From then on it could only get better. We had lost a lot of time and, being the owner of the car, I was not going to risk all in trying to make it up. Towards the end, doing moderately well, all things taken into account, a unanimous instruction was received to turn left.

'Are you sure?' I double checked.

'Are we ever wrong?'

The road looked like a cart track, but I knew the twisted minds of the planners of these rallies; dammit, I'd done the same kind of deceptive trick myself. We turned down the snow-covered bumpy track with no more argument. The twin tyre marks of a tractor stretched before us and within 100yd they descended into the River Frome. With a bang and a big splash, so did we!

Happily this was a recognised ford, recognised by others but not by club navigators. Driving across the bed of the river, wishing that off-road vehicles had been invented, we charged at the other bank. Having regained the track there was nowhere to go but press on to what was supposed to be the finish, only to be met with fence posts and barbed wire across our path. It was time to stop and take stock. The tractor tracks went straight through. It was no mirage, as the posts were firmly in the ground and the wire was firmly stapled to posts on both sides as well as those embedded in the road. The navigators never solved that mystery. There was nothing for it but to apply the same pushing technique as before and retrace our steps yet again.

Previous practice had improved our performance immensely. The car was turned round with relative ease and splashed into the Frome again. The far bank was higher and accounted for the loud bang of bottoming suspensions and chassis, so it became necessary to charge the bank to climb out. Turning on to the road that we had recently left, the navigating team found by accident that we were on a nice straight road to the finish: it was icy, but straight.

Some distance behind, and going relatively slowly for him, we were followed into the finish by Brown from the Full Scale Loft. The car was a 'Brown Special', having a large engine, a wheel at each corner, no comfort and no weather protection. His navigator was Jack Parker, one of the best in the club. Jack navigated by means of a torch and a large luminous alarm clock tied with a bit of string around his neck. He usually came in the first three in the expert's category. However, tonight something had gone wrong as driver and navigator were not their usual talkative selves and avoided one another in the general discussion groups. Unaware of this atmosphere I walked around the car to see what modifications Brown had incorporated since the last rally. He was always changing something to better the performance.

'I see that you have changed the radiator to a Vee shape,' I pointed out. 'What was the purpose of that?'

Brown exploded. 'The silly bugger said straight on to the finish, so I put my foot down! But we were on the wrong road, weren't we? It had a right angle bend in it and we went off and hit this stone gatepost dead centre!'

'Well I must say it looks better than a flat one. Does it still work?'

He gave a suffering-fools-lightly look and opened the bonnet. Melting snow dripped slowly from all around the engine, where it had been packed after the accident. Leaving me to look at the mess, he began to wander around the growing band of finishers asking for chewing gum as a temporary measure to stop up the large leaks in the radiator. The small sticky mess that he came back with was insufficient to plug the gaps so he began to pick up more snow and pack it on the under tray in the engine compartment for the journey home. The idea of a tow on an icy road appealed to no one, least of all himself. It was pointed out to him that another prang would not make much difference to the front of the car. However, it would possibly modify the backside of the car in front.

'It does not pay to believe everything that your navigators tell you!' I said, with feeling.

The Motor Club was now gaining in size and status, and the chairman had persuaded the owner of one of the local engineering firms, Cross Engineering, famous for its piston rings – including the massive ring around Concorde's intake – to sponsor a trophy for the new all-night rally to be held in the near future. This was going to be the first 'big un' and we had managed to get the services of Jack Parker and John Flower as navigators. While one plotted, the other would read the route. Jack had never navigated in such luxury before. Gone was the open top of Brown's Special. Gone was the need for the luminous alarm and the torch. He had his own adjustable map light, heater, leather seat and stopwatch, plus a man to plot the reference points. The Sunbeam Talbot 90 had a good reliable engine despite its aluminium con rods, and a massive chassis through which the propshaft and exhaust passed, leaving nothing protruding underneath. (A Mini driver later said that he was always pleased to get behind this car on rough, rutted roads as it tended to level the bumps sticking out of the surface.) The main disadvantages were an awkward column gear change and brakes which began to fade after trying to stop its twenty-seven hundredweight too many times.

The 300 odd miles of journey gave no particular problems until our brakes began to fade after two-thirds of the distance. Jack had been having a field day and had had time to crack jokes. However, these witticisms were interspersed with detailed instructions concerning the road ahead. Never before had I had every corner read out to me in detail from the Ordinance Survey map. However, the rally organisers would try to find places where the maps were wrong and so care was still needed. We had come down from the Quantocks, where the sight of a large Wolseley, a TR2 and a Sunbeam Talbot drifting round a tight bend in too close proximity, down the open hillside, on a pitch dark night, had reduced everyone to white silence. We were approaching the Somerset Levels on a relatively straight road, having negotiated a fairly full ford. Meanwhile, Jack was into another of his jokes:

'… So I said to this fellow … Turn right. TURN RIGHT!!'

We just made the turn and found ourselves going down to a section where another stream flowed onto the road, so we went along it for some distance before turning off to the other side.

'The map was wrong there,' said Jack. 'The stream is shown running beside the road.'

John agreed. The water was fairly deep as the road at this point was in a hollow. In consequence, the brakes were even less effective when we emerged. Nevertheless, we managed to finish without further mishap. At the finish we noticed a group was standing listening to a tall, thin individual having an altercation with the chief marshal.

'You had no right to use a section where the map was wrong!'

Ian McLeod, one of the club's expert navigators, was beside himself with anger. There was a bruise at the side of his head, his jacket was torn and his spectacles were held together with sticky tape.

'But you yourself used the ploy when organising the last evening rally!' was the riposte.

No quarter was going to be given here. We asked one of the spectators what had happened. He had tears in his eyes as he told us:

'Apparently his driver, Tippen, drove the Volkswagen through the first ford and the hot air heating system drew water as well as air over the cylinders and blew steam onto the windscreen. They nearly crashed. So when they came to the stream on the road they opened the doors. This time the water was even deeper and it came in over the sills. As the VW is waterproof, the water swilled about the cabin. Ian could not stand it slopping from side to side and fore and aft as they cornered, braked and accelerated, so he opened his door and Tippen swung the car from side to side to throw the water out. Whereupon Ian was thrown out with the water!'

Very few cars had seatbelts in that era. Now that they have, there are few such club rallies. Two days later my telephone rang in the office.

'Congratulations, you came fourth!' said Mike Manning, the rally organiser. 'Geoff Mabbs came first.' (Mabbs won the Tulip Rally in the following year.) 'Tippen and Ian McLeod came second despite the water incident, the TR2 was third, and he'd just come back from the Continental rally, you were fourth in front of Tiny Lewis.' Tiny drove for the Sunbeam Talbot team and won a Coupe des Alpes that year. But more was to come: 'Oh, and by the way, out of the thirty-six starters there were only nine finishers and the last man was in your team, so Tippen, you and he have won the team prize!'

On mature reflection I mused that, if we had known the strength of the opposition beforehand, I would probably have offered to be a route marshal, instead of entering as a competitor.

In Aeroplanes

On the other hand, flying around in a small aircraft, although carried out at a higher speed, was paradoxically a much more leisurely pursuit. My training had been done at the College of Aeronautics at Cranfield under the wing of Bert Russell, an ex-Lancaster pilot. His methods of teaching were somewhat unorthodox, in that on take-off he would sometimes shout 'I've got it!' and the pupil would know that he had seen a rabbit and had decided to chase it, and would realise that the next few seconds were going to be hairy to say the least. They got even hairier after the rabbit dived down the nearest hole. With the aircraft at a high angle of bank and the lower wing tip a foot or two off the ground, the command would come back 'It's all yours!' Pupils liked to believe that they had extricated themselves out of the ensuing mess by dint of their own flying skills.

Boredom could never be associated with flying training. Bert had a phobia about small clouds and would attack them at any given opportunity, climbing, spinning and diving through them to try to disperse them. During recovery from spin instruction he would ask the pupil after the n'th spin if he were feeling sick. Word had got round that it was advisable to say 'Yes', otherwise he would do several more. One student with a cast-iron constitution said 'No' until Bert had to say that *he* was! The student had free beer for a week.

Narrowboats were surprised to see a Tiger Moth coming at them seemingly under an impossibly small bridge, only to pull up over it at the last second and buzz past. Students who tried to emulate these manoeuvres and were seen to do so received a roasting of the 'Don't do as I do, do as I say!' variety.

Nevertheless, Dalton Minty, a Canadian student and ex-Dakota pilot, did succeed in knocking bits out of the newly paved runway with the Tiger Moth propeller, and Benson, a naval officer student, flew to the wrong side of the control tower and was arrested in mid-air by the festoon of aerials. On this occasion the port wing snapped back and its trailing edge stopped about a quarter of an inch into his nose. Six inches further on and he would have been headless.

However, having gone solo we were at Bristol flying Austers and, whenever one was free, the beloved Tiger. Balmy days were spent doing aerobatics, flying up and down Coombes and, very infrequently, dam busting. The latter consisted of picking up a friend and a couple of ice cream tubs. After eating the ice cream whilst buzzing over Somerset, the plan was to fly low over the Chew Valley lakes and drop an empty ice-cream tub on the cars whose occupants were basking in the sun on the road on top of the dam. The second time, with backup from the 'second wave' (another Moth), was the last time as the tub fell on a police car. In those days police cars did not have numbers on top and from that aspect were anonymous to a predatory pilot. Following the cry of 'Bombs away!' the Tiger Moth was flown over the Mendips to look for pre-Roman sites, before returning to base to be met by the Chief Flying Instructor. He didn't look happy.

In the office he turned puce and drew himself up to his full 5ft 5in.

'I've had the police here with a complaint against low flying by you!' he roared.

'How do they know that it was me?' I asked, as we had seen no one whilst flying up Burrington Coombe, nor noticed a police car at Chew Valley.

'Because the blasted plane has registration letters on it, of course, dimwit! And I assume that this has your fingerprints on it!' he said, producing the ice-cream tub from his desk drawer.

Forensic science was in its infancy, but faced with these two bits of evidence there was no denying it.

'What happens now?' I asked, visualising the civil equivalent of a court martial, yet wondering why the tub was not encased in a plastic bag sporting an exhibit number. My worry was losing my flying licence.

'I asked them what height you were flying at and, when they told me, I thought that even you would not be that daft! When I tried to get them to estimate the height of one of the aircraft approaching the airfield they were miles out! So they compromised. The police are getting an hour's free flying and you are paying for it! Stick to the 500ft minimum in future! Clear out!'

Following an offer to buy him an evening snifter the office was empty.

In Gliders

To get some proper soaring, as opposed to the short hops around the airfield at Cranfield, the college gliding club took two of its gliders to the Long Mynd, near Church Stretton in Shropshire, during the holidays. These gliders were not the high-performance fibreglass-and-composite machines of today, but were the wood and fabric pre-war designs with low performance. Those with an even lower performance were left behind, one of them being a Dagling – a kind of five-barred gate with wings. It was this one that gave the real sensation of battling with the elements as the pilot sat in the open in a small bucket seat with the joystick between his legs and his feet resting on the wooden rudder bar control. On cold days it was imperative to have your trouser legs tucked into your socks to prevent a gale affecting the nether regions. On the other hand, shorts, worn on a warm summer day, would provide an additional pleasure to the trip. The contraption would be hauled across the ground at just below flying speed by an ex-barrage balloon winch, with the pilot trying to keep it straight and level. Once he had mastered this he would be allowed to coax it into the air in progressively higher and higher hops, eventually being allowed to release the towing cable into free flight. The next obstacle would be the controlled crash, euphemistically called a 'landing'.

The aircraft that we took with us in the college lorry was the single-seat Slingsby Tutor, the next stage but one between the Dagling and the Grunau Baby. The latter had been used initially for primary Luftwaffe training during the Second World War and was appropriated by the Royal Navy after the war, eventually finding itself at the college. Apart from the two gliders, the convoy of ex-WD lorry and several old motorbikes carried a selection of students and college secretaries uncertainly along Watling Street towards Church Stretton.

Navigation was uncertain, despite the map drawn on the wall of my room. The cavalcade missed the turn-off and nearly invaded Wales by mistake. At one point the locals were entertained by an attempt to turn a 30ft lorry in a 15ft lane. However, some cross-examination of the locals, aided by the local brew, enabled the group to locate their target. After a stiff climb with a boiling engine and a smoking clutch, our convoy arrived intact on the top of the Long Mynd.

In front of the larger of the two hangars, several gliders rested with one wing tip into wind, each being held down with a car tyre or a bag of sand. They were brightly painted and contrasted with the greens and browns of the rather bumpy landing area. On the far side of the hangars, the hilltop disappeared abruptly down to the valley below. The hillside faced into the prevailing wind and the combination of hillside and wind would produce the conditions of uplift, which would sometimes keep gliders airborne for hours. The views across the low-lying land to the Black Mountains of Wales were magnificent. Why, I wondered, were the hills in Wales named in English and those in England named in Welsh?

On the evening of our arrival, the resident club's gliders were being put to bed in the larger of the two hangars. At Cranfield the gliders were housed in the large ex-RAF hangars with plenty of room to walk around each one. Here at the Mynd, many more gliders were to be put into an impossibly small space by those who had not sneaked off home. The new arrivals' musings were brought into focus by a cry from inside the hangar.

'Anodder vings higher plis jentlemens!' shouted the resident ground engineer, Teddy Prohl.

He and his few helpers had installed the first glider inside the hangar with its wing tip and nose over the enclosure that formed the clubroom. The tail and opposite tip of the long slender wing were propped upon boxes. The second glider had been moved inside and was being threaded under the first.

Wishing to establish a good rapport with our hosts, we removed the tyre holding down the wing tip of the nearest glider and started to push it into the hangar.

'No! Not dat von. Anodder von over dere!'

In the days to come we were to learn what went where, how, and in what sequence to stow everything inside. At that time the resulting complex pattern of colourful interwoven gliders could easily be passed off as modern art. During the next hour, having helped our hosts, we lifted our own two gliders off the lorry and assembled them and pitched the tents. Unfortunately, the heavens decided to open in traditional fashion and the experience of that night convinced everyone that it would be much better to sleep in the old hangar, small as it was, with the aircraft. The girls slept in the bunkhouse.

The gravel floor of the hangar looked uninviting so the plentiful bracken crop was called into use, covered by whatever was to hand, resulting in the observation next morning from our navy representative (of tangled aerial fame) that 'he never realised that he could become so attached to a pile of damp heather and rotting sacking'.

Although, at first, the gravel from the floor featured prominently in the menus, the excellence of the food became one of the outstanding features of the camp. The main meal of the day was supervised by Yvonne, a very pretty secretary, and after the day's activities we dined at between 10 p.m. and midnight. We then retired to our respective nooks and crannies in, on and around the aircraft. There would be the nightly call from Dudman, sleeping under the tailplane of the Tutor aircraft:

'Pull the joystick back will you? I want to go to bed!'

Few volunteers could be found for the first job in the morning as this involved a descent by motorcycle to one of the farms in the valley, followed by a climb back with a full milk pail slung around one's neck. Waterproofs were essential.

Gliding started apace, with good winds providing our first experiences of bungee launches, in which the glider was perched on the edge of the hill with one holding each wing tip and two holding the tail. The middle of a length of bungee elastic would then be attached to the towing hook of the glider. Two teams would take up the ends and, at a given signal, would run down the hillside. At a second signal those restraining the glider would let go. As a result the aircraft would be catapulted into the lifting airstream and would turn along the ridge to gain height. A second result would be that, as the load on the bungee was released, the launch teams would go somersaulting down the hillside.

As the wind strength grew, it became possible to dispense with the bungee. The aircraft would be pushed so close to the edge in the stronger wind that it was almost airborne. To prevent an uncontrolled departure, two people on each wing support strut, and two on the rear fuselage, would hold it down. At the given signal all six would heave the straining machine above their shoulders and throw it forwards, remembering to fall flat immediately until the tailplane had passed by. There exists a picture in someone's album of the one who did not let go. One hand still clutches the glider strut and his legs are far apart. Realising that the ground was departing he let go quickly and, hitting the ground in a positive manner, was last seen rolling down the hill towards the bushes.

But there would also be times when the wind dropped to such a level that the only way to get airborne was to use the winch. On one such day, when all was absolutely still, with no cloud in the sky and no prospect of soaring, it was decided that as we had all come this far we might as well at least do a circuit each, even though we had to pay the hosts half a crown (2*s* 6*d*) for each one. (It could have been even more expensive if the participants in this venture, being in the majority on the club's committee, had not passed a motion waiving all launch fees whilst away from base.)

I drew first straw and climbed in.

The cable in front slowly snaked across the ground and then tightened as the signaller at the side of the glider raised and lowered the circular bat in his right hand.

'All out!' was called.

Both bats were moved up and down in an increasing frequency as the signaller tried unconsciously to match the increasing speed of the aircraft. The nose rose gently at first in order to be able to recover if the cable broke. Then it was pitched into the exhilarating climb sensation that seems to match that of powerful aircraft. All too soon the point was reached where the climb almost petered out and there was a danger of any more delay causing the cable to be dropped on the winch after it was released from the aircraft. As the climb rate diminished the cable was released, but the aircraft still continued to climb rapidly. To make sure the cable was released the toggle was given another pull. Fantastic! In clear air we were climbing like the clappers! In gentle circling 1,000ft, 2,000ft, 3,000ft, 4,000ft above ground level, we rose and rose. It was now getting murky as the rising column of moist warm air that we had stumbled into started to cool and form a cloud. Well, as there was no one else about, this was the time to do our first bit of cloud flying – even though there was only an airspeed indicator, a bubble turn indicator and an altimeter to help!

After what seemed to be about fifteen minutes, it was deemed prudent to pop out of the cloud to see where we were and who was about. Down below could be seen the north end of the Mynd, but no aircraft, and so back into the cloud we went to continue the lesson.

After another few minutes I was thinking of the possibility of the first cross-country flight and was preparing to go out for another look around when there was a mighty roar, and the glider reared and tried to turn over. Adrenalin surged around the system as the automatic responses tried to set things straight. The lack of a horizon and any useful instrumentation did not help; the airbrakes were operated to avoid excessive speed build-up. Almost immediately I broke cloud on a fairly even keel, just in time to see the rear view of an RAF four-engined Shackleton heading back to Shawbury for a late lunch.

The realisation of what might have been then dawned on me and the solution was to head as rapidly as possible in the opposite direction towards the landing ground. My reception as the aircraft came to a shaky stop, with my stomach still some miles above and behind, was not what I had been expecting.

Activities progressed at a rapid pace, with those in the Tutor picking up bracken on their wing tips as they flew too close to the hillside in their attempts to find lift; charging full tilt towards trailers on landing, but managing to rub off the speed on the landing skid before they reached the obstacle; finding the hill was higher than it was supposed to be and, in trying to reach the top, landing on the slope, thereby doing a tailslide before coming to rest in an ignominious position in full view of the gallery. Our thoughts then were that it would have been better to have risked the frustration of the next in line for a flight and landed in the designated field in the valley and paid the standard half-crown landing fee to the owner.

That field came into use several times during the fortnight. One notable case occurred when Bill Bedford, later to become a test pilot for the vertical take-off Hawker Kestrel and Harrier, arrived on the Mynd in the Hawker Tomtit. He parked the tiny biplane and walked over to a one-off, twin-seat glider that he was to test for the builder. On his walk around inspection he observed that it had no altimeter. Gwen, the third secretary to join the Cranfield group, noted for her high-speed flying in her attempts to avoid the 'dreaded stall', offered (or was persuaded) to hold a hastily found spare for him. Checks completed, the aircraft was winched into the air, whereupon the rudder pedal promptly jammed behind a structural member. No amount of kicking or probing could release it, his efforts being limited by the need to assert what control remained and the inadequate height of a rapidly descending aircraft. Happily there was just enough aileron control to prevent the glider from descending in a rapidly increasing spiral, from which there would be no escape. By employing all the skills that made him a successful test pilot, Bill managed to pull off an unorthodox landing in the field down in the valley. The aircraft was a little bent and strained. The occupants were only strained, judging by their expressions.

Dave Sharp, another of the Cranfield group, had an overall view from the cockpit of the Tutor as he flew up and down the ridge. When he landed he faced a deserted airfield and had to sit in the cockpit for another half hour before the ground crew arrived. In no time Bill Bedford was back up the hill, into the Tomtit and airborne.

'Well that's our excitement over for the week!' someone said. How wrong she was.

Later that week the weather changed and cloud descended on the hill to such an extent that the cloud base was reported to be 'at the third telegraph pole down the hill'. This gave the team time to carry out unscheduled inspections on the gliders, do some much-needed washing, and spend more time enjoying the excellent results produced by Yvonne and her team of culinary irregulars. Nevertheless, as soon as the weather showed signs of clearing we were ready for action. But the wind wasn't. It had started to blow from the north-west and the uplift on the face of the hill had changed to down-thrust. The attempts at circuits only produced downdraughts all round. There was only one thing to do – shop for essentials and visit the pub.

That evening, on the way back, we noticed that the wind had not changed but there now was a cloud stretching out from the south edge of the hill towards the north-west. These clouds form at the top of waves in the wind as it comes off the hills. The clouds often form in a lenticular shape and lie side-by-side crosswind as the air currents rise and fall. Their edges are well defined and they indicate the position of reliable lift for gliders on their windward side. It was too late to do anything that night, so we went to bed early to greet the morrow.

'It's gone!' said the person who was first out of bed.

Bleary eyes looked out of the window and confirmed that the cloud was no longer there.

'But the wind is still there at the same strength. Maybe the air is a bit warmer,' someone added hopefully. 'Let's go for it!'

That was easy to say as he was a Tutor pilot and would not be 'going for it'. Those who were going to 'go for it' were hoping to have to land in the field in the valley if they missed this road in the sky where the gods had demolished the signpost.

Straws were drawn and, again, I drew the short one. The cable was paid out as far as possible so as to give a good high launch. This meant a slight crosswind on take-off, necessitating the right wing to be kept low in the early stages. After taking a deep breath, the cable was released at the top of the launch and we turned away from the hill. Immediately the altimeter started to unwind rapidly as the glider crossed the valley. Looking back it was clear that there was no hope of returning to the hill against this wind so we were committed to a landing in the field if there was no lift. The landing field was easy to spot – it was full of cows. The immediate prayer for lift, and plenty of it, was answered just as rapidly. So there *was* someone up there who was listening.

A slight nudge on the base of my spine became a steady pressure. There was no bucking accompanied by the changes in the rushing sound of the air currents encountered in the thermal lift of the last significant climb. This time it was beautifully smooth and almost silent as the altimeter wound steadily upwards. The time passed probing the wave, trying to assess its extent, to see where the lift was and where it wasn't. This was a sample of flying as it should be. Life was great, but, I thought, better let someone else have a go.

Approaching the hill I found a small thermal and circled around in that until I noticed a buzzard climbing inside the track of the glider. The buzzard looked along its wing at me looking along the wing of the aircraft at him. There was a look of disdain on the face of the bird as, without any instruments and without moving a feather, it climbed faster than its poor imitation. The glider had a climb and descent gauge on the pilot's instrument panel. This consisted of two vertical glass tubes, one containing a red ball and the other a green ball. If the red ball rose from the bottom of the tube, the aircraft was descending. If the green ball rose the aircraft was ascending. We often wondered if the buzzard had a green one, which itched when going up, and a red one, which indicated the opposite. Maybe the females used their intuition instead.

It was time to break out of the thermal and make a bad landing in the deep re-forestation troughs cut into the hillside. Cursing and swearing, the recovery crew pulled the glider to the launch point and the next pilot was briefed briefly:

'It's out there somewhere.'

'Thanks, I could see that from here!'

'When you pass the landing field you should find it at about 300ft above hill level. If you don't, do a quick pass over the landing field to scatter the cows in it.'

This pilot didn't find the lift and didn't have enough height to line up for a pass over the field. However, he did manage to land without hitting any cows. Those watching from the hilltop witnessed everything and were already hitching the glider trailer to the towing lorry well before the Grunau touched down. By the time the recovery crew arrived, the cows were investigating the construction of the glider by scratching their necks on the flying surfaces, ignoring the shouts of the pilot who had to remain in the machine: relieved of his weight it could possibly have been blown over. Luckily no horns had yet penetrated the fabric. They entered the field by climbing over a five-barred gate secured by a chain and padlock. The cows were shooed away to one side of the aircraft. At that point one of the experts in such matters (he'd been on a farm camp during the war) pointed out that one of the cows in front of us was, in fact, a bull. As one, we all retreated to the opposite side of the glider.

'Not there!' shouted the Chief Flying Instructor. 'If he charges he will go straight through it! Round them up in groups, starting at the back and drive them into the next field.'

'Lead on, we'll follow!' we replied.

Within about twenty minutes all animals except the bull were in the other field, being kept there by a man who resembled a dancing dervish, because he was having to perform the function of the missing gate. After a few uncertain minutes the bull followed the herd. The dervish saw him coming and disappeared behind the hedge. Hurriedly the glider was pulled to the opposite hedge near the road, disassembled in record time and the separate parts lifted over the locked gate. The cows and the bull emerged as the frantic lifting came to an end and, with some relief, the emotionally and physically exhausted recovery crew vacated the field and reached the safety of the hilltop. After a swift bout of tea drinking we reassembled the glider – almost. One of the two wing support struts was missing. The next to fly 'provided he didn't try to find the wave cloud', plus an unsuspecting character that had not been in the recovery crew, were volunteered to go back to the field to recover the missing strut. It was not there despite a careful search. Neither were the cows.

'Have you seen a strut from our glider?' they asked the farmer who owned the field as he leaned over the gate to his farmyard. They could see the cows were now in their stalls ready for milking. There was no sign of the bull.

'Yes, it's here,' said the farmer. 'I'll get it. By the way, there's a half-a-crown landing fee.'

'We had a problem with the bull.'

'Yes, so I saw.'

'Why didn't you give us a hand if you saw what was going on?'

'Not me. I allus send the boy as he can run faster. It's had me out of the field several times. That's why I allus keep the gate locked to stop strangers going in!'

24

A VERY BUMPY ROAD

As would be expected in such a complex aircraft, the service life was not uneventful. Take the intake as an example.

A TECHNIBIT

One of the most significant problems with the structure of the engine intake was the effect of the dynamic loads on the support mechanism operating the two ramps which control both the inlet shock system, and the shape of the subsonic diffuser leading from the shocks to the engine.

Each ramp is hinged, the front (shock) ramp at its leading edge, and the rear (diffuser) ramp at its trailing edge. At the opposite ends of the two ramps are links, attached to arms fitted to two common torque tubes, one on the left side and one on the right. A centrally located actuator moves a separate arm on each tube to provide a small degree of rotation, thereby moving the ramps up or down, as required.

In the early days static and dynamic loads were difficult to derive, as there was a paucity of generalised data, and what existed was usually specific to particular installations. Thus, with the torque tubes acting as stiff springs, and the stiff ramps having their own vibration modes, the dynamics were, to say the least, interesting. It should be remembered that these were the sixties, when large calculating engines were limited in capacity. Even if they were improved, the results would only be as good as the suspect loads permitted.

A positive manifestation of a dormant problem was exposed in the early supersonic days of Aircraft 001's test programme, when flying up the Bay of Biscay towards southern Ireland. With a loud bang, followed by subsequent heavy vibration, an intake front ramp tore itself away from its links and the front hinge. In a tumbling motion, it flew forward, against the Mach 2 airstream, exited the entry of the intake, went under the nacelle, and hit the exhaust nozzle and the rear fuselage before heading towards Cork. The ventral scope, fitted to both prototypes, provided the shock-of-the-month to the test observer when he saw the dark void in one of the intakes.

An analysis of the final sequence of events was carried out by Jones of the Accident Investigation Branch. However, the forcing mode left a lot to conjecture and Lionel Howarth of the engine company came up to advise. We explained the problem to him, but that was his only contribution. Nevertheless, corrective modifications (extensive reinforcing) were carried out to such an extent that the intakes and their mechanisms survived over 500 deliberate single and double surge events in the ensuing Flight Test programmes. If they were maintained properly the intakes demonstrated adequate strength. If they were not then one incident demonstrated how problems could arise.

An aircraft flying on the westerly run suffered a hydraulic failure in one lane of a duplicated spill system on an inboard intake. The changeover to the standby system was automatic, to be followed up by a confirmatory selection as indicated on the flight engineer's control panel. Unfortunately, there was a dormant failure on the standby hydraulic lane, which must have occurred following the automatic checking action immediately after engine start-up. This was indicated to the flight engineer, who responded by switching back to the first lane. In order to check the adequacy of the newly selected lane, the control system releases the brakes on the appropriate system and checks for the correct sense of movement. The ramps moved for the second time in the wrong sense and the control system reapplied the brakes. Contrary to the instructions in the *Flight Manual*, further re-selections were made, with the ramp moving in the wrong sense each time. The consequent deterioration in the intake flow pattern caused the engine to surge.

As the aircraft was flying at Mach 2 at the time, the flow disturbance this surge caused at the intake entry disturbed the shocks of the adjacent intake, causing that intake to surge in sympathy. (Because of this known phenomenon Concorde had been certified aerodynamically as a twin-engine aircraft above Mach 1.6.) The surge in this intake resulted in the front ramp departing forwards, exiting the aircraft, and the rear ramp to fall across the flow, blanketing the engine.

The first general reaction was that the Brits had not got it right, even now.

Analysis of the meagre recorded data showed that it was just sufficient to indicate that, consequent to the first failure, everything had behaved as expected, taking into account the crew's actions. The double surge event should not have caused such an abnormal reaction. Suspicion ultimately fell on the possible absence of some vital part. In particular, there were split trunnion shells in the bearing between the ramp actuator jack and the torque tube arm. This unit was held together by a bolt, which was capable of taking normal intake running loads, but not surge loads. Strength tests verified this fact, and so the suspicion fell on the maintenance process, especially as it was learned during the investigation that the actuator had been replaced immediately prior to this flight.

Aerospatiale were worried that BAC was trying to direct the blame towards the airline and requested a meeting to examine the 'facts'. Just as the explanations were coming to an end, Don Exell, the engineer charged with in-service contact with the airlines, was called to the telephone. The caller was from the airline, with the information that the required trunnion elements had been located in their stores, wired on to the actuator that had been replaced the day before the flight. He returned to the meeting with the news.

'They have just found the missing items in their stores,' Don explained.

Suspicion still remained in the minds of the visitors.

'When did you receive this information?'

Don looked slightly hurt.

'Just this minute.'

On their return to Toulouse the visitors telephoned the airline and confirmed the timing of Don's information. They were then convinced that the diagnosis, based on the small amount of information available, had been well conducted in identifying such an improbable result. They were good enough to telephone Filton to congratulate us on an excellent diagnosis.

The failure was the result of a remarkable sequence of events. It started with a simple hydraulic failure, followed by a dormant failure, then an incorrect crew action, then an induced surge, followed finally by a maintenance error. There is no method of design forecasting which could counter such a series of events and the probabilities of repetition were minimal.

We concluded that the flight engineer's action had saved the pilot from having to carry out the difficult fixed-intake drills, for the first time in service history, but had given him a lot more grief.

Then Again, Take the Engine Itself

The Rolls-Royce (ex-Bristol Siddeley) Olympus is generally considered to be at the peak of the world's outstanding pure-jet engines. In its many forms it has powered ships, generating units, and subsonic and supersonic aircraft.

A TECHNIBIT

The ultimate development of this engine, as installed in the Concorde, is almost unique, in that for the greater part of its operating life it operates at, or very close to, its maximum potential thrust. In cruising mode the four Olympus engines are developing a total of 160,000hp and air is entering the compressors at over 100°C and leaving at around 550°C. In consequence, both the high pressure compressor blades and the outer casing are constructed in titanium. This can cause a severe 3,000°C fire problem should a damaged blade rub against the casing.

Tests specific to this problem were carried out by Bristol Siddeley and BAe in an attempt to find some form of protection against the consequences. Protection was absolutely essential with the engine being in close proximity to the wing. The solution was found by using layers of carbon cloth, impregnated with resin, mounted on the section of wing heat shield located immediately above the compressor. The under-wing heat shields extended the length and width of the engine nacelles. They consisted of 10 thou. (thousandths of an inch) of stainless steel supporting about ½in of Microbestos.

In one particular instance a broken final stage blade, as a result of damage from the fracture of a first stage low-pressure compressor blade, was carried round the outer casing by the remaining blades. The heat generated between the blade and the casing caused the titanium to ignite. The net result was a complete circumferential separation of the casing, extending axially for about 3in, plus burn-through of that row of rotor blades for half their length. The severance of the previous row of stators, by the same mechanism, led to their being pushed halfway out of the hole in the casing. When the doors were opened, it was found that the two parts of the engine had been resting their unsupported ends on the nacelle doors.

A three-engine ferry flight returned the aircraft to base at Heathrow. With some trepidation, Tom Madgwick and I travelled from Filton to the British Airways hangars to inspect the damage. Tom was responsible for defining and approving all zonal fire analyses on all BAe aircraft, and methods of protection, including anything that an engine could throw at the structure of an aircraft, such as titanium fires, fuel fires and the possibility of a torching flame: a breakout from the combustion chamber giving an 8ft-long, 2,000°C flame at high pressure (Aircraft 002 survived one of these).

With the engine removed, the extent of the damage was clearly visible. The extensive 3,000°C titanium fire had removed only about 30 sq in of the stainless steel/carbon cloth/resin protection, and above that only about 3 sq in of lower wing surface could be seen through the residue of the Microbestos.

We stood under the nacelle from which the engine had been removed, trying to avoid a group of business-suited Americans who jostled us as we inspected the damage. Looking up into the nacelle, one of the more perspicacious of that group remarked, with a degree of admiration:

'Those boys got it just about right!'

This remark caused us to move aside to let them have a better look.

Then Again, There was the Crash at Gonesse (Paris)

As we boarded the coach to leave the Farnborough Display, another of the retirees said that he had heard that a Concord had crashed in Paris. I told him not to be so bloody silly. Unfortunately, it turned out to be true.

Within a short time I was back at work in company with Tom Madgwick in my old office of the Concorde days, which had been opened up to form a conference room by taking in what had been David Moakes' office. Brian Trubshaw was already there, but he was destined not to finish the course as the Good Lord called him to higher levels shortly afterwards.

Perhaps he got a better view from up there than the engineers down below, as, contrary to international agreement, the judiciary took over the process of investigation instead of the local civil investigators. Technical investigations, made whilst Concordes were still flying, were slower than usual in such circumstances because crash evidence was bagged up immediately and access protected, making detailed analysis difficult and delaying its availability.

International agreement would have given ownership of evidence to the civil investigators of the country where the crash had occurred and they would immediately co-opt their counterparts from the countries where the appropriate aircraft, engine, equipment manufacturers and airline were based. In Britain it would be the Air Accidents Investigation Branch.

An excellent description of the events in and following the incident are given in Captain Christopher Orlebar's *The Concorde Story: 21 Years in Service* (Osprey). The various legal arguments as to who is to blame for this accident have now lasted for twelve years, and counting.

25

ONE-UPMANSHIP IN DESIGN

Many of the failures on these high-speed projects were associated with the power plants, the combinations of air inlet, engine and exhaust nozzle and surrounding bits of the aircraft that were so critical to good, efficient and safe operation of the aircraft as a whole. The Bristol Type 188 was no exception to this rule.

Some truly supersonic projects could only be counted as failures. This list would include aircraft such as the B-70 – a large six-engined aircraft with three engines on each side of a single inlet. Hence it had built-in problems from the start. The four-engined B-58 Hustler supersonic bomber was limited to regular supersonic flights only in time of hostilities, because the loss of one of the four low-slung engines with their off-set thrust could cause serious deviations from the line of flight and result in loss of the aircraft. One-third of these were unfortunately lost in peacetime flying – losses which would be very worrying even in wartime.

The SR-71 Blackbird was an exception: it just had to be a success. It had remarkable, but sensitive, power plants. Should the aircraft depart from the design condition at high speed and cause an oscillation to occur in one or other engine, the resulting rapid changes in thrust would be magnified at the cockpit end of the long fuselage to such an extent that some pilots' helmets would impact against the sides of the cockpit structure and would occasionally split. In a pressure suit, this event was one to be avoided. There was a small elite band of intrepid aviators in America who belonged to 'The Split Helmet Club'.

Even the later aircraft, the B-1, originally designed for Mach 2, had failed to be qualified for regular operation above Mach 1.2. Few of these problems even made the technical press.

The American attempt to make a civil supersonic aircraft failed to get further than a wooden mock-up in the full glare of national publicity. The

Russian Tupolev Tu-144, christened the Concordski in the West, had crashed in full view of the crowds at the Le Bourget Air Show. Because of its restricted performance, it had been limited to domestic medium-range flights from Moscow to Alma Ata. If it had been flown over its true design distance it would probably have been limited to the role of a mail plane (but perhaps only carrying verbal messages?).

So how had these Europeans succeeded in producing a reportedly safe and docile machine – with better handling characteristics than the current civil transports – capable of transporting a hundred old dears across the Atlantic delicately sipping their champagne, whilst covering each mile in less than three seconds, and without a space suit in sight? The advent of a co-operation between British Airways and the American airline Braniff gave the American Military and Civil Authorities the opportunity to find out.

For the Braniff task the Concorde would be picked up in New York by Braniff pilots after BA had flown it from London. Being now flown by American pilots to the Southern States it had to be registered in the US. Therefore a Federal Airworthiness Authority (FAA) team would have to be despatched to assess it. As the FAA had no supersonic background, it turned to the NASA military assessors from the Hugh Dryden Research Centre at Edwards Air Force Base (AFB) in the Mojave Desert for their design and test experience.

A TECHNIBIT

The FAA also had to raise a new breed of civil assessors who had to depart from the black and white (or failing that, 'Old Boy') approach to airworthiness and consider the extensively adopted probability approach accepted for Concorde by the British and French officials. This latter approach grew out of the wide use of complex electronic and hydro-mechanical systems and is now used extensively for the new breeds of civil aircraft. The probability approach involved looking at the effect of each item's failure mode, in isolation or in combination, and assessing the probability of causing a hazard, or catastrophe. If the results were sufficiently remote then no precautions would be taken. (In a discussion with an American lawyer his comment was that if we worked this way, then in court we would be on our own!)

The only instance that they could find in their requirements which might have been applied to the variable geometry intake and control system was the carburettor air intake to piston engines.

These gentlemen descended on Filton, Fairford and Toulouse, probing, flying and assessing. The pilots and power plant engineers in this team from Edwards Air Force Base who had dealt with the Hustler, the B-70 and derivatives of the Blackbird were now flight testing the B-1 bomber, it being the nearest thing in the West to Concorde.

Amongst other manoeuvres, BAC pilots insisted in demonstrating the effects of one and two engines failing at speeds above Mach 2 as they pointed the aircraft down the aerodynamic slope towards the maximum operating speed. Whilst doing this test, it was flown 'hands off', to the consternation of the visitors. These hardened NASA engineers, used to violent aircraft misbehaviour in such circumstances, were visibly apprehensive as the time to chop the engines approached, but Concorde demonstrated her good manners, rolling slightly in the wrong sense, and sideslipping a degree or so as automatic rudder inputs set her on the new path. There was no suggestion of misbehaviour from the other engines, no bits of the aircraft flew off, and there was no need for the military test pilots to feel for the triggers for the non-existent ejector seats.

A TECHNIBIT

When an engine fails on a multi-engined subsonic aircraft, the associated wing drops as the opposite wing advances, due to the asymmetric thrust now obtaining. The wing dihedral and the small differential in airspeed across the wings will generate the extra momentum, causing the aircraft to roll. Unwanted air in front of the dead engine is spilled radially around the cowling, adding to the asymmetry.

In the case of the Concorde, the automatic intake control system spills the bulk of the unwanted air vertically downwards, thereby thrusting the affected wing upward. This input, combined with an automatic corrective input into the rudder, minimises any adverse effect, as outlined by David Davies in the Postscript.

The exercises were repeated and still they gazed, and still the wonder grew. They flew, probed and discussed, and were impressed to the extent that the most significant question left to the American Authorities was what American registration numbers should be painted where on the aircraft. These important decisions were left to the experts.

Sometime later, an invitation arrived from one of the assessors, Bill Schweikard, Director of Performance and Propulsion at the Hugh Dryden Research Establishment on Edwards AFB, to give a joint paper at the International Astronautical Federation at Anaheim, California, on the experience of Upper Atmosphere Transients (air turbulence at high altitudes) derived from the SR-71 and Concorde. At Filton, Bill had been initiated into the complex intake control system, the associated engine controls and flight controls, which gave the well-behaved overall aircraft temperament beyond that yet to be achieved in the US.

The SR-71 operates at much higher altitude than Concorde, which in turn operates at much higher altitude than conventional jets, but this lecture was to be given to the space rocket boys and it was difficult to see what help could be given in this field. However, because of his contacts, giving astronauts some theoretical background, Bill had a clue and the additional invitation of two days at Edwards AFB was the most powerful incentive ever conceived. Terry and I worked with the Americans on the paper.

With the intention of visiting relations after the lecture, Ann and I flew to Los Angeles. The hotel at nearby Anaheim turned out to be an outsized Disneyfied version of a Tudor Manor, with featureless surrounds for a block or two until the outskirts of Disneyland itself were encountered.

Our first mistake was to go for a walk, when it became quite clear that the only people who walked here in temperatures of a humid 93° were the down-and-outs and the British. The buses were occupied by the next level up the social strata. So the obvious answer was to hire a car. Basing the experience that had accumulated in the cut-and-thrust of macho driving in France, a small, racy Japanese car was chosen. In Europe in those days, few small hire cars had such luxuries as air-conditioning and the car would have been nippy had it not been for the over-large air-conditioning plant on board. It was quickly established that as soon as the air-conditioning cut in, the power to the wheels diminished significantly.

With little experience of large, left-hand drive, multi-lane highways, we plunged into the traffic from the depot and decided to do a bit of straight-and-level before 'making any rights', or more seriously, any lefts. Heading towards the coast in a straight line whilst watching the technique of those turning left was fairly easy, so I decided to have a go. However, at the instant of my decision, the many lanes on each side merged into one lane each way, both disappearing into a newly formed fog. This was no time to try more experiments. By dint of pulling into the side, listening for traffic through the open windows of the car, and then accelerating across to the other side, we headed back to the hotel. That was enough excitement for one day, and with some relief that night we ate a meal in a pensioned-off railway coach, and prepared for the next technical highlight – Disneyland.

Disneyland turned out to be all that we had anticipated and far too good for kids. However, the main business of the visit beckoned and early the next morning the massive auditorium opened up for the registration of attendees.

Bill Schweikard delivered the paper explaining the types of atmospheric ups and downs encountered at high altitude by the SR-71 Blackbird and the Concorde. It was not immediately apparent to me how this data could affect the rocket fraternity, but affect them it did when the questions came in thick and fast:

'Where the hell did you get all that data from?'

'All over the world,' he replied (and this included Russia and China!)

'Is it verified?' someone else asked. 'Where can we get hold of it?'

A group of agitated rocketeers had realised that, if this data was true, then the predictions that they had made for good weather window criteria for the forthcoming launches of the space shuttle at Cape Kennedy needed considerable revision. They had made their observations using weather balloons, which drifted slowly upwards and had not picked up any hiccups. On the other hand, the aircraft had covered a mile every two or three seconds at high altitude in the tropics and had picked up quite a lot. The rocketeers were promised more data and left in deep gloom. However, as the space vehicles have now flown many times we can suppose that they eased their consciences or tightened their 'launch windows' somehow.

'Ted, there's a message for you on the notice board,' one of the Dryden men told me.

Clearly these people thought nothing of being paged 3,000 miles from home. However, this call was from the Los Angeles representative of General Electric that had been instructed to get in touch and invite me over to their headquarters 'for a look around and a talk'. This seemed unusual and a bit suspicious, especially as BAC had had no dealings with this particular firm at that time. My mention of Ann brought no additional invitation in response, so it looked like a lone excursion for me, if I went at all.

It transpired that this firm had phoned the Head of Fire Precautions, Tom Madgwick, at Filton asking about precautions taken against titanium fires and would not expand on their reasons for asking. With that reticence Tom would not answer any more questions without further clarification and clearance from his executive. And where was he? In LA.

Not knowing this and thanking the rep for the offer, I got back to the business in hand.

Bill Schweikard had taught various subjects to the astronauts and, in one session here, they were together with the Russian cosmonauts with whom they had linked up in space. After a lively seminar there were questions from the audience. An aggressive American woman reporter praised the Russians for their English (which unknown to her was really American) and berated the Americans for not bothering to learn Russian. She was taken to task by the lead American astronaut, speaking in Russian, for not reading the press handout.

The time had come to go to Edwards AFB. Between LA and Lancaster, near Edwards in the Mojave Desert, lay the San Gabriel Mountains and several thousand feet of hot mountainous highway. And the little Japanese car hated every hot foot of it. It did not like the hot, flat desert either. However, we eventually made Lancaster, as different from its English namesake as it could possibly be with its straight roads, well-spaced houses, 94° heat and a desert next door. As soon as we read the note at the reception desk of the small hotel, we realised that things were done differently in America.

'You will both be picked up at 7.30 a.m.' was contrary to the Filton policy of picking visitors up at 9.00 a.m. to get in an hour or so of work before meeting outsiders. In addition, Ann was also in the party as well. Bang went her day's sunbathing and her eventual hope of even slightly changing the tone of her pale skin, a legacy of her Norse ancestors. Someone had been working hard behind the security screen to get her a pass in a very short time. They did ask me what she did and, not knowing the American for midwife, I said medicine and I suppose that they took it to be Aviation Medicine.

For those not used to such things, the base and its surrounds was a shock to the senses both in size and activity. A flat plain of glaringly white salt stretched for miles in all directions towards mountains on distant horizons. The runway approaches, thresholds and limits were painted in black on the white salt. If ever it rained the slight ripples formed on the salt were graded and the paintwork renewed. This surface would then support very high bearing loads. In the near field, row upon row of F-111 aircraft and a miscellany of others stood in front of large groups of massive hangars. Lined up outside their respective test hangars were the USA's latest prototypes with their respective test pilots nearby, ready to answer any questions.

'Help yourself,' was the surprising instruction, 'the test pilots will be standing by.'

At this point we realised what impact the technical advances of Concorde had made on our hosts. There would have been little chance of an invitation to visit the base and even less of a chance to 'help ourselves' had they not been massively impressed. The next two hours or so were spent with our heads into every hole in every new aircraft, discussing everything with little held back. Ann had the attention of two nauseatingly handsome blue-eyed senior air force officers (Base Commander and Adjutant, no less) while this tour was taking place. The range of research machinery was mind boggling, but it slowly became apparent why there was so much interest in Concorde technology. Concorde already incorporated a lot of the technology that they were now investigating.

This included intakes and engines with electronic control integrated into power plants and then into the aircraft (as Concorde had from the outset and the TSR-2 beforehand), as well as F-8 Crusaders with 'fly by wire' (Concorde, a civil aircraft, had flown with the analogue version seven years before).

However, the most significant example came as we entered a hangar in a remote area of the field. Whereas the others had been huge, this was massive. Entering at one corner it was possible to see a B-1 Mach 2 aircraft in each of the other three corners. These supersonic bombers were only slightly smaller than the Concorde and were being readied for tests. For this part of the visit we were accompanied by the B-1 test pilot, Doug Benefield, their 'low level pilot' who, because of his experience with this machine and others, had assessed the Concorde for the American Airworthiness Authorities. As we stood in the doorway and looked at the form and lines of these sleek aircraft 40ft or so away, I felt a frisson of excitement and chanced my arm by saying:

'You're going to have trouble with those intakes at around Mach 2!'

A TECHNIBIT

Even from that distance it was possible to see that the wedges, which diverted the slow-moving wing surface boundary-layer air around the nacelle between the wing and the engine intakes, looked like the front of a Bull-Nose Morris and were a much worse shape than those that had caused so much trouble on the Concorde prototypes at the higher supersonic speeds. The British and French firms had to effect a significant revision on the later aircraft. Added to this the intakes were on their side and the formative shocks would sweep over the thickening boundary layer as the aircraft accelerated above Mach 1.

'How do you get past Mach 1.6?' I asked.

Doug looked at me hard and long. Obviously this unprecedented freedom of inspection was only afforded whilst bound around with limitations on access to secret information.

'With difficulty!' came the laconic answer.

Approaching closer it was possible to see that there were sensors on the outside of the intakes, presumably located there because of the unsuitability of the transonic porridge of airflows inside.

'Oh! I see that you *have* had trouble with the intakes!'

Strangely enough this remark opened up the conversation. When I climbed into the cockpit it became clear how they were getting the programme watchers off their backs for a while and were aiming for Mach 2. The three control surfaces in each of the four intakes were monitored in the cockpit by small dials calibrated, not in surface position, but in Mach number. Each dial had a small knob underneath and as the speed of the aircraft was increased, each of the four knobs was moved in increments up the dial, so repositioning each of the control surfaces. Engines would not be adjusted at all, once a given Mach number was achieved. Slowing down was an even more delicate operation. This served to show how determination and a little risk can temporarily overcome a setback and, presumably, secure a milepost in terms of the budget. However, it was not acceptable for continued service operation. On Concorde the intake automatically follows the engine and aircraft behaviour faithfully in any aircraft attitude, with any transient atmospheric and speed hiccup and any engine condition with no interaction by the crew. Hence it is in conformance with the requirement that it must handle like any conventional subsonic aircraft, which does not have a complex intake in front of the engine.

No wonder they had been impressed with the handling qualities of the Concorde power plants as they dived to the maximum supersonic speed, slamming the four throttles to and fro in any combination without having to touch anything else and, similarly, how the effect of double engine failure at these speeds could be controlled.

As an interesting digression, I should mention that many years later there was a sequel to this part of the visit. By then Filton had a contract to do major servicing of all USAF F-111s in the European theatre. On one of his frequent visits to the States, the project manager, John Dickens, was shown into a large hangar by a US general where B-1 aircraft were being converted to a reduced speed role, having failed at Mach 2. He turned to John and said: 'Some time ago one of your men took one look at these aircraft and said, "These bastards will never get to Mach 2!" – he's a legend here now!' The official line was that high level Mach 2 was now missile country. Had we persisted with the TSR-2 they could have saved a lot of money and bought that.

After an inspection of the cockpit, with every question answered, it was Ann's turn to have a look at things. She, in turn, was inspected by the technicians standing around as she climbed the steep ladder into the cockpit. Once inside she felt the confining effects of the four-man cockpit.

'How do you get out in a hurry?' she asked.

The three remaining crew members immediately launched into a demonstration of the systems shutdown and escape drill, stopping short of blowing off the entire front end escape capsule. Long afterwards I often wondered whether the escape parachute would have worked had they gone too far and blown the front end through the hangar roof. Meanwhile, I was concentrating on the outside of the aircraft. Of particular interest were the two small wings sticking out under the chin of the aircraft which had the objective of reducing the loads and smoothing the ride in gusty conditions.

'Do those "Easy Riders" actually show a benefit at high speed at low level?' I asked.

'Of course!' said the structural technician in the party. 'Don't you have them on your aircraft?'

This convinced me that they must design their aircraft whilst encased in a cocoon. I would not put it down to sportsmanship as they did not play cricket. The Russians knew every detail of our aircraft, usually before it flew.

'No,' I replied.

'Then what is the ride like under gusty conditions at low level?'

'A f★★★★★★ sight better than this one!' muttered Doug as he walked away.

Some while later the Filton Flight Test team were devastated to learn that Doug was killed whilst flying that particular aircraft at low level. A great loss of a real engineer's pilot and a gentleman to boot.

Meanwhile, the tour continued: the new, as yet unproven space shuttle; an F-111 converted to be totally un-pilotable without electronic wizardry, but highly manoeuvrable with it; a remotely piloted small aircraft to help soldiers do their scouting without exposing themselves; an aircraft which flew low over the alfalfa grass in the bug season to see how the squashed bugs affected the airflow on carefully contoured wings; and a highly manoeuvrable dog-fighting aircraft. They were all lined up for inspection and manned by prime experts.

This was being treated how I always imagined that I should be treated, but never expected to be. And then there was the A-10: a stubby, squat, completely functional Tank Buster of an aircraft with a test pilot to match.

Major Zang, of oriental extraction, had the same approach to offending mechanised armour that Genghis Khan must have had had to the opposing infantry of his era. There was only a small stretch of imagination needed to visualise his forebears in the same image as the stocky major, with thick black hair unimpeded by its military cut flying behind them, as, mounted on sturdy stallions, they charged over the Kirghiz Steppes to lay waste to some unfortunate opponents.

His prime consideration was the powerful cannon, which started in the bowels of the aeroplane, passed under his legs and stuck out of the front of the aircraft. It had six 30mm barrels which rotated rapidly on the Gatling principle and fired sixty shells every second. Rearward thrust from the cannon must have been significant. All spent shell cases were collected and fed back to a drum during the firing process.

'After devastating a line of tanks I suppose that these spent shell cases are collected so as not to affect the environment adversely?' I suggested.

Major Zang dealt only in facts.

'Hell no! We don't want them flying into the engine!'

Man and machine in unison.

During the afternoon a test had been held over for special viewing. The plan was to fly two YF-12s (smaller versions of the SR-71 Blackbird) side-by-side at Mach 3, a dozen or so miles high, and advance one slowly forward so that the shock wave from its pointed nose would play down the intake of the other aircraft's engines. The net result should be unsettling on the engines' behaviour and possibly also on the pilots' helmets. All the important results should be telemetered back to the console in the test laboratory around which we, and the engineers, would be sitting. There was a long wait as the tension grew. Finally, a technician tiptoed in and whispered into the ear of the engineer in charge. With remarkable control he turned round and announced:

'Gen'lemen, I'm sorry to say that we have FOD!'

Foreign Object Damage, as mentioned earlier, is the bane of an aircraft engineer's life, and means that the engine has sucked up something that does it a power of no good, be it a stone, a nut, bolt or washer or, mercifully infrequently, a mechanic. Any of these are usually held as a black mark against the maintenance team, since the ensuing expense is usually enormous. However, with only five engines between two twin-engine aircraft and the spare being in Maintenance, there was nothing that could be done in the timescale. Plan B was made operational.

'We will take you to see the rocket testing base.'

There had been no sign of rockets anywhere. Anyway, the post-war Civil side of Filton had had very little knowledge of rockets in this particular branch of aeronautics. There had been a time when, as a boy, I had made a rocket from two soldered No 8 battery cases and gunpowder. The first 3ft of vertical flight were perfect, but then it departed from the vertical, turned through 90° and launched itself horizontally through the neighbour's greenhouse.

'Where is that?' I asked.

'Oh! It's not far . You can see it from here.'

He walked to the window and pointed across the airfield. The salt flats shimmered glaring white from horizon to horizon in the 97° midday heat. He pointed.

'You see those hills on the other side of the base?'

The other side of the base was on the far horizon.

'Yes, just.'

'Well, there are some small lumps sticking up. Those are the test sites. There is a car outside for you both.'

As with most of the roads on the flats around there, the highway to the rocket site was fairly straight until it began to climb into the foothills. At the gate the guard inspected our passes and the two of us were shown into a large lecture room, where we were introduced to the director of the site, who promptly launched into a description of his site and his rockets. Several years ago BAC had fitted an adaptation of one of the little attitude adjusting rockets used on space capsules to provide emergency power for Concorde 01. The tiny rocket fired at a turbine wheel which generated power for hydraulics and electrics. The monofuel was so unstable that it was a menace to everything in its vicinity. We were told that it had the characteristics akin to a nerve gas and had to be handled by trained personnel in special suits. During one of the test runs at night when installed on the aircraft (which we found later to be ahead of the bed tests in America), a safety diaphragm cracked, allowing the fuel to drip on to the ground. The test took place on a very wet and windy night on the end of the airfield at Filton. The alien drip was spotted by a sharp-eyed fitter who walked forward to carry out the standard foreign substance identification test. He licked his finger and held it out to catch a drip, intending to have a smell and a taste. Before contact could be made Holman had stopped him and hauled him out of the way, saving many embarrassing questions and possibly a post-mortem.

At a later date, an extraneous signal had been picked up by the starting system and had caused the unit to fire up, blowing a fitter working near the tail off his platform, The device was an absolute disaster, with every component giving trouble to the extent that the technical director threatened the supplier with exposure to the press for the responsibility of delaying the first flight of the pre-production aircraft. This was my sole recent practical experience of rocketry on the civil side. However, it provided more than enough background for me to ask a few questions after the rocket director's dissertation. After about half an hour's questioning the director called a halt:

'I'll say, you know your rockets! Let's do a tour of the test sites and I'll see if there are any more questions!'

As with everything else in this corner of the world, things were on a mammoth scale, with rigs capable of testing rockets from 5lb thrust to 600,000lb. With some relief on both sides we eventually shook hands and left unfamiliar but interesting territory for a return across the hot salt flats to the aircraft, passing the 'largest borax mine in the world' on the way. Taking note of everything else around this area, the opencast had to be massively in keeping with its surroundings. It was. Under this sun the temperature at the bottom must have been unbearable. Way down below in the depths of the gigantic hole the earthmovers, looking like small Dinky toys, started their long, slow, laborious climb to the upper world, eventually emerging at their true size, akin to a small house.

The day could have gone on and on, but there was a commitment to talk to the local branch of the American Institute of Aeronautics and Astronautics (AIAA). This was scheduled for 6.30 p.m. and here again things were done differently. We were ushered back to the hotel at high speed (about 55mph) and then collected by the local branch president and again rushed to a restaurant 20 miles away for the first two courses, and told: 'We can come back for the dessert!'

This was the lowlight of the tour, as the audience was mainly family and the lecture, so painfully prepared, was pitched at too high a level. We did not go back for the dessert but studied the president's family hobby of cutting and mounting ornate fossil stones.

Next day was technician's day at the base. I was invited to 'Come and talk to the boys.'

Envisioning a technitalk session around a table I walked through the nearby door and found myself on stage. In the auditorium were some of Edwards' engineers, technicians and pilots, sitting in rows. There was only one course of action: panic. Last night's slides, plus a few more, were hastily put into a carousel and assembled into the projector, which did not work. However, after a few minutes order was restored and I gave a semi-rehearsed talk, which seemed to go down reasonably well – it was certainly more suited to the audience than that of the previous night. Having plugged the safe ground concerning the power plant handling characteristics in areas at and around maximum aircraft speed, where we knew they had strict limitations, prudence dictated that this was the time to stop.

'Any questions?' I asked in the hope that the talk had either been fully comprehensive or, alternatively, completely incomprehensible and that there would be none. No such luck.

'Ah we've got a question,' I said.

A tall figure stood up in the dimmed auditorium. I tried to smile but it was a weak effort, and the fingers on both my hands were firmly crossed. The questioner leaned forward towards another person on his left and said quietly: 'Whaa cain't we do that?'

To this day I swear that I cannot remember any more of the questions.

After a lunch, taken in a unilevel canteen sitting opposite to the director who had recently returned from the moon, amongst technicians, astronauts, secretaries and the like, the heavy technical discussions began. The visit to Filton and Fairford had clearly produced a significant change in the American attitude towards collaboration in that they realised how far ahead the need to meet civil aircraft requirements had taken the Europeans, while the Americans were still coping with the limiting ejector-seat mentality of the military. The amusing aspect of the meeting was that the secrecy of their military and research projects prevented their discussion, even in areas where solutions had been achieved on the other side of the pond, and a lot of help was available.

'There are a lot of questions we would like to ask and know that you have the answers, but we are not allowed to discuss these,' someone said.

It was difficult to see how asking the question would infringe any security aspects, but it is possible that some remote autocrat might concoct some farfetched reason based on a completely warped analysis of an inadequately understood subject. It might affect his promotional hopes to admit to those at higher levels that some other researchers in other countries with much smaller budgets might be ahead. Finding and suggesting common fields of research was going to be very difficult, especially as all the money would now have to come from them – Filton had none. However, common ground was soon established and we were racing ahead.

'When you saw the B-1 yesterday you mentioned the trouble we were experiencing,' I was asked. 'How did you know?'

As none of the people in this meeting were on that part of yesterday's tour they must have had a briefing meeting in between times.

'Your boundary layer diverters were a much worse shape than our original ones,' I answered. 'Not enough respect had been paid to the supersonic part of the boundary layer in a critical area. Add to that the fact that with your design the shocks from the main intakes would slide over the wing surface as the speed increases and also adversely affect the boundary layer. The amount of test probes in that area suggested a few problems. And when I assessed from the visit to the cockpit (the crew were a bit evasive) how they managed to reach Mach 2 it was clear that the intake control system could not find a reliable operating source.'

'Did you use test probes like ours to find the solution?' (Their test instrumentation was superb. It included probes of near hypodermic size fitted with micro high-frequency sensors which would cause minimum disruption to the flow that they were trying to measure.)

I reasoned, when you are on top you can take a few liberties, as the actress said to the bishop:

'No, we used a bucket, castor oil and some oil lamps.'

'Excuse me?'

Without putting too fine a point on it I now had their undivided attention.

'A what?'

'A bucket. We did not have the sophisticated instrumentation that you now have, so we adapted the old wind tunnel test technique of using 'slush'. We half-filled a bucket with lamp black and mixed in some castor oil until it became a very thick black slush. We then painted it on the white aircraft in front of the engines and flew off smartly to Mach 2. The slush would not move when it was cold, but when it got very warm at Mach 2 it flowed in the direction of the airflow and showed quite clearly where the shock waves were and that they were in the wrong places. The picture was 'frozen' by slowing down quickly in the sub-zero air at high altitude. We had a permanent pictorial record of the location of the problem shock waves, unassailable in accuracy, in a tenth of the time it would take to install and calibrate your instrumentation, even if we had had it! The later test aircraft were cleared to use thrust reverse at idle on the inner engines at Mach 2, too late for this test but OK for future emergencies.' (I just threw this in to impress!)

The traditional adaptability of the Brits had triumphed here. As a joke it was suggested that they should develop their technique by painting a British Airways Concorde in New York and BAC would mark them out of ten when it landed in London. The trouble with that suggestion was that it very nearly got serious backing! Eventually time came to leave.

'It's been great having you here,' someone said to me. 'From what the British Aircraft Corporation publishes it appears that they know nothing. From what we (NASA) know their experience is in excess of anyone. Why the hell don't they get around more?'

'Let's put the answer down to Europe's introverted politicians and heads of industry.'

'Oh, and by the way, please give these to Michael and Richard.'

'These' were two examples of American Public Relations at their best. Attached to fat packs of aerospace goodies were personally addressed good wishes to my two children. They were signed under a picture of the ex-astronaut director of the research centre, Dave Scott, with whom we had had lunch.

The next week was occupied with a visit to Florida to see Aunt Georgiana, who was noted for keeping up a continuous supply of boiled sweets moving across the Atlantic during the war and for driving all over the place in her eighties. The house was in Fort Lauderdale. A substantial part of the visit was occupied with warnings such as:

'Some people don't close the sluices after they sail through so there is a risk of meeting an alligator!' or alternatively, 'Don't lie on the grass, dear. The bug man hasn't been round with his spray yet this week.'

With some relief we left the humidity of Florida separately, Ann to Washington and me to this mysterious meeting with GE.

In Washington Ann stayed in a hotel which was hosting a nurses' convention, so worries about her being lonely were unfounded. In my case the first question I was asked was 'where is your wife?' and the real technical question was never asked explicitly. They did not wish to say that they had severe troubles with titanium blades rubbing on their surface treatments, causing explosions inside the engines. I did not want to say that we knew that they had these troubles, or I might have to say how we knew and what had been done about titanium fires on Concorde. We got nowhere. Even the freebee ball pen did not work.

Back in Washington after a frustrating scheduled morning meeting with the Federal Aviation Authorities, who did not want to have a meeting, Ann and I met up, did a quick tour, and left overnight for London, arriving on the redeye shift early in the morning. On leaving the plane we passed through Customs and Immigration and then waited beside the baggage carousel while the baggage handlers wrestled with the access door to the plane's hold. Someone had jammed it.

Some years before, when the then BAe Director, Dr Russell, had a similar experience with a de Havilland Comet, he immediately got on the telephone in the baggage claim hall to register a friendly barb with Ron Bishop, the Comet Chief Designer, himself. Regrettably I was not in the same elevated circle of the Boeing top brass.

Not until two hours later did the carousel start to move and the baggage came through. And only when we reached the Avis car hire desk did we find that my wallet with cards and licence had last been seen on the plane, which by now had been cleaned, serviced and turned round to go back. This was explained to the Avis receptionist, together with the facts that one Avis car had been used to reach London and another to tour parts of America and the tab was being picked up by BAe. The explanations all fell on stony ground. No licence equals no car, so we came back to Bristol using Ann's licence.

This final experience left me with two lasting impressions. One was that if you undertake a morning flight from Cincinnati to Washington, have a meeting with a government establishment which does not want to see you, tour Washington, take the evening flight to London with uncontrollable kids running up and down the aisles, find out that you have lost your wallet after waiting two hours for baggage because some idiot of a ground handler has jammed the baggage door locking mechanism, then it is wrong to try to drive 130 miles under the influence of jetlag, even if the babysitter has a pre-planned appointment to get to only four minutes after you arrive home.

The other is that no matter how many years one may spend trying to design faster modes of transport to get passengers to their eventual destination as quickly as possible, some careless, ham-fisted bugger will eventually set it all to nought.

26

TWO-UPMANSHIP, OR GAME, SET AND MATCH

Well into the period of Concorde passenger operation the bogey of 'Overfuelling Surge' raised its ominous head.

A TECHNIBIT

Overfuelling Surge was a phenomenon wherein one fuel valve in an engine fuel control might stick temporarily and a second would open wide to compensate. Nothing untoward would happen unless the first valve suddenly became free. Then all hell would be let loose as the engine tried to cope with the sudden onslaught of excess fuel. The surge pressures could be greater than any previously contemplated.

The design office went into overdrive during this overfuelling crisis. Everyone became an instant overfuelling expert, even those who thought it was something to do with putting too much fuel in the tanks.

There were two approaches to the problem. One was to do a carefully controlled set of flight tests, advancing up the speed range in small steps and checking the resultant structural stresses at each step. The other was to get as much information as possible from elsewhere. We did both.

Once the bench and Flight Test programmes were well advanced, a party of one Rolls-Royce engine specialist, Alan Lewis, and two aircraft engineers, Terry and I, left for the US to talk to experts in engine surge pressures, whose reports we had read over the past few weeks. As before, the problem of security got in the way. But as we were possibly in trouble, we decided to eat humble pie and take any scraps that could be picked up. On the plane over to the NASA engine research laboratories, the three of us puzzled our brains on the results shown in the NASA main report and decided that this must form the basis of all questions.

Of the four NASA engineers in the meeting next morning, one was the author of that report and who, mysteriously, had a Russian-type name and spoke with a thick Russian-type accent. Not to appear the country cousins in this game, we outlined the background to the problem and a summary of the total history of Concorde power plant flying and testing. One thing that had not been appreciated at that time was that the total flying time for Concorde at Mach 2 was close to that of the whole of the US Air Force. At this juncture the chairman sent for a couple of reinforcements.

Terry then started questioning the Russian-named, Russian-accented expert on the background behind the test reports. It was a delight to hear Terry, this technical genius, take the report and gently dig pits for the author to fall into:

'We had compared over twenty engines of the same breed, and found marked differences, even with the same type of engine. How many did you investigate?' Terry asked.

'Two.'

'Of the same type?'

'No.'

'Our range of results spans those of yours, so we could argue that your claimed differences between engine types could be negligible, or two or three times as much!'

'Yes, possibly.'

'We compared tunnel with flight tests, as shown here. Have you done any flight tests?' Terry continued.

'No, not yet.'

After more discussion it was obvious that the net was beginning to close in. Terry went on:

'We suggest that, with more results, your curves would look like this.'

'I zuppose zo.'

The camouflage had been removed from over the pit and the trap exposed.

'So perhaps we could draw other conclusions?'

'I t'ink I r-rewrite.'

It was clear that little could be gained from further in-depth questioning, as a greater depth to their knowledge was not present. It was not buried under a protective shroud of security. So we proceeded to adopt Plan B and flew to the Rockwell base, the home of the supersonic long-range bomber, the B-1, in California.

Here again the not-the-country-cousins ploy was adopted and we mentioned the 2,500 hours of testing at Mach 2 and the 450 deliberate surges on twenty engines on three different airframes. At this juncture the aerodynamicist in their party left the room, not to return. This departure was thought to be a sign of impatience in having to deal with people with begging bowls and little experience. After all, they had designed the impressive B-1, and had enjoyed the support of NASA and their years of experience.

In the silence that followed the Americans were reluctant to talk and to kick-start the discussion we asked how many surges they had encountered.

'Not many.'

'How many deliberate surges were induced?'

'None deliberately induced.'

In other words, any surges that were encountered were unintentional and no operating envelopes had been investigated, i.e. signs of big trouble. Very few vital questions could now be asked.

'And how many hours at Mach 2 in total?' I asked, hoping that Concorde's 2,500 hours devoted to power plant testing alone was not insignificant.

There was a significant pause. The B-1 Project Manager looked each of us in turn straight in the eye.

'Fifty-six minutes!' he said.

Which made the next question impossible to answer – so it wasn't asked. We then understood how prophetic the comment made about the B-1's potential a few years before at Edwards AFB had become.

EPILOGUE

'Ann, your name has come out of the hat!'

'What do you mean?'

'The Works are having an open day and those who wanted tickets to fly on Concorde had to put their name in for the draw. I put yours in and you have got one – that's the good news.'

'And the bad?'

'It costs one hundred and sixty pounds.'

'Ouch!'

A new wind was now blowing through Filton. After the decline following the end of the Concorde era and the steadying influence of re-equipping VC 10s as flying refuelling tanks for the RAF, work, work and more work was descending upon the depleted numbers in the design office. Under new management there was an effort being made to revive an interest in all things aeronautical. Perhaps one day there would even be a grant to do private flying again?

The second of the new annual open days was planned with the intention of getting up to a thousand people airborne. Two Concorde flights were planned, together with three Airbus A310 flights and innumerable journeys in an ageing DC-3 Dakota – the wartime workhorse – and a helicopter. Exhibitions, tours of the works and sideshows were to supplement the flying display for the ground-bound visitors.

The first Concorde flight was scheduled from Heathrow via the Bay of Biscay to Filton and the second one from Filton, via the Bay of Biscay, to Heathrow. Buses to and from Heathrow would complete the round trip for each group of passengers. Ann was booked on the Concorde flight out of Filton.

A few days before the flight, I had contacted the Senior Flight Engineer on the British Airways Concorde staff and asked if he could arrange that, during the flight, a call over the passenger address system would announce that the intake control system had developed a fault and would Mrs T. come and fix it? After living with this, and other things technical for the last twenty-five years, some relevant knowledge was likely to have rubbed off.

'Good God man! We can't announce failures like that! – But leave it to me – we have ways and means,' he said, implying some other ploy, but not elaborating.

Weather, on that summer of 1985, was all around as the open day dawned wet, cloudy and windy. Nevertheless, the pre-flight party in the office enjoyed the prospect of cold meats, cold wine and salads. Ann, who always concentrated on a book during take-off and landing, was somewhat apprehensive, whilst Shirley, the wife of our neighbour Roy, was the only one who was unaware that she had been booked on one of the Airbus A310 flights.

When the time came Ann was taken by shuttle to the Airfield Departure Lounge (in reality the Rolls-Royce sales lounge). With a parting peck on the cheek, she was away. At the appointed hour the passengers were taken by bus to the far end of the runway where Aircraft 14 stood serene in its new livery. (This was the livery, recognisable as a British derivative, before British Airways went universally unrecognisable, incurring the wrath of all true Brits including, most noteworthily, the Iron Lady herself.) Ann boarded the aircraft by the same stairs that had been used for many a North African campaign and settled herself in her window seat.

The PA system cleared its throat.

'Will Mrs T make herself known to the cabin staff?'

'My God, what is the matter now?' Ann thought.

She signalled an air hostess.

'That call was for me.'

'I think that you are to go up,' said the hostess, and busied herself taking photographs of the passengers using their own cameras. When one starts they all start!

Well, Ann thought, that's what I'm on this plane for! But a germ of doubt made her have another attempt to find out what was going on. Possibly Ted had had a heart attack? She got up.

'Are you Mrs T?' asked a steward who had emerged from the forward galley next to the corridor of electrical equipment that led to the cockpit. 'You have got to go up,' he said, pointing to the front end.

A tall figure met her at the entrance to the cockpit.

'Hello, I'm David,' said the Senior Flight Engineer. 'Please sit down here,' he said, indicating a crew seat.

Panic set in.

'It is serious,' she thought, 'they're taking me aside to tell me that it's worse!'

The next move convinced her that it was even more serious than that bit of news could be because she then found that the reason the man was feeling below her skirt was that he was trying to find the strap to anchor her into the fourth crew member's seat right behind the captain. Instead of some heart-stopping announcement, she was then introduced to the crew and a headset was placed on her head. Over the headphones she heard the captain say, 'Watch your language, gentlemen, there is a lady present.'

The dawning of a realisation brought a surge of totally different emotions as the crew went through the pre-taxi drills and Concorde AG slowly turned into the runway. Pre take-off drills were completed with Ann trying to locate the owner of each voice heard over the headset. Once the differential sounds indicating directions had been eliminated by the earphones, this task was reduced to seeing which mouth was moving.

Reheat was selected, the brakes released and the throttle levers pushed forwards to their maximum travel. Many thousands of horsepower put their shoulders behind the aircraft and pushed as only many thousand can. Over the brow of the hump in the runway it went, where the village of Charlton had been razed to accommodate the Brabazon, and up into the murk of a summer's day. Cloud blotted out the view while pilots and ground control discussed and co-ordinated 'making a right'.

'Do they say things like that in normal conditions?' Ann thought. 'What has happened to ports and starboards? And "make a right again to do a fly past".'

A crew member called out the altitude as the aircraft descended on instruments through the murk towards Filton Aerodrome.

'Fourteen hundred – twelve hundred – one thousand – eight hundred.'

'We're going to crash, they are all mad,' she thought.

'Seven…'

On the ground the commentator told the crowd to look to its right. The aircraft was visible under the low cloud, coming in fast. It was, as always, an elegantly impressive sight which still turned heads, even in its middle age. After his turn to approach the airfield, the pilot had turned the wick up again and, to the onlookers, the flypast became a spectacle, a sound, and then a memory.

Ann was released from her seat when Concorde had reached supersonic speeds in the stratosphere and it was suggested that she made her way back to the cabin for champagne and food. The passengers looked at her through respectful eyes.

'Who was she?' was asked in hushed tones.

'She must be important.'

The firm's creeps came up and introduced themselves. Through mouthfuls of caviar and smoked salmon and sips of champagne she acknowledged their homage.

While the lesser lights were given a brief glimpse of the cockpit and marvelled that anyone could read all those instruments at once, Ann and the girl in the next seat were deep in conversation. The girl had just come back from the same town in Corfu where we were intending to stay at in two weeks' time, so very soon Ann knew what to expect before we went there.

During the flight the cabin crew appeared to have a standard cure for everything.

'Miss, I've got hiccups. Could I have a glass of water, please?'

'Here, have some champagne instead!'

'Where are the toilets?'

'I think that they are occupied. Have some champagne while you wait.'

Ann, still musing over the whole experience, walked off the aircraft and into the disembarkation lounge at Heathrow with a half-full glass.

'Will Concorde passengers please follow me?' said the hostess.

Feeling superior in every way, they put their noses in the air and followed her through the common herd of subsonic travellers to the buses waiting to take them down the M4 back to Filton. After a flight round the Bay of Biscay, at a speed of a mile in under three seconds, champagne and chatter made the return from Mach Two-and-a-Bit feel just like any other flight, but a bit special. Which, come to think of it, was what had been intended from the start.

What added to the feeling was that the Queen Mother sat in the same seat on that aircraft's next flight. Would the Lady in Waiting have been delegated with the task of strapping her in?

POSTSCRIPT

The Achievement

In the extract below, David Davies, Head of Flight Department, Civil Airworthiness Authority, considers that, 'A boy of 16 could do it':

> The effective control of the air-intake geometry was another important success – certainly as significant as the good flying qualities of the 'naked' aeroplane. As you might know, it is generally accepted that the Russian aeroplane has fallen down primarily because they can't get the intakes right, and the Americans are not doing all that well in terms of intakes either. The knowledge of the Concorde intake control system is hopefully locked in the UK and France. It would be worth a fortune to any other country. This 1.6 is a sort of magic Mach number. You can fly up to 1.6 on fixed intakes; they're not frightfully efficient, but at least they will operate. But to get up to Mach 2 you've got to have a variable intake. And the Concorde one works – really very well.
>
> The most comforting things about Concorde, were first its behaviour at high incidence … and the fact that the machine would accept a simultaneous double failure of two engines on one side at Mach 2. That's the thing that would destroy some other aircraft in seconds. It's a very critical thing to do, to be able to shut down two engines simultaneously at Mach 2. American pilots have flown Concorde and a lot of them have had military experience at Mach 2 and they're frankly nervous of this test, but when they see it they can't believe their eyes … on this Concorde at Mach 2, you can just sit there and cut two engines on one side; of course the machine will begin to roll – it rolls the wrong way, compared with the conventional way of a subsonic – but it doesn't matter. Then it will yaw and because the true airspeed is so high, you're actually pushed over to the side of the cockpit. You don't need to touch the controls for five seconds.

> Imagine! And then after the end of five seconds you just get hold of the wheel, level the wings, and get rid of the sideslip with the rudder. A boy of 16 could do it. That is a remarkable achievement. (Owen, K.T., *Concorde: New Shape in the Sky*, HMSO Janes, 1982)

And, from the other end of the scale, the letdown: 'He goes down holes, and turns taps on' (Michael Talbot – age 5 – when asked by the teacher what his father did for a living, after seeing him dealing with a domestic plumbing problem).

VALEDICTION

Two major tragedies in quick succession contributed to the demise of Concorde's service life. The tragedy that occurred on take-off from Charles de Gaulle airport, Paris, combined with the effect of the tragedy of the Twin Towers in New York, was more than sufficient to dissuade a significant section of the travelling public not to fly, particularly to fly in expensive style.

The low number of Concordes actually flying, coupled with Concorde's worldwide fame, and the catastrophic consequences of the accident, made it less difficult for the authorities to withdraw the certificates with relatively little opposition, apart from that of British Airways engineers and the majority of the British public. This is to be compared with the effect that the grounding of the large fleets of Boeing 747 would have had on the world's air transport, following the tank malfunction, which downed one of that type of aircraft with heavy loss of life, when it was flying out of New York.

The feelings of those who designed and built this beautiful aircraft, in the knowledge that something that they had lovingly created had, by a combination of circumstances, resulted in the deaths of over 100 people, cannot be described. It was as though we were part of the families who had suffered this great loss, and to whom our sincerest sympathies are extended.

APPENDIX

PRINCIPAL POWER PLANT VARIATIONS

Aircraft	Intakes	Engines	Secondary Nozzles
Prototypes	Basic Geometry	Bristol Siddeley Olympus 593	SNECMA (Circular)
(001 & 002)			
Electronics	Analogue	Analogue	Analogue
Actuation	Hydraulic	'HP' Fuel system	Pneumatic
Design	2-Hinge Spill/ Aux. Inlets	Cannular Flame Tubes	Cascade Reversers
Pre-Production	Cutback Lower Lip	Olympus 593	New Circular
(101 only)			
Electronics	Digital Law Generation	Analogue	Analogue
Actuation	Hydraulic	'LP' Fuel System	Pneumatic
Design	Blow-in Aux. Inlets	Annular Flame Tubes	Cascade Reversers

Pre-Production	As 101	As 101	New 'TV' Exit
(102 only)			Pneumatic Actuation, 'Bucket' Reversers
Production*	As 102**	Bristol Siddeley Olympus	As 102
(201 & 202)		Mark 601	

* The first two Production Aircraft, 201 and 202, were retained for the Certification process and did not enter service. They had sufficient instrumentation installed for that purpose.

** After being in service for a few years, an In-Service Aircraft modification for a thinned lower lip with less inner curvature was developed on a commercial basis. This gave less drag and hence less fuel load with negligible loss in intake/engine performance.

INDEX